Bride OF THE HIGH PLACES

Discipleship and Devotionals

A WOMAN'S INNER HEART
as seen through
Hannah Hurnard's

Allegory

Hinds' Feet on High Places

for women who mostly know
and men seeking clues

Karl Duff

A Division of WINEPRESS PUBLISHING

Note to the Reader

All text on the left-hand side is from *Hinds' Feet on High Places*, by Hannah Hurnard.

All text on the right-hand side is by Karl Duff and pertains to this set of devotional studies. Each devotional study is placed on the page opposite the related text of *Hinds' Feet....*to which it applies. Copyright of *Bride of the High Places* applies only to devotional text.

Scripture quoted by Hannah Hurnard is from the King James Version of the Bible.

Scripture quoted by Karl Duff is from the New American Standard Bible © 1960, 1963, 1968, 1971, 1972, 1973, 1975, 1977 by The Lockman Foundation. Used by permission.

ISBN 1-57921-518-1
Library of Congress Catalog Card Number: 2002114632

Author's Preface

"The LORD your God is in your midst, a victorious warrior.
He will exult over you with joy, He will be quiet in His love, He will
rejoice over you with shouts of joy." —Zephaniah 3:17

A zillion or so classic novels and movies have been written to portray what God writes on a young girl's heart; a brave man who will face death to gain her love, fight dragons and set her free from curse or imprisonment. She recognizes him as her true love and lives with him "happily ever after." There are many more details. This "imprint" of God's plan of salvation is no accident and has application in the world as well as in the Kingdom of God. The details of this vision should aid a woman's recognition of the gospel of Jesus Christ and His conquest of Satan on behalf of His chosen eternal Bride. They also confirm the biblical portraits of gender roles on earth, in courtship, marriage and in reproduction of Godly seed.

Many boys consider the above vision to be nonsense and contribute greatly to its damage. Yet they have another vision, dim and elusive. What is it? They have a general sense of their destiny for "greatness". They know they are purposed to accomplish something mighty in their lives. Yet most grow old and die without discovering what this "greatness" was meant to be (reflected in "mid-life crisis" for millions.) What goes wrong?

Answers to these questions are hidden in the mystery of love. Boys don't comprehend these things until they have discovered a love worth dying for. They become men *through* the process. Love discovered must be refined and proven by fire and water; established on a firm foundation. A ransom must be paid. The same is true between Christ and His Bride. The Bride is won by a love which conquers all.

Hannah Hurnard's famous allegory, *Hinds' Feet on High Places*, offers a classic portrait of discipleship in Christ, worth serious study and personal application. In addition, perhaps unwittingly, Hurnard also portrays her own female heart and soul through her heroine, "Much-Afraid", brilliantly capturing things unique to the hearts of girls and women but mostly hidden to men. Many of her expressions of emotions, perplexity, fear and the circumstances which induce these things are female gender specific. Many of Hurnard's portraits of how women naturally view the issues of life, relationships and happiness are simply stunning! Reviewing the allegory offers opportunity to apply lessons of discipleship into our own lives, drawing both men and women into conformance with Christ, in the fashion of Hurnard's heroine "Much Afraid", to rid themselves of the deformities that keep them from more effectual service.

Text is formatted to enable devotional study, prayer and personal decision making. Limited space is provided for notes; however, a journal notebook for note-taking, recording prayers and discipleship decisions would be helpful. Extensive scriptures not referenced in Hurnard's work have been added to the commentary to strengthen and validate Hurnard's portraits. It is recommended they all be incorporated into the study, but this is ultimately the reader's choice.

KMD

Preface to the Allegory

One morning during the daily Bible reading on our mission compound in Palestine, our little Arab nurse read from Daily Light a quotation from the Song of Songs, "The voice of my Beloved! behold, he cometh leaping upon the mountains, skipping upon the hills" (Song of Solomon 2:8). When asked what the verse meant, she looked up with a happy smile of understanding and said, "It means there are no obstacles which our Savior's love cannot overcome, and that to him, mountains of difficulty are as easy as an asphalt road!"

From the garden at the back of the mission house at the foot of Mount Gerizim we could often watch the gazelles bounding up the mountainside, leaping from rock to rock with extraordinary grace and agility. Their motion was one of the most beautiful examples of exultant and apparently effortless ease in surmounting obstacles which I have ever seen.

How deeply we who love the Lord of Love and desire to follow Him long for the power to surmount all difficulties and tests and conflicts in life in the same exultant and triumphant way. To learn the secret of victorious living has been the heart's desire of those who love the Lord, in every generation.

We feel we would give anything if only we could, in actual experience, live on the High Places of love and victory here on this earth and during this life—able always to react to evil, tribulation, sorrow, pain and every wrong thing in such a way that they would be overcome and transformed into something to the praise and glory of God forever. As Christians we know, in theory at least, that in the life of a child of God there are no second causes, that even the most unjust and cruel things, as well as all seemingly pointless and undeserved sufferings, have been permitted by God as a glorious opportunity for us to react to them in such a way that our Lord and Savior is able to produce in us, little by little, His own lovely character.

The Song of Songs expresses the desire implanted in every human heart, to be reunited with God Himself, and to know perfect and unbroken union with Him. He has made us for Himself, and our hearts can never know rest and perfect satisfaction until they find it in Him.

It is God's will that some of His children should learn this deep union with Himself through the perfect flowering of natural human love in marriage. For others it is equally His will that the same perfect union should be learned through the experience of learning to lay down completely this natural and instinctive desire for marriage and parenthood, and accept the circumstances of life which deny them this experience. This instinct for love, so firmly implanted in the human heart, is the supreme way by which we learn to desire and love God Himself above all else.

But the High Places of victory and union with Christ cannot be reached by any mental reckoning of self to be dead to sin, or by seeking to devise some way or discipline by which the will can be crucified. The only way is by learning to accept, day by day, the actual conditions and tests permitted by God, by a continually repeated laying down of our own will and acceptance of His as it is presented to us in the form of the people with whom we have to live and work, and in the things which happen to us. Every acceptance of His will becomes an altar of sacrifice, and every such surrender and abandonment of ourselves to His will is a means of furthering us on the way to the High Places to which He desires to bring every child of His while they are still living on earth.

The lessons of accepting and triumphing over evil, of becoming acquainted with grief, and pain, and ultimately, of finding them transformed into something incomparably precious; of learning through constant glad surrender to know the Lord of Love Himself in a new way and to experience unbroken union with Him—these are the lessons of the allegory in this book. The High Places and the hinds' feet do not refer to heavenly places after death, but are meant to be the glorious experience of God's children here and now—if they will follow the path He chooses for them.

Perhaps the Lord will use it to speak comfort to some of His loved ones who are finding themselves forced to keep company with Sorrow and Suffering, or who walk in darkness and have no light or feel themselves tossed with tempest and not comforted. It may help them to understand a new meaning in what is happening, for the experiences through which they are passing are all part of the wonderful process by which the Lord is making real in their lives the same experience which made David and Habakkuk cry out exultantly, "The Lord God maketh my feet like hinds' feet, and setteth me upon mine High Places" (Psa. 18:33 and Hab. 3:19).

Allegories and Parables

READ: Hinds' Feet, Preface to the Allegory & **Matthew 13:1–53**

"And He said, 'Go, and tell this people: "Keep on listening, but do not perceive;
keep on looking, but do not understand. Render the hearts of this people insensitive,
their ears dull and their eyes dim, lest they see with their eyes, hear with their ears,
understand with their hearts, and return and be healed."'
—Isaiah 6:9–10

Webster's New World Dictionary defines allegory as "a story in which people, things, and happenings have a hidden or symbolic meaning; used for teaching or explaining ideas, moral principles, etc." It is also "the presenting of ideas by means of such stories".

In walking with Much-Afraid through her journey with the Chief Shepherd, we read the allegory by Hannah Hurnard to teach and explain ideas applicable to our own lives. In using the words "walking" and "journey" in the last sentence, we are using allegorical terms. Jesus used parables (simple allegoric relations and analogies) to teach, and quoted Isaiah to show that truth is best taught in this manner to separate those able to hear from those unable to hear.

Both Hurnard and her allegorical disciple are female, important because there are differences in how men and women see God. In the relationship between the Bridegroom, Jesus Christ, and his bride, we are all female. Yet men must also be conformed to the Bridegroom in order to minister to their wives. Women remain brides in both cases and God is given headship through their fathers, then their husbands. Women see God and experience value and uniqueness primarily through men who love them, while the reverse is not identically true. Men experience Christ's headship while dying for their wives (I Cor. 11:1–3, 8–12, Eph. 5:21–33). One goal of this study is to give men deeper perceptions of the unique heart of women and the mysteries of the husband-wife (and father-daughter) relationships.

May the grace of God be upon this text and the prayers of each person who undertakes its study. (Zech. 12:10–14, Eph. 3:1–10). Amen.

QUESTIONS AND PRAYER: What are your goals in this study? Would you please write them down below at this time? *To understand the book of Song of Solomon better and to study the lessons of the High Places that I might better love my Shepherd.*

Part One

"Weeping may endure for a night"
(Psalm 30:5)

CHAPTER 1

Invitation to the High Places

This is the story of how Much-Afraid escaped from her Fearing relatives and went with the Shepherd to the High Places where "perfect love casteth out fear." For several years Much-Afraid had been in the service of the Chief Shepherd, Whose great flocks were pastured down in the Valley of Humiliation. She lived with her friends and fellow workers Mercy and Peace in a tranquil little white cottage in the village of Much-Trembling. She loved her work and desired intensely to please the Chief Shepherd, but happy as she was in most ways, she was conscious of several things which hindered her in her work and caused her much secret distress and shame.

In the first place she was a cripple, with feet so crooked that they often caused her to limp and stumble as she went about her work. She had also the very unsightly blemish of a crooked mouth which greatly disfigured both expression and speech, and was sadly conscious that these ugly blemishes must be a cause of astonishment and offense to many who knew that she was in the service of the great Shepherd.

Most earnestly she longed to be completely delivered from these shortcomings and to be made beautiful, gracious, and strong as were so many of the Shepherd's other workers, and above all to be made like the Chief Shepherd Himself. But she feared that there could be no deliverance from these two crippling disfigurements and that they must continue to mar her service always.

Deformities

READ: Page 1 of Hinds' Feet....(facing page) & **Romans 8:26–39**

"Strengthen the hands that are weak and the knees that are feeble."
—Hebrews 12:12

"But we have renounced the things hidden because of shame, not walking in
craftiness or adulterating the word of God, but by manifestation of the truth
commending ourselves to every man's conscience in the sight of God."
—II Corinthians 4:2

Much-Afraid has two serious deformities which cause her distress and shame. One has
to do with her "walk" and the other with her "talk". Do you see the analogy this is pointing
out? All of us have major problems in our inability to act and speak according to what we
know to be right, because of sin in our mind and in our flesh. In a moment you will be asked
to identify some areas in your own life. Our mind and flesh is influenced by the prince of
power of the air (Eph.2:2–3) who seeks to ruin the work of the Prince of Peace. This is
Much-Afraid's problem and ours, too.

Also, we have both visible and hidden disfigurements; some behavior so vile we would
be ashamed of having other people see it and other behavior which is accepted by others
only because they love us (or tolerate us.) Many of us didn't notice these things until we
came into service of the True Shepherd. Now, like Much-Afraid, we are as "sadly conscious"
as she is of her deformities. Have you become aware of your deformities and an earnest
desire to become free of them?

There is a characteristic in all of us; we would like to be attractive and gracious, drawing people to us because of our character and wisdom. We want *to be regarded* as righteous,
but have little *power to be* righteous! Much-Afraid is no different and, tormented by all sorts
of fears and doubts regarding her value, is to be challenged to leave her world and walk
with the Shepherd in order to be changed.

The press of the "relatives" of fear are driving Much-Afraid toward action. Though she
abhors Craven Fear, she is not able to be free of him and is being further pressured to come
into closer relationship—to marry him! If she succumbs to that choice, he will be her master! And our bad habits will only get worse if we are not rid of them.

**QUESTIONS AND PRAYER: Please list your deformities which make it
difficult for you to serve Christ. Talk to God about your desire to please Him.**

*My lack of self-discipline; my neglect of
private prayer; my struggle with stress from
school + schedule; my desire to do BIG things
that overtakes little faithfulness*

There was, however, another and even greater trouble in her life. She was a member of the Family of Fearings, and her relatives were scattered all over the valley, so that she could never really escape from them. An orphan, she had been brought up in the home of her aunt, poor Mrs. Dismal Forebodings, with her two cousins Gloomy and Spiteful and their brother Craven Fear, a great bully who habitually tormented and persecuted her in a really dreadful way.

Like most of the other families who lived in the Valley of Humiliation, all the Fearings hated the Chief Shepherd and tried to boycott His servants, and naturally it was a great offense to them that one of their own family should have entered His service. Consequently they did all they could both by threats and persuasions to get her out of His employment, and one dreadful day they laid before her the family dictum that she must immediately marry her cousin Craven Fear and settle down respectably among her own people. If she refused to do this of her own free will, they threatened to use force and compel her.

Poor Much-Afraid was, of course, overwhelmed with horror at the mere idea, but her relatives always terrified her, and she had never learned to resist or ignore their threats, so she simply sat cowering before them, repeating again and again that nothing would induce her to marry Craven Fear, but she was quite unable to escape from their presence.

The unhappy interview therefore lasted a long time, and when finally they did leave her for awhile, it was already early evening. With a surge of relief, Much-Afraid remembered that the Chief Shepherd would then be leading His flocks to their accustomed watering place beside a lovely cascade and pool on the outskirts of the village. To this place she was in the habit of going very early

10

Longing Desire

READ: Hind's Feet... facing page & II Corinthians 7 & 8

"Delight yourself in the LORD; and He will give you the desires of your heart." —Psalm 37:4

"...they also, by prayer on your behalf, yearn for you because of the surpassing grace of God in you." —II Corinthians 9:14

Much-Afraid grieves about her disfigurement and desire to be like the Chief Shepherd. She thinks that her disfigurements will always mar her service for Him. Yet she yearns to serve Him better. Do you see how the enemy can use this to torment a servant? It is true that our disfigurements do mar our service, but it is also true that God changes us as we walk with Him (Romans 8:29).

Paul wrote that an important thing for the Corinthians to discover was their own "earnestness". This is true for all of us. Much-Afraid will find that the Chief Shepherd is waiting for her own expression of "earnestness" to walk with Him to the high places. Is your personal earnestness for the LORD still in the future? Does it relate to these daily devotions?

Notice the particular nature of Much-Afraid's relatives; pessimism (Dismal Forebodings and Gloomy), personal wounding (Spiteful) and perverted manhood (Craven Fear). They denote both circumstantial and relationship problems, typical for all of us. Men should be especially attentive to how the author of this allegory (a woman) portrays the behavior of the bully (Craven Fear) who torments Much-Afraid. Do you see a relationship between fear and bullying? Does the behavior of men also relate to the well being of girls and women?

Do you think it is only Much-Afraid's service to the Chief Shepherd that makes her unwilling to marry Craven Fear? Or do you think there are deeper things written into a girl's heart that cause her to look for particular things in the man she wants to marry? These things relate directly to the things to which God is calling men in His service.

QUESTIONS AND PRAYER: With whom do we identify in this story? Is it Much-Afraid? Should we also identify with protecting her against Craven Fear? What members of our family need such protection? *Primarily w/ Much Afraid, (which was the author's intention) I find it intriguing how all the enemy relatives are still in the family of "Fearings" most sins find root in well disguised Fear or Pride*

11

every morning to meet Him and learn His wishes and commands for the day, and again in the evenings to give her report on the day's work. It was now time to meet Him there beside the pool, and she felt sure He would help her and not permit her relatives to kidnap her and force her to leave His service for the dreadful slavery of marriage with Craven Fear.

Still shaking with fear and without pausing to wash the tears from her face, Much-Afraid shut the door of the cottage and started off for the cascade and the pool.

The quiet evening light was filling the Valley of Humiliation with a golden glow as she left the village and started to cross the fields. Beyond the river, the mountains which bounded the eastern side of the Valley like towering ramparts were already tinged with pink, and their deep gorges were filled with lovely and mysterious shadows.

Through the quiet and peace of this tranquil evening, poor, terrified Much-Afraid came to the pool where the Shepherd was waiting for her, and told Him of her dreadful plight.

"What shall I do?" she cried as she ended the recital. "How can I escape? They can't really force me to marry my cousin Craven, can they? OH!" cried she, over-whelmed again at the very thought of such a prospect, "it is dreadful enough to be Much-Afraid, but to think of having to be Mrs. Craven Fear for the rest of my life and never be able to escape from the torment of it is more than I can bear."

"Don't be afraid," said the Shepherd gently. "You are in My service, and if you will trust Me they will not be able to force you against your will into any family alliance. But you ought never to have let your Fearing relatives into your cottage, because they are enemies of the King who has taken you into His employment."

"I know, oh, I know," cried Much-Afraid, "but whenever I meet any of my relatives I seem to lose all my strength and simply cannot resist them, no matter how I strive. As long

Time with God

READ: Hind's Feet... facing page & **Psalm 23**

"Rejoice in the LORD always; ag ain I will say, rejoice! Let your forbearing spirit be known to all men. The LORD is near. Be anxious for nothing, but in everything, by prayer and supplication, let your requests be made known to God."—Philippians 4:6

"Grant those who mourn in Zion, ...the oil of gladness instead of mourning, the mantle of praise instead of a spirit of fainting."—Isaiah 61:3

Much-Afraid remembers the meeting place with the Chief Shepherd, right after getting "beat up" by her relatives. He admonishes her for letting them into her cottage in the first place. How many times have we heard the word of God and yet been unable to find power to obey! Would you agree with Much-Afraid's words, "I know, oh, I know, but......"?

The LORD draws us to His meeting place where we can pour out our problems, reviewing all of our grief to our Savior, who gives us pasture and water. The scriptures give us directions regarding removal of the spirits of our hurtful "relatives" in exchange for the wonderful presence of the LORD. We praise Him and express gratitude for His works.

The beautiful sunset suggests that Much-Afraid sees and appreciates the work of God over the Valley of Humiliation. Possibly her relatives didn't notice it at all. God pours out His blessings on all alike, with no partiality. But only some see and appreciate it. Only one leper returned to thank Jesus after ten were healed on the road from Samaria to Galilee (Luke 17:11–17).

Upon what does Much-Afraid's deliverance depend? The Shepherd tells her, "...*if you will trust in Me* they will not be able to force you against your will into any family alliance." John 10:27–30 tells us the same thing. At the same time, the warning is clear; we are not to entertain the enemy under our roof and we must learn to put unwelcome "relatives" not of God out of the house.

QUESTIONS AND PRAYER: Name some enemy relatives that you "entertain" in your "house". Discuss with the LORD how you want to resolve this. Please make notes of any you renounce, in Christ. Self pity (esp. about my illness/weakeness), Pride (and the fear of disappointing others by not living up to a certain reputation), Depraved Ignorance (ignoring feelings/stressors b/c I'm overwhelmed & want to pick "the best" "the most..." etc.)

as I live in the Valley I cannot escape meeting them. They are everywhere and now that they are determined to get me into their power again I shall never dare venture outside my cottage alone for fear of being kidnapped."

As she spoke she lifted her eyes and looked across the Valley and the river to the lovely sunset-lighted peaks of the mountains, then cried out in desperate longing, "Oh, if only I could escape from this Valley of Humiliation altogether and go to the High Places, completely out of reach of all the Fearings and my other relatives."

No sooner were these words uttered when to her complete astonishment the Shepherd answered, "I have waited a long time to hear you make that suggestion, Much-Afraid. It would indeed be best for you to leave the Valley for the High Places, and I will very willingly take you there Myself. The lower slopes of those mountains on the other side of the river are the borderland of My Father's Kingdom, the Realm of Love. No Fears of any kind are able to live there because 'perfect love casteth out fear and everything that torments.' "

Much-Afraid stared at Him in amazement. "Go to the High Places," she exclaimed, "and live there? Oh, if only I could! For months past the longing has never left me. I think of it day and night, but it is not possible. I could never get there. I am too lame." She looked down at her malformed feet as she spoke, and her eyes again filled with tears and despair and self-pity. "These mountains are so steep and dangerous. I have been told that only the hinds and the deer can move on them safely."

"It is quite true that the way up to the High Places is both difficult and dangerous," said the shepherd. "It has to be, so that nothing which is an enemy of Love can make the ascent and invade the Kingdom. Nothing blemished or in any way imperfect is allowed there, and the inhabitants of the High Places do not need 'hinds' feet. I have them Myself," He added with a smile, "and like a young hart or a roebuck I can

14

Invitation to High Places

READ: Hind's Feet... facing page & **Exodus 3–4:15**

"The mouth speaks out of that which fills the heart." —Matthew 12:34

**"For everyone who asks receives, and he who seeks finds, and to
him who knocks it shall be opened." —Matthew 7:8**

Why does God want us to speak to Him of our desires? He says He knows our needs before we ask (Isaiah 65:24). Yet He often waits until we ask before He provides them. Maybe it is because He wants more personal relationship with us (which requires talking). Possibly also, more of God's glory is revealed when we specifically request His provisions. God's purpose is to build our faith, *He wants us to know Him in all of His character, power and beauty to the greatest extent possible.*

Much-Afraid experiences dreadful circumstances that bring her to great despair. Her heart is filled with longing that she can no longer contain. She now speaks and the LORD instantly grants her request!

Do you suppose Moses had a similar yearning desire during the forty years since he had fled from Egypt— to set his people free?

The things that inhibit Much-Afraid's response are the very types of spirits that also weigh us down. We often argue with God as Moses did, as though God is not able to heal our mouths or fix our lame feet. In the comfort of our home, would we respond as Moses, or Much-Afraid? But God does not confront us in our comfort areas, does He? He confronts us in our weaknesses, where comfort or strength are lacking. Like Moses and Much-Afraid, He uses those weaknesses for His glory.

In responding to her doubts and fears, the Shepherd begins to lead Much-Afraid, like He led Moses, into deeper understanding of His provisions, the nature of His Kingdom and His ability to handle all of its steepest terrain with ease.

QUESTIONS AND PRAYER: Please identify a time where you felt led to walk with God and discovered you had excuses regarding why you "couldn't". If this wasn't resolved in God's favor, please take it to Him now and attempt to do so. If you can't recall such an instance, would you invite God to call you in this way?

_____

_____

_____

go leaping on the mountains and skipping on the hills with the greatest ease and pleasure.

"But, Much-Afraid, I could make yours like hinds' feet also, and set you upon the High Places. You could serve Me then much more fully and be out of reach of all your enemies. I am delighted to hear that you have been longing to go there, for, as I said before, I have been waiting for you to make that suggestion. Then," He added, with another smile, "you would never have to meet Craven Fear again."

Much-Afraid stared at Him in bewilderment. "Make my feet like hinds' feet," she repeated. "How is that possible? And what would the inhabitants of the Kingdom of Love say to the presence of a wretched little cripple with an ugly face and a twisted mouth, if nothing blemished and imperfect may dwell there?"

"It is true," said the Shepherd, "that you would have to be changed before you could live on the High Places, but if you are willing to go with Me, I promise to help you develop hinds' feet. Up there on the mountains, as you get near the real High Places, the air is fresh and invigorating. It strengthens the whole body and there are streams with wonderful healing properties, so that those who bathe in them find all their blemishes and disfigurements washed away.

"But there is another thing I must tell you. Not only would I have to make your feet like hinds' feet, but you would have to receive another name, for it would be as impossible for a Much-Afraid to enter the Kingdom of Love as for any other member of the Fearing family. Are you willing to be changed completely, Much-Afraid, and to be made like the new name which you will receive if you become a citizen in the Kingdom of Love?"

She nodded her head and then said very earnestly, "Yes, I am."

Again he smiled, but added gravely, "There is still one thing more, the most important of all. No one is allowed to dwell in the Kingdom of Love,

Promise of Transformation

READ: Hind's Feet... facing page & **Luke 9:57–62**

"...He also predestined to become conformed to the image of His Son..." — Romans 8:29

" ...and I will give him a white stone, and a new name written on the stone which no one knows but he who receives it." —Revelation 2:17

The Shepherd continues to reveal His provisions and promises to Much-Afraid while dealing with her fears. She has already been in His service for some years and so is not dealing with the problem of resolving to "follow Jesus". The kind of intimate understanding and fellowship Much-Afraid is now receiving is a result of having already entered that door. It is a door we must all enter, perhaps without much supporting explanation from God. He knows what is sufficient for those who have been called.

Much-Afraid does not know she has already been predestined to be conformed to His image. The decisions she still faces are of much the same nature of yearning for God's provisions. She still faces fear and her personal problems. The LORD deals with them, revealing He already has provisions for healing her deformities and also to change her name and nature. Some of the changes are to be "miraculous", through healing with divine waters; others are to be through exercise and practice—and will take time. These are promises for us, as well.

Notice that the same "earnestness", previously studied, is still expressed in Much-Afraid's responses to the Shepherd.

In your walk with Christ, you can probably identify both areas where miraculous healing and change have already taken place and other areas where you struggle to overcome weaknesses and failure. Do you see that the latter areas are for the purpose of developing your dependence upon Him to walk with Him in to the "High Places", while he transforms you?

QUESTIONS AND PRAYER: Do God's miracles of love and power give you a deeper desire to follow Him? Is this true where your weaknesses are exposed to God and others? Do you express gratitude? What is your attitude with Christ today regarding exposing your serious weaknesses? _____

_____

_____

_____

unless they have the flower of Love already blooming in their hearts. Has Love been planted in your heart, Much-Afraid?"

As the Shepherd said this He looked at her very steadily and she realized that His eyes were searching into the depths of her heart and knew all that was there far better than she did herself. She did not answer for a long time, because she was not sure what to say, but she looked rather flinchingly into the eyes which were gazing at her so penetratingly and became aware that they had the power of reflecting what they looked upon.

She could thus really see her own heart as He saw it, so after a long pause she answered, "I think that what is growing there is a great longing to experience the joy of natural, human love and to learn to love supremely one person who will love me in return. But perhaps that desire, natural and right as it seems, is not the Love of which you are speaking?" She paused and then added honestly and almost tremblingly, "I see the longing to be loved and admired growing in my heart, Shepherd, but I don't think I see the kind of Love that you are talking about, at least, nothing like the love which I see in You."

"Then will you let Me plant the seed of true Love there now?" asked the Shepherd. "It will take you some time to develop hinds' feet and to climb to the High Places, and if I put the seed in your heart now it will be ready to bloom by the time you get there."

Much-Afraid shrank back, "I am afraid," she said, "I have been told that if you really love someone you give that loved one the power to hurt and pain you in a way nothing else can."

"That is true," agreed the Shepherd. "To love does mean to put yourself into the power of the loved one and to become very vulnerable to pain, and you are very Much-Afraid of pain, are you not?"

The Pain of Love

READ: Hind's Feet... facing page & John 15:1–13

"Love does not act unbecomingly; it does not seek its own, is not provoked, does not take into account a wrong suffered, does not rejoice in unrighteousness, but rejoices with the truth; bears all things, believes all things, hopes all things, endures all things. Love never fails; ..." —I Corinthians 13:5–8

"...I will greatly multiply your pain in childbirth....." —Genesis 3:16

The Shepherd gives Much-Afraid a penetrating question and gaze regarding whether she has had Love placed in her heart. She is able to give an answer many of us would not admit; that she wants to be loved and admired, but does not have love like that of the Shepherd.

In looking at pain and love, we can see that scripture's curse upon Eve of pain at childbirth is likely not limited only to the moment of birth. It may apply also to the multiplied pain a mother feels throughout the life of a sinful child in a sinful world due to her unique bonding to the child at childbirth. This bonded love gives her little choice but to be committed to the child. Dependable love like this is the love God is talking about. It is love that will not fail and does not depend upon the "lovability" of the loved one.

Few men today achieve this type of bonded love for their wives before marriage. Nothing akin to Christ's death for us or the difficulty of carrying a baby through the pain of childbirth is usually required for a man to win his wife. Has he yet discovered that she is worth any price unto death? If not, the marriage is insecure. Husbands, are you willing to die for your wife as described by Ephesians 5:25–29? Does she know that she will always be most important in your eyes and that your love will never fail them? Single men, are you willing to be bonded to a woman like this?

Can we anticipate what the "bloom of love" is that the Shepherd promises will be ready when Much-Afraid gets to the High Places?

QUESTIONS AND PRAYER: Might God have means of natural "bonding", which draw husband and wife to each other for life?_____

_____

How did God bond Himself to us through Christ?_____

_____

How did we bond to Christ?_____

_____

She nodded miserably and then said shamefacedly, "Yes, very much afraid of it."

"But it is so happy to love," said the Shepherd quietly. "It is happy to love even if you are not loved in return. There is pain too, certainly, but Love does not think that very significant."

Much-Afraid thought suddenly that He had the most patient eyes she had ever seen. At the same time there was something in them that hurt her to the heart, though she could not have said why, but she still shrank back in fear and said (bringing the words out very quickly because somehow she was ashamed to say them), "I would never dare to love unless I were sure of being loved in return. If I let You plant the seed of Love in my heart will You give me the promise that I shall be loved in return? I couldn't bear it otherwise."

The smile He turned on her then was the gentlest and kindest she had ever seen, yet once again, and for the same indefinable reason as before, it cut her to the quick. "Yes," He said, without hesitation, "I promise you, Much-Afraid, that when the plant of Love is ready to bloom in your heart and when you are ready to change your name, then you will be loved in return."

A thrill of joy went through her from heat to foot. It seemed too wonderful to be believed, but the Shepherd Himself was making the promise, and of one thing she was quite sure. He could not lie. "Please plant Love in my heart now," she said faintly. Poor little soul, she was still Much-Afraid even when promised the greatest thing in the world.

The Shepherd put His hand in His bosom, drew something forth, and laid it in the palm of His hand. He held His hand out toward Much-Afraid. "Here is the seed of Love," He said.

She bent forward to look, then gave a startled little cry and drew back. There was indeed a seed lying in the palm of His hand, but it was shaped exactly like a long, sharply-pointed

Love in Return

READ: Hind's Feet... facing page & **John 14:15–24**

"I will put enmity between your seed and her seed; He shall bruise you on the
head, and you shall bruise him on the heel." —Genesis 3:15

"I the LORD your God, am a jealous God, visiting the iniquity of the fathers
on the children, and on the third and the fourth generations
of those who hate Me. —Deuteronomy 5:9

One of God's attributes is reproduction. In both His creation and redemption He reveals that He is a reproducing God and has built this feature into His design of all living
things. Starting with the early verses of Genesis (Genesis 1:20–25) and the creation of man
(Genesis 1:26–28), reproduction of seed "in kind" is a key feature. The first name given to
the Messiah, the redeemer of mankind, is also "her Seed". God also stresses that "whatever
a man sows, this he will also reap" (Galatians 6:7). Love, mercy and all the fruits of the
Spirit reproduce themselves. So does iniquity.

The promise in John 14 is that God, the LORD Jesus Christ and our Father in heaven
respond to our love with their love. Doesn't this seem shocking? Hasn't God already loved
us first? Yes! But there is a greater promise in terms of personal relationship and intimacy
that God promises when we're obedient to Him. Now Much-Afraid is hearing this wonderful promise for the first time.

Husband and wife were made differently from each other in order to mutually comple-
ment each other and support their spouses' weaknesses. Love given to us might not be in
the form we would ask for it, but in areas of our weakness. We are frequently blind to our
weaknesses and don't appreciate how God loves us through parents, spouses, the body of
Christ or others. But a special intimate love is also revealed by God to all who obey Him.
He has promised it.

QUESTIONS AND PRAYER: Do you long to be loved in your areas of need?
How do you respond to the needs of others?_____

_____

How might God reproduce love in your life and in your situation?_____

_____

Who are you truly serving—yourself, God, or others?_____

_____

thorn. Much-Afraid had often noticed that the Shepherd's hands were scarred and wounded, but now she saw that the scar in the palm of the hand held out to her was the exact shape and size of the seed of Love lying beside it.

"The seed looks very sharp," she said shrinkingly. "Won't it hurt if You put it into my heart?"

He answered gently, "It is so sharp that it slips in very quickly. But Much-Afraid, I have already warned you that Love and Pain go together, for a time at least. If you would know Love, you must know Pain, too."

Much-Afraid looked at the thorn and shrank from it. Then she looked at the Shepherd's face and repeated His words to herself. "When the seed of Love in your heart is ready to bloom, you will be loved in return," and a strange new courage entered into her. She suddenly stepped forward, bared her heart, and said, "Please plant the seed here in my heart."

His face lit up with a glad smile and He said with a note of joy in His voice, "Now you will be able to go with Me to the High Places and be a citizen of the Kingdom of My Father."

Then He pressed the thorn into her heart. It was true, just as He had said, it did cause a piercing pain, but it slipped in quickly and then, suddenly, a sweetness she had never felt or imagined before tingled through her. It was bittersweet, but the sweetness was the stronger. She thought of the Shepherd's words, "It is so happy to love," and her pale, sallow cheeks suddenly glowed pink and her eyes shone. For a moment, Much-Afraid did not look afraid at all. The twisted mouth had relaxed into a happy curve, and the shining eyes and pink cheeks made her almost beautiful.

"Thank you, thank you," she cried, and knelt at the Shepherd's feet. "How good You are. How patient You are. There is no one in the whole world as good and kind as You. I will go with You to the mountains. I will trust You to make my feet like hinds' feet, and to set me, even me, upon the High Places."

22

Step of Faith

READ: Hind's Feet... facing page & Hebrews 11:1–6

"For whoever wishes to save his life shall lose it; and whoever loses his life for My sake and the gospel's shall save it." —Mark 8:35

He who loves his life loses it; and he who hates his life in this world shall keep it to life eternal." —John 12:25

Much-Afraid sees the association between the seed of Love and the scars of the Shepherd's hand as He extends it to her. She shrinks at first from its thorny appearance and promise of pain until He answers gently and repeats the association between love and pain—the very thing she has noticed between the scar and the seed. Then, suddenly she *steps forward* and bares her heart to Him! It is a step of faith. His words have overcome her fear and brought her to trust Him.

She has also consciously decided to bear pain, even as all the saints of the Bible have, in faith, in order to respond to God's call. It is however, not a fearful, begrudging response. It is one which has overcome fear and gone beyond compulsion (II Cor.9:7).

There is immediate joy expressed on the part of the Shepherd. Then, following the pain of the seed's insertion, she notices a bitter-sweetness in her she has never felt before. Possibly this is related to a similar effect recorded with Ezekiel (Ezekiel 3:3, 3:14) and John (Revelation 10:8–11) where bitterness is present in the digesting of the word, but sweetness in yielding to it.

Now Much-Afraid portrays all the supernatural effects of receiving God's reproductive "seed", *whenever we receive it in our hearts.* She shows health and beauty; her cheeks glow and eyes shine. She enters into gratitude. Her faith becomes her new reality. All of her emotions also follow obediently.

QUESTIONS AND PRAYER: Does the LORD currently have a promise and call to you that you are reluctant to act upon? What does God say about your concerns in responding? Would it be worthwhile to research this in the scriptures and in prayer? Possibly some follow-up counseling with your brothers or sisters in Christ or with your pastor could resolve this._____

_____

_____

_____

"I am more glad even than you," said the Shepherd, "and now you really act as though you are going to change your name already. But there is one thing more I must tell you. I shall take you to the foot of the mountains Myself, so that there will be no danger from your enemies. After that, two special companions I have chosen will guide and help you on all the steep and difficult places while your feet are still lame and while you can only limp and go slowly.

"You will not see Me all the time, Much-Afraid, for as I told you, I shall be leaping on the mountains and skipping on the hills, and you will not at first be able to accompany Me or keep up with Me. That will come later. However, you must remember that as soon as you reach the slopes of the mountains there is a wonderful system of communication from end to end of the Kingdom of Love, and I shall be able to hear you whenever you speak to Me. Whenever you call for help I promise to come to you at once.

"At the foot of the mountains My two servants whom I have chosen to be your guides will be waiting for you. Remember, I have chosen them Myself, with great care, as the two who are most able to help you and assist you in developing hinds' feet. You will accept them with joy and allow them to be your helpers, will you not?"

"Oh, yes," she answered at once, smiling at Him happily. "Of course I am quite certain that You know best and that whatever You choose is right." Then she added joyfully, "I feel as though I shall never be afraid again."

He looked very kindly at the little shepherdess who had just received the seed of Love into her heart and was preparing to go with Him to the High Places, but also with full understanding. He knew her through and through, in all the intricate labyrinth of her lonely heart, better far than she knew herself. No one understood better than He, that growing into the likeness of a new name is a long process, but He did not say this. He looked with a certain tender pity and compassion

24

Joy Follows Obedience

READ: Hind's Feet... facing page & **Matthew 2:1–10**

"Those who sow in tears shall reap with joyful shouting." —Psalm 126:5

"A joyful heart is good medicine.." —Proverbs 17:22

The story of the three magi (wise men) who came seeking the King of the Jews at the time of His birth is a classic story in faith and joy. They must have come many hundreds of miles and had many doubts and uncertainties regarding the prophecies of the stars, the appearance of the new star in the east, their understanding and obedience to the Spirit of God that was moving them. Then they had to go through political intrigue and danger, as well. Finally, God honored their faith in a rich and personal way. "The star, which they had seen in the east, went on before them, until it came and stood over where the Child was."

Then, "when they saw the star, they rejoiced exceedingly with great joy." This is not a routine type of joy as when your favorite team wins or even possibly as when a child is born. It is fist pounding, hand-slapping, teeth gritting, tear weeping glory!! "Joy inexpressible and full of glory", as Peter put it (I Peter 1:8). No one who has experienced it is ever quite satisfied again without again finding the same obedience and joy with God. Jesus tells us that "joy" is why He came. It is what He taught the disciples in John, chapter 15 about death in loving (John 15:11).

The Shepherd advises Much-Afraid about two companions selected to go with her during her trip to the High Places. Who are these specially chosen companions and why? In addition, it is made clear that the Shepherd does not reveal all that He knows about Much-Afraid, her heart and the process she will go through to grow into the likeness of her new name.

QUESTIONS AND PRAYER: Do you have testimony regarding some extreme moment of joy that God gave you in response to your obedience; a "moment of truth" that tested your faith? Would you write this story below and share it with someone?_____

_____

How do you generally respond to new experiences in trusting God?

_____

_____

at the glowing cheeks and shining eyes which had so suddenly transformed the appearance of plain little Much-Afraid.

Then He said, "Now you may go home and make your preparations for leaving. You are not to take anything with you, only leave everything in order. Do not tell anyone about it, for a journey to the High Places needs to be a secret matter. I cannot now give you the exact time when we are to start for the mountains, but it will be soon, and you must be ready to follow Me whenever I come to the cottage and call. I will give you a secret sign. I shall sing one of the Shepherd's songs as I pass the cottage, and it will contain a special message for you. When you hear it, come at once and follow Me to the trysting place."

Then, as the sun had already gone down in a blaze of red and gold, and the eastern mountains were now veiled in misty mauve and grey, and the shadows were lengthening, He turned and led His flock away toward the sheepfolds.

Much-Afraid turned her face homeward, her heart full of happiness and excitement, but still feeling as though she would never be frightened again. As she started back across the fields she sang to herself one of the songs from an old book of songs which the shepherds often used. Never before had it seemed to her so sweet, so applicable.

"The Song of Songs," the loveliest song,
The song of Love the King,
No joy on earth compares to his,
But seems a broken thing.
His Name as ointment is poured forth,
And all his lovers sing.

Draw me—I will run after thee,
Thou art my heart's one choice,
Oh, bring me to thy royal house,
To dwell there and rejoice.
There in thy presence, O my King,

Patient Love

READ: Hind's Feet... facing page & **Song of Solomon 2:1–13**

"Rejoice, ...for the marriage of the Lamb has come and
His bride has made herself ready." —Revelation 19:7

"To him the doorkeeper opens, and the sheep hear his voice, and He calls
his own sheep by name, and leads them out." —John 10:3

The preparation of the bride of Christ is still in progress and scripture says she, like all brides, is to make herself ready while the Shepherd sets a path for us to follow. His patience to let love develop and draw us; not to overwhelm or force love upon us is a marvel of His character.

We read in verses from Song of Solomon, "I adjure you, O daughters of Jerusalem, by the gazelles or by the hinds of the field, that you will not arouse or awaken my love until she pleases" (2:7, 3:5). We see the whole portrait of gentle wooing, and learning to know each other taking place both in the Song of Solomon and between the Shepherd and Much-Afraid. It is very much a male-female thing. All believers are His Bride. But in this world, men must also emulate the Bridegroom.

Men should appreciate the process by which love comes to full bloom in the heart of a girl —free to love according to the love and trust that is in her heart. Many men have violated the trust of the girls they married because they were not patient or had other priorities. The damage needs to be repaired. Men are involved in the building of a Free Woman.

QUESTIONS AND PRAYER: If you are a man, did (will) your bride see in you prior to marriage the patience and self-denial of the Bridegroom of the Song of Solomon? Of the Shepherd?_____

_____

_____

Are there things in your past you would like to correct? Please discuss these and receive direction from the Lord._____.

_____

What specific things can you recall in your life for which you could praise God right now? _____

_____

To feast and hear thy voice.

Look not upon me with contempt,
Though soiled and marred I be,
The King found me—an outcast thing—-
And set his love on me.
I shall be perfected by Love,
Made fair as day to see.

(Cant. 1:1–6)

She walked singing across the first field and was halfway over the next when suddenly she saw Craven Fear himself coming toward her. Poor Much-Afraid: for a little while she had completely forgotten the existence of her dreadful relatives, and now here was the most dreaded and detested of them all slouching toward her. Her heart filled with a terrible panic. She looked right and left, but there was no hiding place anywhere, and besides it was all too obvious that he was actually coming to meet her, for as soon as he saw her he quickened his pace and in a moment or two was right beside her.

With a horror that sickened her very heart she heard him say, "Well, here you are at last, little Cousin Much-Afraid. So we are to be married, eh, what do you think of that" and he pinched her, presumably in a playful manner, but viciously enough to make her gasp and bite her lips to keep back a cry of pain.

She shrank away from him and shook with terror and loathing. Unfortunately this was the worst thing she could have done, for it was always her obvious fear which encouraged him to continue tormenting her. If only she could have ignored him, he soon would have tired of teasing and of her company and would have wandered off to look for other prey. In all her life, however, Much-Afraid had never been able to ignore Fear. Now it was absolutely beyond her power to conceal the dread which she felt.

28

After the Mountaintop

READ: Hind's Feet... facing page & **Matthew 3:13–4:11**

"Beloved, do not be surprised at the fiery ordeal among you, which comes upon you for your testing, as though some strange things were happening to you." —I Peter 4:12

"But I warn you whom to fear: fear the One who after He has killed has authority to cast into hell; yes, I tell you, fear Him!" —Luke 12:5

There is a cycle of confrontation with evil which occurs following "mountain top" experiences with God. This is reported in scripture and is common in the lives of believers active in their discipleship. Moses experienced extreme trials following his "burning bush" experience. Jesus Christ was painfully tested by Satan following His baptism by John and anointing by the Holy Spirit. When this occurs, don't be dismayed and do not fear (Matt. 10:26, 10:31, John 14:27).

Much-Afraid now has this experience, not realizing that her true desire is not "victory over" fear, but to be rid of circumstances that cause her to fear. She quickly becomes helpless.

What triggers fear? Why do we fear? Jesus identifies fear of death at the root. In the scripture from Luke, above, He says we should only fear God, who alone has authority to give eternal death or life. Fear of death is identified in Hebrews, chapter 2, as the problem finally resolved by the defeat of Satan, who by the work of Christ "has been rendered powerless". We have been delivered from slavery to fear of death.

Beyond this, though, we have lesser things which can lead to fear; fear of pain, loss, insecurity, change, bondage, etc. where we believe we cannot truly "live" in such circumstances. Being controlled by Craven Fear (with the prospects of being married to him and his torment!) causes fear in Much-Afraid. Can we identify with her? She becomes powerless, even to the point of being unable to conceal her dread.

QUESTIONS AND PRAYER: What would you do in Much-Afraid's situation? If you had power to pray what would you pray? _____

_____

Does Jesus have promises for this situation that apply to you? Your family?_____

_____

Her white face and terrified eyes immediately had the effect of stimulating Craven's desire to bait her. Here she was, alone and completely in his power. He caught hold of her, and poor Much-Afraid uttered one frenzied cry of terror and pain. At that moment Craven Fear loosed his grasp and cringed away.

The Shepherd had approached them unperceived and was standing beside them. One look at His stern face and flashing eyes and the stout Shepherd's cudgel grasped in His strong, uplifted hand was more than enough for the bully. Craven Fear slunk away like a whipped cur, actually running from the village instead of toward it, not knowing where he was going, urged by one instinct alone, to find a place of safety.

Much-Afraid burst into tears. Of course she ought to have known that Craven was a coward and that if only she had lifted her voice and called for the Shepherd, he would have fled at once. Now her dress was torn and disordered, and her arms bruised by the bully's grip, yet that was the least part of her distress. She was overwhelmed with shame that she had so quickly acted like her old name and nature, which she had hoped was beginning to be changed already.

It seemed so impossible to ignore the Fearings, still less to resist them. She did not dare look at the Shepherd, but had she done so she would have seen with what compassion He was regarding her. She did not realize that the Prince of Love is "of very tender compassions to them that are afraid." She supposed that, like everybody else, He was despising her for her silly fears, so she muttered a shamed "thank you."

Then, still without looking at Him, she limped painfully toward the village, weeping bitterly as she went and saying over and over again to herself, "What is the use of even thinking of going to the High Places? I could never reach them, for the least little thing is enough to turn me back."

Fear

READ: Hind's Feet... facing page & **Genesis 14–15:1**

"But Thou, O LORD, art a shield about me, My glory and the One who lifts my head."
—Psalm 3:3

"Behold, the LORD's hand is not so short that it cannot save;
neither is His ear so dull that it cannot hear." —Isaiah 59:1

The Chief Shepherd appears at the INSTANT where Craven Fear lays his hand on Much-Afraid. He is a Shield of protection. This is how he also announced Himself to Abraham after Abraham's mountain-top experience in the rescue of Lot and meeting with Melchizedek. Then he was tempted by the King of Sodom to taint the whole victory by a "gift" of the spoils. Abraham risked his life by rejecting the offer—from a King who had already had his pride crushed and was then rescued by a shepherd! However, God soon appeared to Abraham and confirmed Himself as His shield (Gen. 15:1)

The relationship of bullying to fear is evident. It is a characteristic of Satan to bully us through fear, because he has now been defeated and is fearful. All his "demons believe and shudder" (James 2:19) and use fear as a tactic to keep us "frozen", not exercising our authority as children of God. In learning who we are, we should respond just like Much-Afraid, "Of course (I) ought to have known that (Satan) was a coward, and if (I) had only lifted (my) voice and called for the Shepherd, he would have fled at once." There is an important condition, though, which we often fail to meet. Do you know what it is?

The condition is that we must be humbly submitted to God, just like Much-Afraid. Read again James 4:7 and I Peter 5:6–11. The relationship between submittal to God and the power to resist the devil are clear throughout the Bible!

QUESTIONS AND PRAYER: In the first question of the preceding devotional, did you correctly call on the Shepherd? Did you recognize the need to be submitted to God? _____

_____

_____

Is there an area in your life possibly tormented by fear? If so, will you now submit yourself to the LORD in this?_____

_____

However, when at last she reached the security of the cottage she began to feel better, and by the time she had drunk a cup of tea and taken her evening meal she had recovered so far that she was able to remind herself of all that had happened there beside the cascade and the pool. Suddenly she remembered, with a thrill of wonder and delight, that the seed of Love had been planted in her heart. As she thought about it, the same almost intolerable sweetness stole over her, the bittersweet, indefinable but wholly delightful ecstasy of a new happiness.

"It is happy to love," said little Much-Afraid to herself and then she repeated: "It is happy to love." After putting the cottage in order for the night, because she was utterly tired out with all the conflicting emotions of that strange day, she went to bed. Lying there before falling asleep, she sang over and over again to herself another of the lovely songs from the old song book.

> *O thou whom my soul loveth,*
> *Tell me where thou dost feed,*
> *And where thy flocks at noonday*
> *To rest and browse dost lead.*
> *For why should I*
> *By others be,*
> *And not by thee?*
>
> *O fairest among women,*
> *Dost thou indeed not know?*
> *Then lead my little flocklet*
> *The way that my flocks go;*
> *And be to me,*
> *As I to thee,*
> *Sweet company.*

> *(Cant. 1:7,8)*

Then she fell into a heavy, dreamless sleep.

32

Remembrances

READ: Hind's Feet... facing page & **Malachi 3:16–18**

"It is more blessed to give than to receive." —Acts 20:35

"If I give all my possessions to feed the poor, and if I deliver my body to be burned, but do not have love, it profits me nothing." —II Corinthians 13:3

Following her confrontation with Fear and rescue by the Shepherd, Much-Afraid is now drawn into a period of remembrances of "all that had happened" in her mountain top experience. It brings thrills of wonderment and delight, even including a repeat of her emotions and their "almost intolerable sweetness". This is a normal thing for those who take time to meditate on the LORD and His works in their life. It is frequently recorded in the Psalms as well as in the testimony of the apostles in their letters. The written word of the authors frequently breaks out into spontaneous praise of God! Does this describe experiences you have had? How good it is to specifically recall our blessings!

"It is happy to love," says Much-Afraid to herself. The words of God sink into her heart as she meditates upon them. It has been a "strange" day of contrasts and conflicting emotions, a day in which she has made a covenant with the LORD and has the seed of Love now planted in her heart.

A recurring theme with Much-Afraid is her taking the position of "bride" in the biblical Song of Solomon (Canticles) and fellowshipping with the Shepherd portrayed in that book. Men do well to join in fellowship with our Shepherd and Bridegroom in the same fashion. Christ is our Lover of lovers, the "Seed", who has been planted in our heart. In addition, men need to portray the love of Christ to the women and girls He has placed in our protection. Christ desires to love them through the flesh and blood of godly shepherds. This does not come easily, but you may be sure that God does not intend women to live with their visions as figments of their imaginations! Daughters and wives who do not find this in their fathers and husbands are easily tempted to look for it elsewhere.

QUESTIONS AND PRAYER: Men, are you applying what Christ has done in your life to the treatment of your wife? Children? Girl friend? Is I Peter 3:7 your guide?_____

_____

Ask God to show you how a woman views "her Shepherd" in her most vivid visions of a man for her life._____

_____

CHAPTER 2

Fearing Invasion

Much-Afraid woke early the next morning and all her fears were gone. Her first thought was, "Probably sometime today I am to start for the High Places with the Shepherd." This so excited her that she could hardly eat her breakfast, and as she began making arrangements for her departure, she could not help singing.

It seemed to her that ever since the seed of Love had been planted in her heart, songs of joy were welling up in her innermost being. And the songs which best expressed this new happiness and thankfulness were from the old book which the shepherds so loved to use as they worked among the flocks and led them to the pastures. As she carried out the simple arrangements the Shepherd had told her to make, she sang another of these songs.

> *Now when the King at the table sits,*
> *My spikenard smelleth sweet,*
> *And myrrh and camphire from my store*
> *I pour upon his feet,*
> *My thankful love must be displayed,*
> *He loved and wooed a beggar maid.*
>
> *Ye daughters of Jerusalem,*
> *I'm black to look upon*
> *As goatskin tents; but also as*
> *The tent of Solomon.*
> *Without, I bear the marks of sin,*
> *But Love's adorning is within.*

A Bride's Joyful Anticipation

READ: Hind's Feet... facing page & **Song of Solomon 1**

"But whoever drinks of the water that I shall give him shall never thirst; but the water that I shall give him shall become in him a well of water springing up to eternal life." —John 4:14

"Then we who are alive and remain shall be caught up together with them in the clouds to meet the LORD in the air, and thus we shall always be with the LORD." —I Thessalonians 4:17

Jewish marriage customs had the bride betrothed to her bridegroom an extended period prior to the wedding. Then he would come for her, usually during the night at a time she did not know. She was to be prepared and ready for the call of the bridegroom. This picture is used in Jesus' parable of the wise and foolish maidens (Matthew 25:1–13) and is also a picture of how Christ will come for his bride, the church, at the end of the age. He will come for us at a time we do not know, but we are to be prepared in happy anticipation!

The Song of Solomon is a depiction of the heart's greatest affections of love, expressed as rapturous human love. It was probably written by Solomon, in association with one of the few women he married with whom he had truly rapturous romantic love. His marvelous poetry is also recognized as prophetic and descriptive of the longing between Christ and His bride and is to be fulfilled at our calling away and at the marriage supper of the Lamb. It is this somewhat modified poetry that Hannah Hurnard uses in her allegory of Much-Afraid's simple, joyful preparations and singing in happy anticipation of the Shepherd's call.

The LORD has told us to prepare by making disciples of the nations (including ourselves; Matt. 28:19), purifying ourselves (II Cor.7:1, Rev.19:7–8) and in happy thanksgivings to God (Phil. 4:4–7). For He Himself has called us and sent the Holy Spirit working in us to perfect us (II Tim. 1:9, Phil. 1:6).

QUESTIONS AND PRAYER: Do you agree that girls carry this poetic vision of matrimony in their own hearts? Where do you think it comes from?_____ ____

_____

_____

How can we enhance and protect it from damage? Do you have girls whom you need to protect or for whom you could intercede in prayer?_____

_____

Despise me not that I am black,
The sun hath burned my face,
My mother's children hated me,
And drove me from my place.
In their vineyards I toiled and wept.
But mine own vineyard have not kept.

I am not fair save to the King,
Though fair my royal dress,
His kingly grace is lavished on
My need and worthlessness.
My blemishes he will not see
But loves the beauty that shall be.

(Cant. 1:12–15,5,6)

From time to time as she went about her work her heart fluttered, half with excitement, half with dread of the unknown, but whenever she remembered the thorn in her heart, she tingled from head to foot with the same mysterious sweetness. Love was for her, too, even for her, crippled little Much-Afraid. When she reached the High Places she was to lose her humiliating disfigurements and be made beautiful, and when the plant in her heart was ready to bloom she was to be loved in return. Even as she thought of this, doubt mingled with the sweetness. Surely it could not possibly be true; just a beautiful dream, but not reality.

"Oh, I am afraid it won't ever happen," she would say to herself, and then, when she thought of the Shepherd, her heart quickened again and she would run to the door or window to see if He were coming to call her.

The morning wore on and still He had not come, but just after midday something else came: an invasion by her terrible relatives. All of a sudden, before she realized what was happening, they were upon her. There was tramping of feet and a clamor of voices and then she was surrounded by a whole army of aunts and uncles and cousins.

Expectations

READ: Hind's Feet... facing page & James 1:1–8

"Behold, I tell you a mystery; we shall not all sleep, but we shall all be changed, in a moment, in the twinkling of an eye, at the last trumpet; for the trumpet will sound, and the dead will be raised imperishable, and we shall be changed."
—I Corinthians 15:51–52

Much-Afraid continues excitedly in her work in preparation for the call of the Chief Shepherd, reviewing all the wonderful promises He has made to her. She marvels that Love is for her, too and that she will be loved in return. In the midst of her thoughts, doubt enters. "Surely it could not possibly be true; just a beautiful dream, but not reality."

Doubts rob us of the power of our faith. A double-minded man cannot expect to "receive anything from the LORD." This particular doubt of Much-Afraid inhibits (1) the power of faith of a believer to receive the promises of God and (2) the power of a young woman to believe that God has a special man of her dreams who will be her "knight-in-shining-armor". This is the vision that she has dreamed about since she was a little girl. God is able to fulfill this dream for her, but it can easily be shattered by failure to protect the daughter and the dream from doubts and destruction. Giving up on this vision will cause the girl to settle for second or third best from men who do not have her best interests at heart. It is important for fathers to build the expectation of this vision and to be the guide and protector of their daughters during their years of expectation and preparation. Girls should have no doubt that they have a bridegroom from God who will come for them, and that their dads are on their side in assuring success both before and after he appears.

QUESTIONS AND PRAYER: How did you respond to the movies, "Beauty and the Beast", "Snow White", or other stories which depict the girl being rescued at the risk of death (or actual death) by a man who demonstrates his love for her?_____

_____

_____

Do you agree that this actually depicts the story of the gospel written in a girl's heart? Do you have girls for whom you can apply this?_____

_____

_____

Other thoughts?_____

_____

Craven, however, was not with them. The family, hearing of his reception the evening before, and realizing that she shrank from him with peculiar dread and terror, had decided that it would not be wise to take him with them.

They were determined to overrule Much-Afraid's objections to the marriage, and if possible get her out of the cottage and into one of their own dwelling places. Their plan was to make a bold attack while she would be alone in the cottage and the Shepherd far away with his flocks, so they hoped she would be at their mercy. She could not be forcibly abducted in broad daylight; there were too many of the Shepherd's servants in the village who would instantly come to her assistance.

However, they knew Much-Afraid's timidity and weakness and they believed that, if there were enough of them present, they could cow her into consenting to go with them to the Mansion of old Lord Fearing. Then they would have her in their power.

The old Lord himself was actually with them, assuring her in a fatherly tone of voice that they had come with the kindness and friendliest intentions. He understood that she had some objections to the proposed marriage, and he wanted to have the opportunity of quietly talking them over with her, to see if he could set them at rest. It seemed to him that it was a suitable and attractive match in every way and that there must be some extraordinary misconceptions in her mind which a little understanding talk together would set right. If not, he assured her kindly, he would not permit her to be married against her will.

When he had finished, a babble of other Fearing voices broke in, reasoning with her and making all sorts of suggestions. The fact was, they told her, that she had cut herself off from her relatives for so long, it was now quite apparent that she had all kinds of strange notions about their feelings and intentions toward her. It was really only right that she should now spend a little time with them and thus give them the opportunity of proving that she had misjudged and misunderstood them.

The Assault of the World

READ: Hind's Feet... facing page & I Corinthians 2

"His speech was smoother than butter, but his heart was war; his words were
softer than oil, yet they were drawn swords." —Psalm 55:21

"See to it that no one takes you captive through empty deception,
according to the tradition of men, according to the elementary principles
of the world, rather than according to Christ." —Colossians 2:8

The entry of Much-Afraid's family and their ensuing persuasions to bring her into their
power portray techniques and strategy of the evil one to distract, deceive and draw us away
from our decisions for Christ—our many decisions and goals that are part of our discipleship and walk with Him. Tongues "dripping with oil" talk to her with "sweet reasonable-
ness" according to the ways of the world. How easy it would be to compromise and reduce
confrontation. A "babel of other voices" compete to "reason" and "suggest" alternatives. But
we are warned that such wisdom is of the world, and though it may seem right, it produces
death (Proverbs 14:12).

Subtle speech "smoother than butter" by the enemy posing as a gentle father, tempt
her to depart from her decision to follow the Shepherd. "It's now quite apparent that she
had all kinds of strange notions about their feelings and intentions toward her." Wouldn't it
would only be "right" that she should now spend a little time with them and give them the
opportunity to prove she has misjudged them. Does that sound similar to words and persuasions that have diverted you from your decisions and dedication to Christ? Have they
dulled your effectiveness or availability for Him?

As the bride of Christ, we are like Eve; only too easy to deceive with words, especially
when we have no protecting "shield"; no confirmation of truth through multiple witnesses
or without support of others.

QUESTIONS AND PRAYER: What means have you established for using the
wisdom and strength of others to sort truth from lies? To pray? To stand firm?_____

_____

_____

What steps can you take to protect your discipleship through confirming "everything through two or three witnesses"? _____

_____

_____

Craven might not be just as handsome and pleasing in appearance as a prince in a fairy tale, and it was true that he had, unfortunately, rather a rough manner, but that was because he had known nothing of the softening and refining influences of marriage. Certainly the responsibilities and joys of married life would quickly alter this, and would indeed effect a transformation in him. It was to be her delightful privilege to assist as principal mover in bringing about this reformation which they all so eagerly wished to see.

The whole gang talked on and on, while poor Much-Afraid sat cowering in their midst, almost too dazed to know what they were saying and suggesting. Just as they had hoped, they were gradually bringing her to a state of bewilderment and incoherent fear. It looked as though they would soon be able to persuade her that it was her duty to attempt the impossible task of trying to convert Craven Fear into something less objectionable than he really was. Suddenly there came an interruption from without.

The Fearings had carefully closed the door when they entered the cottage and even contrived to bolt it, so that Much-Afraid could not escape. Now came the distant sound of a man's voice raised in song, singing one of the songs from the old book which Much-Afraid knew and loved so well. Then the singer Himself came in view, slowly passing along the lane. It was the Chief Shepherd, already leading His flock to the watering place. The words floated in through the open window, accompanied by the soft bleating of the sheep and the scuffling of many little dusty feet as they pattered after Him.

It seemed as though all other sounds were hushed to stillness on that quiet summer afternoon as the Shepherd sang while passing the cottage. Inside, the clamor of voices had ceased instantly and was succeeded by a silence which could be felt. This is what He sang:

The Voice of my Beloved!
Through all my heart it thrills,
He leaps upon the mountains,
And skips upon the hills.

40

Testing

READ: Hind's Feet... facing page & **I Samuel 17:1–50**

"And we know that God causes all things to work together for good to those who love God, to those who are called according to His purpose." —Romans 8:28

"For it is God who is at work in you, both to will and to work for His good pleasure." —Philippians 2:13

The fearful scene continues with the "Fearing Family" tormenting Much-Afraid with their reasoning and persuasions. We anticipate already that deliverance may soon be at hand for Much-Afraid, but have no idea how it might come. We also have a ringside seat to observe closely a process by which evil is illustrated to be limited by God while being used for good in shaping Much-Afraid into the image of the Shepherd.

We observe that Much-Afraid is completely overwhelmed by events and does not perceive that the Shepherd might have a hand in these affairs. The reader may have some perception of limits upon evil which threatens her and of Much-Afraid's inability to "see" through the eye of faith. Nevertheless, we identify with her because we know we are like her and often interpret circumstances in a way that leaves God's sovereignty, purposes, power and love completely out of the picture.

One temptation given to Much-Afraid is a common lie believed by many women; that they have the "delightful privilege" to reform their husbands. Some enter marriage with this deception. Many would deny they ever have believed this lie, but it is a common error in marriage to think one can change a spouse. Only God can change people (much more difficult than changing circumstances!). Yet he does promise to change the hearts of our enemies when our ways become pleasing to Him (Proverbs 16:7).

When Much-Afraid is almost lost in her helplessness, comes the Shepherd walking through the valley with His sheep. He sings His song of love, at which all else stills.

QUESTIONS AND PRAYER: Describe your perceptions that God is in control of events and people, even the evil, that is allowed into your life?_____

_____

_____

How might you improve your attitude and prayers when severe pain or hardship arises?_____

_____

For like a roe or young hart,
So swift and strong is he,
He looketh through my window,
And beckoneth unto me.

"Rise up, my love, fair one,
And come away with me,
Gone are the snows of winter,
The rains no more we see.

"The flowers are appearing,
The little birds will sing,
The turtle dove is calling,
Through all the land 'tis spring.

"The shoots are on the grapevines,
The figs are on the tree,
Arise, my love, my fair one,
And come away with me.

"Why is my dove still hiding?
When all things else rejoice,
Oh, let me see thee, fair one,
Oh let me hear thy voice."

(Cant. 2:8–14)

As she sat listening at the cottage, Much-Afraid knew with a pang of agonizing pain that the Shepherd was calling her to go with Him to the mountains. This was the secret signal He had promised, and He had said that she must be ready to leave instantly, the moment she heard it. Now here she was, locked inside her own cottage, beleaguered by her terrible Fears and unable to respond in any way to His call or even to give any sign of her need.

There was one moment indeed, when the song first started and everyone was startled into silence, when she might have called to Him to come and help her.

42

Song of Love

READ: Hind's Feet... facing page & **Ephesians 1**

"He encircled him, He cared for him, He guarded him as the
pupil of His eye." —Deuteronomy 32:10

The LORD is my light and my salvation; whom shall I fear? The LORD
is the defense of my life; whom shall I dread?" —Psalm 27:1

All rescue is accomplished by the extension of love in mercy. We seldom comprehend love; it is perhaps impossible to even conceive of love until we have received it in a form which delivers us from something in which we are trapped and helpless. Sin is the most insidious trap because it lies about its own character and its consequences. Nevertheless, it is in salvation alone that we may come to fully comprehend (touch and lay hold of) the strong love and kind intentions of God for each of us through Jesus Christ. That surpassing knowledge (Ephesians 3:19) sets us free.

How little God receives from us for all His songs of love through the ages and in our every-day moments. Yet how great is His love that He continues to pour it out upon us and find full joy and satisfaction in it! Hear the poetic beauty and hearken as the bride to the song of our Lover. We are the apple of His eye; the most precious part of His creation and Being!

How many moments can we recall where we have experienced a miraculous deliverance from death or serious catastrophe? Or providential help that was too specific and timely to call a mere "coincidence"? Can we recall the specific moment of salvation when we realized that God was alive and loved us?

Much-Afraid hears the call of her Shepherd and agonizes over her helplessness. She carries for a brief moment a mere mustard "seed" of an idea of escape that occurs to her, but it quickly vanishes. It appears to her there is no way of escape.

QUESTIONS AND PRAYER: What other scriptures do you know that promise of "escape" from defeat? _____

_____

Can you recall at least one instance where God confirmed such a word in your life through faith in Him?_____

_____

Are there now any circumstances in your life where you need this assurance?_____

_____

She did not realize that the Fearings were holding their breath lest she did call, and had she done so, they would have fled helter-skelter through the door. However, she was too stunned with fear to seize the opportunity, and then it was too late.

The next moment she felt Coward's heavy hand laid tightly over her mouth, then other hands gripped her firmly and held her in the chair. So the Shepherd slowly passed the cottage, "showing Himself at the window," and singing the signal song, but receiving no response of any kind.

When He had passed and the words of the song and the bleating of the sheep had died away in the distance, it was found that Much-Afraid had fainted. Her cousin Coward's gagging hands had half-choked her. Her relatives would dearly have liked to seize this opportunity and carry her off while she was unconscious, but as this was the hour when everybody was returning from work it was too dangerous. The Fearings decided therefore that they would remain in the cottage until darkness fell, then gag Much-Afraid and carry her off unperceived.

When this plan had been decided upon, they laid her upon the bed to recover as best she might, while some of the aunts and cousins went out into the kitchen to see what provisions for refreshing themselves might be plundered. The men sat smoking in the sitting room, and Gloomy was left to guard the half-conscious victim in the bedroom.

Gradually Much-Afraid regained her senses, and as she realized her position she nearly fainted again with horror. She dared not cry out for help, for all her neighbors would be away at their work; but were they? No, it was later than she had thought, for suddenly she heard the voice of Mrs. Valiant, her neighbor in the cottage next door. At the sound, Much-Afraid braced herself for one last desperate bid for escape.

Gloomy was quite unprepared for such a move, and before she realized what was happening, Much-Afraid sprang from the bed and shouted through the window as loudly as

Rescue from Fears

READ: Hind's Feet... facing page & **Psalm 20**

"No temptation has overtaken you but such as is common to man; and God is faithful, who will not allow you to be tempted beyond what you are able, but with the temptation will provide the way of escape also, that you may be able to endure it." —I Corinthians 10:13

"Whoever will call upon the name of the LORD will be saved." —Romans 10:13

The ordeal of testing by fire should not be underestimated or "put down". It is fiery as the testing of Daniel by lions or of Shadrach, Meshach and Abednego by fire. When released, however, all those delivered testified that God had sent help to them during their trial.

All who follow God will be led into tribulation and trials. These are the paths of righteousness (i.e., His, not ours!) which demonstrate the LORD's power, love, purpose, and holiness to the world.

In the two examples above from the book of Daniel, one person underwent trial alone, the other three had each other's company. We can choose to be alone or to be linked together with others. "A cord of three strands is not quickly torn apart" (Ecclesiastes 4:12). Sometimes we have such a choice, but sometimes there are no choices if we are to remain faithful. Establishing such faith is God's major work on the face of the earth and is the key question awaiting resolution in the heavens: "When the Son of Man comes, will He find faith on the earth" (Luke 18:8)?

If deliverance were easy, we could be deceived that it was our own work. But God's promises to deliver are based upon His work in us! Much-Afraid is now drawn by her revived "mustard seed" idea to shout from the window!

QUESTIONS AND PRAYER: In author Hurnard's mind, who or what is it that you think she is attempting to portray as Much-Afraid springs to the window?_____

_____

_____

Do you feel familiar with the Holy Spirit directing your path? Please write down an example you recall._____

_____

_____

her fear permitted, "Valiant! Valiant! Come and help me. Come quickly. Help!"

At the sound of her first cry, Mrs. Valiant looked across the garden and caught a glimpse of Much-Afraid's white, terrified face at the window and of her hand beckoning entreatingly. The next moment the face was jerked away from view and a curtain suddenly drawn across the window. That was enough for Mrs. Valiant, whose name described her exactly. She hurried straight across to her neighbor's cottage and tried the door, but finding it locked, she looked in through a window and saw the room full of Much-Afraid's relatives.

Mrs. Valiant was not the sort of person to be the least intimidated by what she called, "a pack of idle Fears." Thrusting her face right in through the window, she cried in a threatening voice, "Out of this house you go, this minute, every one of you. If you have not left in three seconds, I shall call the Chief Shepherd. This cottage belongs to Him, and won't you catch it if He finds you here."

The effect of her words was magical. The door was unbolted and thrown open and the Fearings poured out pell-mell, tumbling over one another in their haste to get away. Mrs. Valiant smiled grimly as she watched their ignominious flight. When the last one had scuttled away she went into the cottage to Much-Afraid, who seemed quite overcome with fear and distress. Little by little she learned the story of those hours of torment and the plan to kidnap the poor victim after darkness fell.

Mrs. Valiant hardly knew herself what it was to feel fear, and had just routed the whole gang of Fearings single-handed. She felt much inclined to adopt a bracing attitude and to chide the silly girl for not standing up to her relatives at once, boldly repulsing them before they got her into their clutches. But as she looked at the white face and terrified eyes and saw the quaking body of poor Much-Afraid, she checked herself. "What is the use of saying it? She can't act upon it, poor thing; she is one of them herself and has got Fearing in the blood, and when the enemy is within you it's a poor prospect. I think

Valiant and Un-Afraid

READ: Hind's Feet... facing page & **Psalm 91:1–16**

"In God, whose word I praise, In God I have put my trust; I shall
not be afraid. What can mere man do to me?" —Psalm 56:4

"But Jesus, overhearing what was being spoken, said to the synagogue
official, 'Do not be afraid any longer, only believe.' " —Mark 5:36

Much-Afraid calls upon someone with quite a different character toward fear than hers. Mrs. Valiant hardly knows herself what it is to feel fear and routs "the whole gang of Fearings single-handed". She uses some important ideas in her words to the spirits of fear and in her subsequent ministry to Much-Afraid.

One of these is Mrs. Valiant's recognition that the house of Much-Afraid belongs to the Chief Shepherd. This is true for the homes of all believers, but is often unrecognized. Dedication of homes to Christ resolves that they shall be places of peace, restoration and protection, and assists in discerning enemy spirits which enter and disturb. This in turn helps men, in particular, to be alert to the corrective actions needed to insure everything entering "under our roof" is compatible with peace and protection.

Following banishment of fear by Mrs. Valiant, "who hardly knows fear", she discerns that Much-Afraid is in such bondage to fear that it would do no good to chide her, even though her fear is truly silly. She recognizes that Much-Afraid has a 'stronghold' such as Paul describes in II Corinthians 10:4–5, which needs to be torn down with weapons of spiritual warfare and is best left to the Chief Shepherd, rather than undertaking it herself. As a result Mrs. Valiant extends, in effect, "mercy" over "judgment" to Much-Afraid. This is one of the most powerful concepts upon which the Kingdom of God is founded (see James 4:13).

QUESTIONS AND PRAYER: How have you dedicated your home to the LORD
and resolved that it shall be a place of peace and protection?_____

_____

How you would respond if someone were to enter your home and cause strife?_____

_____

How do you regard your own actions that produce tears or anger in your home?____

_____

no one but the Shepherd Himself can really help her," she reflected.

So instead of an admonition, she patted the trembling girl and said with all the kindness of her motherly heart, "Now, my dear, while you are getting over your fright, I'll just pop into the kitchen and make a good cup of tea for both of us and you'll feel better at once. My! If they haven't been in here and put the kettle on for us," she added, as she opened the kitchen door and found the cloth already on the table and the preparations for the plundered meal which the unwanted visitors had so hastily abandoned.

"What a pack of harpies," she muttered angrily to herself, then smiled complacently as she remembered how they had fled before her.

By the time they had drunk their tea and Mrs. Valiant had energetically cleared away the last trace of the unwelcome invaders, Much-Afraid had nearly recovered her composure. Darkness had long since fallen, and now it was much too late for her to go to the pool to keep tryst with the Shepherd and explain why she had not responded to His call. She would have to wait for the morning light.

So at Mrs. Valiant's suggestion, as she was feeling utterly exhausted, she went straight to bed. Her neighbor saw her safely tucked in, and kissed her warmly and reassuringly. Indeed, she offered to sleep in the cottage herself that night, but Much-Afraid, knowing that she had a family waiting for her at home, refused the kind offer. However, before leaving, Mrs. Valiant placed a bell beside the bed and assured her that if anything alarmed her in the night she had only to ring the bell and the whole Valiant family would be over instantly to assist her. Then she went away and Much-Afraid was left alone in the cottage.

Propitiation

READ: Hind's Feet... facing page & **Genesis 45:1–26**

"Therefore, He had to be made like His brethren in all things, that He might become a merciful and faithful high priest in things pertaining to God, to make propitiation for the sins of the people." —Hebrews 2:17

"And He Himself is the propitiation for our sins; and not for ours only, but also for those of the whole world." —I John 2:2

A continuing theme we will see more of in the story of Much-Afraid (and in our own lives) is the great power of God to *propitiate* all things for good. This vital and phenomenal power of God is illustrated in the story of Joseph, where what was meant for evil turned out to have been intended by God from the beginning to extend mercy and save life. A close look at the word shows its root idea is to make something *positive*, as in the case of promotion, provision, progress, etc.. Propitiation therefore reflects much greater power than expiation, which merely means to erase or remove. Yes, God propitiates our sin and its results, using it for good in lives called by God (Romans 8:28). Ours is a God of awesome power, character and glory!

Following the flight of the Fearings, Mrs. Valiant humbly decides to leave work on Much-Afraid's "stronghold" of fear to the Shepherd. Then, as the first of many such examples, she discovers that the preparations of the Fearings to plunder a meal instead ease the effort needed to minister to Much-Afraid. She sees the hand of the LORD on their behalf. How marvelous to walk with eyes such as these!

Before leaving, Mrs. Valiant makes a very practical provision to help Much-Afraid call for help again, if necessary. Much-Afraid begins to nurture the idea that it is "too late" to respond to the Shepherd's call.

QUESTIONS AND PRAYER: How have you been the recipient of help like Much-Afraid received from Mrs. Valiant? _____

_____

How can you reproduce this seed in others?_____

_____

How do you desire to do this?_____

_____

*Note: Many modern translations of the Bible no longer incorporate this word or seem to recognize its significance as an attribute of God on our behalf.

CHAPTER 3

Flight in the Night

For hours poor Much-Afraid lay sleepless on her bed, too bruised in mind and body to rest in one position, but tossing and turning wearily from side to side until long after midnight. Somewhere at the back of her mind was a dreadful uneasiness, as though there was something she ought to remember, but was unable to do so. When at last she fell asleep this thought still haunted her.

She woke suddenly an hour or two later, her mind intensely alert, conscious of an agonizing pain such as she had never known before. The thorn in her heart was throbbing and aching in a manner she could scarcely bear. It was as though the pain was hammering out something which at first she was still too confused to be able to understand. Then, all of a sudden, in a terrible flash, it became clear to her, and she found herself whispering over and over again, "The Shepherd came and called me as He promised, but I didn't go to Him or give any answer. Supposing He thought that I had changed my mind and didn't want to go with Him. Supposing He has gone and left me behind! Gone without me! Yes, left me behind!"

The shock of this thought was awful. This was the thing she had forgotten. He would not be able to understand why she had not gone out to Him as He had told her.

He had urged her to be ready to go with Him the instant that He called, that there must be no delay, that He himself had to go to the mountains on urgent business. She had not been able to go even to the trysting place as usual that evening.

Night Watch

READ: Hind's Feet... facing page & **I Samuel 3**

"When I remember Thee on my bed, I meditate on Thee in the night watches."
—Psalm 63:6

"Nathaniel said to Him, 'How do You know me?' Jesus answered and said to Him, 'Before Philip called you, when you were under the fig tree, I saw you.' " —John 1:48

Instead of sleeping the sleep of the emotionally exhausted, Much-Afraid lies sleepless, with a nagging feeling she has forgotten something. After finally falling asleep, she awakens suddenly. The thorn of love in her heart is throbbing and aching.

God often speaks to us in the "night watches". If, as Samuel, we don't have sheep to tend as did the shepherds of old, the LORD will awaken us to talk to us. Old Eli recognized this and instructed Samuel to respond. Whether or not He is talking to us, He fully understands, knows and loves us. Now the Shepherd is dealing in a brand new way with Much-Afraid, yet without her being aware of the fact that He is with her.

Weaknesses frequently cause us to fall short of the mark, yet God is always propitiating and dealing with us in some fashion that is "exceedingly abundant beyond anything that we ask or think" (Eph.3:20). As a Royal King and perfect gentleman, He never forces Himself upon us, but humbly waits upon us, knowing our poor frames, that "we are but dust" (Ps. 103:14). Yet, He always magnificently works through this, knowing everything about us, as well, and is victorious over our weaknesses.

The love in Much-Afraid's heart convicts her of having failed to respond to the Shepherd. She has mixed conversation with herself, recognizing that He kept His promise, but that she did not. Not appreciating His perfect knowledge, she "thinks" that He might have misunderstood why she did not respond. She "fears" that she has been left behind, but will soon discover the power of this type of love and "Godly fear" to overcome all other fears.

QUESTIONS AND PRAYER: What is the nature of some of the things God has taken up with you during "night watches" in which He has awakened and given you revelation and direction? _____

_____

How does this type of personal attention and love influence you?_____

_____

Of course He would think that she was afraid. Perhaps He was gone already and alone. Much-Afraid turned icy cold and her teeth chattered, but it was the pain in her heart which was the most awful part of her distress. It seemed to suffocate her as she lay there in bed. She sat up, shivering with cold and with the horror of the thought. She could not bear it if He had gone and left her behind.

On the table beside her lay the old song book. Glancing down at it in the light of the lamp, she saw it was open at the page whereon was written a song about another shepherdess. She, just like herself, had failed to respond to the call of love and then found, too late, that Love had gone away.

It had always seemed to her such a sad song that she could hardly read it, but now as she read the words again in the dark loneliness of the night, it seemed as though it was the cry of her own forlorn and terrified heart.

> *By night on my bed I sought him,*
> *He whom my soul loveth so.*
> *I sought—but I could not find him,*
> *And now I will rise and go—-*
>
> *Out in the streets of the city,*
> *And out on the broad highway;*
> *For he whom my soul so loveth,*
> *Hath left me and gone away.*

The page in the little song book ended there, and she did not turn the leaf. Suddenly she could bear the uncertainty no longer. She must see for herself at once if He really had gone away and left her behind. She slipped out of bed, dressed herself as quickly as her shaking fingers would permit, and then unlocked the cottage door. She, too, would go out into the street and the broad highway and would see if she could find Him, would see if He had gone and left her behind, or—oh, if only it were possible—if He had waited to give her another chance.

Love Calls

READ: Hind's Feet... facing page & **I John 4:11–18**

"My beloved responded and said to me, 'Arise, my darling, my beautiful one, and come along.' " —Song of Solomon 2:10

"For now we see in a mirror dimly, but then face to face; now I know in part, but then I shall know fully just as I also have been fully known." —I Corinthians 13:12

Love is working now in Much-Afraid's heart even before she recognizes the relationship between its pain and its power working in her. As a bride, she is responding to her lover's call to her by experiencing and responding to the pain in her heart. This is the common characteristic of all love, starting with first love and carrying all the way through life to mature *agape* in the likeness of God's.

From an early age, a bride's heart is prepared for the love spoken of in Song of Solomon, verse 3:1. Girls seek the true lover that will call them away, who will overcome obstacles and slay a "dragon" to set them free, and who will remain forever faithful. That God has placed the gospel of the Savior in the hearts of girls is a wonderful mystery; one from which men should draw many lessons in what is required of the bridegroom.

One of her first discoveries (although it might not be termed so much her discovery as ours as we observe her), is that this love has cast out her fear of the Fearings. "Perfect love casts out fear."

Provided a girl is pursuing the true Bridegroom, her faith and search for Him will not be disappointed. However, the powerful love response present in the hearts of all girls can lead them into dangerous situations where the risks associated with "a young woman going out to seek her lover", without a man's protection, can result in terrible damage and grief.

QUESTIONS AND PRAYER: How many daughters or younger sisters are you responsible to protect? Please list their names._____

_____

_____

How might you affirm and provide safety and encouragement to them in their search for their bridegroom, without the dangers of their "searching the city at night"?_____

_____

Opening the door, she went out into the darkness. A hundred Craven Fears lurking in the lonely street could not have deterred her at that moment, for the pain in her heart swallowed up fear and everything else and drove her forth. So in the dark hours, just before the dawn, Much-Afraid started off to look for the Shepherd.

She could not go quickly because of her lameness, but limped along the village streets toward the open fields, and the sheepfolds. As she went she whispered to herself, "O Shepherd, when You said that Love and pain go together, how truly You spoke."

Had she but known or even dimly sensed what it would be like, would she, could she, possibly have consented to let Him put the thorn in her heart? It was too late now; it was there. Love was there and pain, too and she must find the Shepherd. At last, limping and breathless, she came to the sheepfolds, still and silent in the dim starlight. One or two undershepherds were there, keeping watch over the flocks through the night, and when they heard footsteps approaching they rose up from the ground and went to meet the intruder.

"Who are you?" they challenged her in the darkness, then stared in amazement as their lanterns flashed on the white face and frightened eyes of Much-Afraid.

"Is the Chief Shepherd here?" She gasped as she leaned against the wall of the sheepfold, panting and trying to recover her breath.

"No," said the watchman, staring at her curiously. "He left the flocks in our charge this night and gave His orders. He said that He had to make a journey to the mountains, as He often does, and did not say when He would be back."

Much-Afraid could not speak. She moaned and pressed her hands to her heart, feeling as though it would break. What could she do now? He was gone. He had thought that she did not want to go and had not waited for her. Then, aching

Death of a Dream

READ: Hind's Feet... facing page & **Genesis 37:1–20**

"Ask, and it shall be given to you; seek, and you shall find; knock,
and it shall be opened to you." —Matthew 7:7

"And without faith it is impossible to please Him, for he who comes to God must
believe that He is, and that He is a rewarder of those who seek Him." —Hebrews 11:6

There is another scriptural pattern that we personally experience in our walk with Christ. That is the "death" of our dreams, wishes and ambitions. Many of these visions, wishes and dreams are actually from the LORD, but we shall not be free to experience God's power in their fulfillment until they are put to death, given up through the crushing weight of circumstances and disillusion. Visions not from God will die forever. Those from Him will be miraculously resurrected!

Joseph is one of many biblical characters who saw their "dreams" die. Abraham, Moses, Daniel, Paul and others experienced it, as did the disciples when Jesus was crucified. But all were resurrected!

Much-Afraid "discovers" that the pain in her heart "swallows" up fear and drives her forth to seek the Shepherd. She "discovers" also the association between love and pain and, (as do all of us) that much of the pain we experience goes far beyond that which we could have guessed or willingly consented to in following commitments to love. This surprise can be said to be one of the true discoveries of love, and a continuing one, starting with marriage and extending into our deeper walk with God and with our spouses and children. More is always demanded in response to love than we bargained for. Love is not a thing to be bargained for!

Much-Afraid comes to her destination and is crushed with the discovery that the Shepherd is not there. He has gone, without her. She feels as though her heart will break. What can she do now?

QUESTIONS AND PRAYER: Do you have a personal vision that has been put to death, perhaps right now? Please write it down. _____
_____

What is God's promise of resurrection to you?_____
_____

How do you bargain for love to attempt to minimize its pain? _____
_____

with despair, as she leaned trembling against the wall of the fold, she remembered the Shepherd's face and the loving-kindness of the look with which He had invited her to accompany him to the mountains.

It came to her mind that He who understood her so well, who knew all about her fears and had compassion on her, would not leave until He was quite sure that she really meant to refuse to go with Him. She lifted her eyes, looked across the Valley toward the eastern mountains and the high places. A faint streak of light was appearing in the east, and she knew that soon the sun would rise. Suddenly she remembered the last verse of the sad song which she had read, the last verse on the page which she had not waited to turn over. It came whispering into her mind just as a little bird began to sing in one of the bushes beside her.

> *And then—in the dawn I saw him,*
> *He whom my heart loveth so.*
> *I found him, held him and told him*
> *I never could let him go.*
>
> (Cant. 3:1–5)

Much-Afraid ceased trembling and said to herself, "I will go to the trysting-place, and see if He is waiting for me there." With scarcely a word to the watch-men she turned and hurried southward, over the field where Craven Fear had met her toward the sheep pool. Almost forgetting that she was lame, she sped toward the distant trees which fringed the pool.

Just as the sky turned red above the mountains, the joyous, babbling sound of cascading water reached her ears, and as she hurried forward Much-Afraid suddenly found a cascade of song pouring forth from her own heart. He was there, standing by the pool, looking toward her with the light of the sunrise shining on His face. As Much-Afraid stumbled toward Him, He stepped quickly to her side and she fell at His feet sobbing, "O my Lord, take me with You as You said. Don't leave me behind."

"I knew you would come," He said gently, "but Much-Afraid, why were you not at the trysting-place last evening? Did you not hear Me when I passed your

Resurrection of a Dream

READ: Hind's Feet... facing page & **Genesis 41 –42:9**

"Finally, brethren, whatever is true, whatever is honorable, whatever is right, whatever is pure, whatever is lovely, whatever is of good repute, if there is any excellence and if anything worthy of praise, let your mind dwell on these things."
—Philippians 4:8

"But on the first day of the week, at early dawn, they came to the tomb, bringing the spices which they had prepared. And they found the stone rolled away from the tomb." —Luke 24:1–2

Following the death of her vision, Much-Afraid begins to think of the Shepherd. She recalls His loving-kindness; the look on His face when He invited her to go with Him to the mountains. Immediately, her mind begins to recall and realize His excellent character, compassion and understanding of her; that He would not go off and leave her without clear understanding with her. He could not possibly act on a misunderstanding. Her mind is further filled with revelation from allegorical scripture —the pictures of the dawn and re-finding her love that are painted in her song of the shepherds.

With all of these revelations given to her after she begins to think upon the Shepherd, she suddenly arrives at an action which is in harmony with the Spirit of God; she will return to the trysting place. Such harmony of action with God's purposes is what the Bible means when it describes "wisdom". Much-Afraid carries out her heart and mind, no longer crushed by disappointment in God, but with confidence in His character and provision for her now restored by faith.

Arriving at the trysting place, she finds her loving Shepherd just as dawn turns the sky red. Her dream is resurrected in tears and she repeats her plea to be taken with Him.

QUESTIONS AND PRAYER: How would you rate your "scorecard" of faith when you have had something important put to death by God? _____

_____

Do you spend time recalling the character and word of God; His work in your life? Or do you tend to carry despair and other negative emotions?_____

_____

What opportunities do you see here for improving your steadfastness to Him who is faithful to you? _____

_____

cottage and called? I wanted to tell you to be ready to start with Me this morning at sunrise." As He spoke the sun rose fully over the peaks of the mountains and bathed them both in a lovely golden light.

"I am here," said Much-Afraid, still kneeling at His feet, "and I will go with You anywhere."

Then the Shepherd took her by the hand and they started for the mountains.

A Bride's Heart

READ: Hind's Feet... facing page & **Song of Solomon 1–3**

"And he said to me, "Write, 'Blessed are those who are invited to the marriage
supper of the Lamb.'" And he said to me, 'These are true words of God.'"
—Revelation 19:9

"For the son of the bondwoman shall not be an heir with the son of
the free woman." —Galatians 4:30

This point of Much-Afraid's beginning of her walk to the High Places with the Shepherd is a fitting point to discuss particular features which distinguish "marriage" between men and women in light of the gospel. We see clearly from the gospel that love, character and faithfulness of the Bridegroom must be proven prior to marriage. But the reverse is not true. From the gospel we can see that a woman is not required to prove her love before marriage. The bridegroom commits first. When a woman discovers a man who loves her at the risk of his own life, she will gladly follow him anywhere, suffering shipwreck and hardship, if necessary, to remain within the covering of his love.

This is quite contrary to many lies given girls this modern day in which girls are impressed to sleep with a man to "prove" their love. Rather than establish the certitude that she is loved, she reaps seeds of destruction.

Sexual abstinence prior to marriage establishes a foundation of love and proof of love by which a man helps establish a free woman. She is a picture on earth of the bride of Christ; the valuable woman who inherits the promises of the vision of the gospel of Jesus Christ given to her as a little girl. God desires for her a husband who will love her as the Shepherd does.

Much-Afraid's vision is validated. Her hand is placed in the Shepherd's, who has just revealed that He intended to leave with her "in the morning at sunrise"! Nothing has been lost! (Did she catch this, or is this only an observation for the reader?) Much-Afraid kneels at her LORD's feet; "I will go with You anywhere." It is the declaration of a loved woman.

**QUESTIONS AND PRAYER: Why is Much-Afraid willing to go anywhere with
the Shepherd?**_____

_____

**How do men fall short in their treatment of girls and wives who have looked to
them as "knights in shining armor"?** _____

_____

CHAPTER 4

Start for the High Places

It was early morning of a beautiful day. The valley lay as though still asleep. The only sounds were the joyful laughter of the running streams and the gay little songs of the birds. The dew sparkled on the grass and the wild flowers glowed like little jewels. Especially lovely were the wild anemones, purple, pink and scarlet, which dotted the pastures everywhere, thrusting their beautiful little faces up through the straggling thorns. Sometimes the Shepherd and Much-Afraid walked over patches of thousands of tiny little pink or mauve blossoms, each minutely small and yet all together forming a brilliant carpet, far richer than any seen in a king's palace.

Once the Shepherd stooped and touched the flowers gently with His fingers, then said to Much-Afraid with a smile, "Humble yourself, and you will find that Love is spreading a carpet of flowers beneath your feet."

Much-Afraid looked at Him earnestly, "I have often wondered about the wild flowers," she said. "It does seem strange that such unnumbered multitudes should bloom in the wild places of the earth where perhaps nobody ever sees them and the goats and the cattle can walk over them and crush them to death. They have so much beauty and sweetness to give and no one on whom to lavish it, nor who will even appreciate it."

The look the Shepherd turned on her was very beautiful. "Nothing My Father and I have made is ever wasted," He said quietly, "and the little wild flowers have a wonderful

Who are the Flowers?

READ: Hind's Feet... facing page & **Job 14**

"...Observe how the lilies of the field grow; they do not toil
nor do they spin." —Matthew 6:28

"I will be like the dew to Israel; he will blossom like the lily, and he will take root
like the cedars of Lebanon. His shoots will sprout, and his beauty will be
like the olive tree, and his fragrance like the cedars of Lebanon.
........they will blossom like the vine. ...." —Hosea 14:5–7

Much-Afraid's journey to the High Places starts through the eye of author Hurnard as she "sees" the beauty of the early morning valley and its streams, flowers and birds. We will see these things identified in the two opening sentences used at greater length later in her allegory. What marvelous insights author Hurnard was given in the Swiss alps, the place of her inspiration and insight for *Hinds' Feet in High Places!*

The comparison of flowers to men by Job was made during a period of extreme torment and suffering for him. He was focused on the particular nature of flowers to be "quickly passing"; briefly temporal in nature (Job 14:2, Isaiah 40:6–8, I Peter 1:24–25). But the allegory of Much-Afraid, like the word of God through Hosea, identifies other characteristics of the flowers; their beauty, their lovely fragrances, their prolific many numbers in company. We see them also being compared with people who have been drawn through repentance to love and fear God.

Much-Afraid begins to meditate aloud to the Shepherd about the mystery of beauty being lavished in areas where there are no people to see or appreciate them. It seems like "such a waste". But the Shepherd responds with words that reflect the thoughts of Isaiah 55:8–11; nothing that proceeds out of God "is ever wasted." There are things to learn and understand in all that God has created. By whom are they to be learned? By His children; for whom He has accomplished it all to His glory.

QUESTIONS AND PRAYER: Do you have ideas on how flowers compare with people who belong to God? What about the idea that their beauty might be wasted? How does your life compare to that of a flower?_____

_____

_____

_____

_____

lesson to teach. They offer themselves so sweetly and confidently and willingly, even if it seems that there is no one to appreciate them. Just as though they sang a joyous little song to themselves, that it is so happy to love, even though one is not loved in return.

"I must tell you a great truth, Much-Afraid, which only a few understand. All the fairest beauties in the human soul, its greatest victories, and its most splendid achievements are always those which no one else knows anything about, or can only dimly guess at. Every inner response of the human heart to Love and every conquest over self-love is a new flower on the tree of Love."

"Many a quiet, ordinary, and hidden life, unknown to the world, is a veritable garden in which Love's flowers and fruits have come to such perfection that it is a place of delight where the King of Love Himself walks and rejoices with His friends. Some of My servants have indeed won great visible victories and are rightly loved and reverenced by other men, but always their greatest victories are like the wild flowers, those which no one knows about. Learn this lesson now, down here in the valley, Much-Afraid, and when you get to the steep places of the mountains it will comfort you."

Then He added, "Come, the birds are all singing so joyously, let us join them too, and the flowers shall suggest the theme of our song." So as they walked down the Valley toward the river, they sang together another of the old songs in the Shepherd's book, singing the parts in turn.

I am the Rose of Sharon,
A wild anemone.
As lily 'mong the thorn trees
So is my love to me.

An apple tree 'mong wild trees,
My Love is in my sight,

Knowledge with Understanding

READ: Hind's Feet... facing page & Proverbs 2:1–11

"Rejoice with those who rejoice and weep with those who weep." —Romans 12:15

"Consider what I say, for the LORD will give you understanding in everything."
—II Timothy 2:7

Much-Afraid comes upon the discovery that there is beauty expressed in the world without others who appreciate it. She grasps the idea that love can be expressed by those who desire to love and will find satisfaction even when it is not returned. Yes, it is so happy to love, regardless!

The Shepherd explains to her a deeper truth that this portrays about people, also, even to the point that it is a "law" of truth that the greatest accomplishments of the human heart are accomplished in secret. Every conquest of Love over self-love "is a new flower on the tree of Life." Oh, how true this is, and how necessary for men who would be bridegrooms in the likeness of Christ to learn it, grasp it and apply it! Yet, no exhortation will ever bring it about. Each discovery of such a secret must be itself learned and resolved in secret with the Shepherd.

Real understanding of the truth is for "the few", the Shepherd says. Proverbs 9:10 identifies understanding as being "the knowledge of the Holy One". We need to ever 'know' Him better by walking with Him. In II Timothy 2, Paul identifies that God will give "understanding in everything" in the context of hardship (v. 3), soldiering (v. 4), competition and rules (v. 5), and the hard labor of the farmer (v. 6). We should recognize that the same 'rules' for attaining understanding apply to us in our walk.

In addition to the Shepherd, Himself, we have other consolation also. Flowers are usually in company with each other. There is some degree of sharing and support we can give to each other in our "aloneness" by coming alongside and sharing in each other's grief and joy.

QUESTIONS AND PRAYER: How do you relate the story of the flowers to Christ's incarnation among mankind?_____

_____

How might it relate to your own discipleship journey? Describe how you might "expect" consolation, admiration and support from others when working on their behalf._____

_____

I sit down in his shadow,
His fruit is my delight.

He brought me to his palace,
And to the banquet hall,
To share with me his greatness,
I, who am least of all.

Oh, give me help and comfort,
For I am sick with shame,
Unfit to be his consort,
Unfit to bear his Name.

I charge you, O ye daughters,
Ye roes among the trees,
Stir not my sleeping loved one,
To love me e'er he please.

(Cant. 2:1–4, 7)

Just as they finished singing this song they came to a place where a rushing stream poured itself across the path they were following and went cascading down the other side. It was running so swiftly and singing so loudly that it seemed to fill the valley around them with its laughing voice.

As the Shepherd lifted Much-Afraid across the slippery, wet stones she said to Him, "I do wish I knew what it is that all running water sings."

"Sometimes in the silence of the night I lie in bed and listen to the voice of the little stream which runs past our cottage garden. It sounds so happy and so eager, and as though it were repeating to itself over and over again some very lovely, secret message. I think all running water seems to be singing the same song, either loud and clear or soft and low. I do wish I knew what the waters were saying. It is quite different from the voice of the sea and of salt waters, but I never can understand it. It is an unknown tongue. Tell me, Shepherd, do you know what the waters sing as they hurry on their way?"

Running Water

READ: Hind's Feet... facing page & **Revelation 1:12–15**

"And they were all filled with the Holy Spirit and began to speak with other tongues, as the Spirit was giving them utterance." —Acts 2:4

"For one who speaks in a tongue does not speak to men, but to God; for no one understands, but in his spirit he speaks mysteries." —I Corinthians 14:2

In the Shepherd's song, a line identifies that the bride feels unworthy to bear the name of her bridegroom. Do men reflect today that identification of the woman with the name of her husband is intended to reflect her coming under protection and identity with his character and power in her behalf, exactly as we do with Jesus Christ? Our society has moved far from that. Now many women refuse to accept their husband's name or to commit to them for life. How does this reflect upon the men of this age?

Now Much-Afraid begins to inquire of the unknown language of running water. It emits beautiful sounds at all times, but without understanding for the hearer. She notes that this is true for all flowing water, whether fast or slow, loud or soft. This is the same phenomenon described in Revelation of the sound of our LORD's speech, "like the sound of many waters". What is the lovely, secret mystery being spoken here that is true for all ages in the character of the voice of our LORD?

We are told in scripture that unknown tongues are a gift available to believers "until the perfect comes", when the partial is done away (I Cor.13:10). The benefit is not for others, unless interpretation is given. It is between the believer and God that mysteries are spoken. In this case, Much-Afraid is about to hear a mystery the Shepherd will reveal to her about the message sung by flowing water.

QUESTIONS AND PRAYER: What is running water doing as it flows, to create noise? Do you see a physical relationship? ... a spiritual relationship? How do you feel this allegory relates to the portraits of the Holy Spirit and "living water" contained in scripture?

_____

_____

_____

_____

_____

The Shepherd smiled again, and they stood silently for a few moments by the little torrent, which seemed to shout even more loudly and exultantly as though it knew they had paused to listen. Suddenly, as Much-Afraid stood beside the Shepherd it seemed as though her eyes and her understanding were open, and bit by bit, the water-language became clear. It is, of course, impossible to write it in water-language, but this is the best I can do to translate it. Of course, it is a very poor effort, for though a water song perhaps may be set to music, words are quite a different matter. But it went something like this."

The Water Song

Come, oh come! let us away—-
Lower, lower every day,
Oh, what joy it is to race
Down to find the lowest place.
This the dearest law we know—-
"It is happy to go low."
Sweetest urge and sweetest will,
"Let us go down lower still."

Hear the summons night and day
Calling us to come away.
From the heights we leap and flow
To the valleys down below.
Always answering to the call,
To the lowest place of all.
Sweetest urge and sweetest pain,
To go low and rise again.

"That is very puzzling," said Much-Afraid, after she had listened for a little and found that this was the refrain, repeated over and over again, though with a thousand variations of little trills and murmurs and bubbles and splashing sighs. "'Let us go down lower still,'" the water seems to be singing so gladly, because it is hurrying to go down to the lowest

66

Running Water's Secret

READ: Hind's Feet... facing page & **Deuteronomy 18:15–19**

"Now the man Moses was very humble, more than any man
who was on the face of the earth." —Numbers 12:3

"And he showed me a river of the water of life, clear as crystal, coming
from the throne of God and of the Lamb." —Revelation 22:1

It should come as no surprise that God, having made man in His own image, should portray the entire creation to reflect Himself and the gospel of Jesus Christ to all man-kind. Nevertheless, it surprises us, over and over, to see the beauty and wealth of this revelation. In Moses, the humblest man on earth, we have one of the strongest "types" of Christ in the Old Testament (including David, Joseph, Judah and others). God said He would send a Messiah like the man whose strongest recorded character trait was his humbleness.

This is what Much-Afraid discovers is the foremost message of the mysterious water song that is now opened to her understanding. The water loves to go lower. "It is happy to go low." An "unending summons night and day" not only to itself, but to those who can understand its message. The Water Song contains the message that height is opportunity and power to go lower only to be lifted up and "rise again". Contained in these words are the power of the resurrection and the power of God to lift up all those who will humble themselves before Him and before men. We are resurrected by being raised from the low-est places, where we have "died" to ourselves, then are brought back to the High Places by God's heavenly power vested in Christ.

Much-Afraid hears thousands of variations of the trills, murmurs and "splashing sighs." She senses the gladness and joy that is inherent in coming down from the High Places. We sense also the fact that this central character feature of our Holy LORD and Savior brought Him down from the High Places of Heaven to be buried and impart His Holy Seed to us.

QUESTIONS AND PRAYER: How might we each rejoice in the beauty of this revelation, asking that we desire it with our own lives through Jesus Christ? _____

_____

_____

_____

_____

place, and yet You are calling me to the High Places. What does it mean?"

"The High Places," answered the Shepherd, "are the starting places for the journey down to the lowest place in the world. When you have hinds' feet and can go 'leaping on the mountains and skipping on the hills,' you will be able, as I am, to run down from the heights in gladdest self-giving and then go up to the mountains again. You will be able to mount to the High Places swifter than eagles, for it is only up on the High Places of Love that anyone can receive the power to pour themselves down in an utter abandonment of self-giving."

This saying seemed very mysterious and strange, but now that her ears had been opened to understand the water song, she heard it repeated over and over again by all the little streams which crossed their pathway or ran beside it. It seemed, too, that the wild flowers were also singing the same sort of song, only in yet another language, a color language, which, like the water tongue, could only be understood by the heart and not by the mind. They seemed to have a little chorus all their own which thousands upon thousands of them were singing in different color notes.

This is the law by which we live—-
It is so sweet to give and give.

After that it seemed to Much-Afraid that all the little birds were chirping and trilling and lilting a tiny theme song also, with unnumbered variations, but still with one chorus breaking in all the time.

This is the joy of all winged life above—-
Happy it is to be able to love.

"I never knew before," said Much-Afraid suddenly, "that the Valley is such a beautiful place and so full of song."

The Shepherd laughed and answered, "Only Love can really understand the music and the beauty and the joy which was planted in the heart of all created things. Have

Power to Love

READ: Hind's Feet... facing page & Isaiah 40:12–31

"And God created man in His own image, in the image of God
He created him; male and female He created them." —Genesis 1:27

"And so, when they had come together, they were asking Him, saying,
'LORD is it at this time You are restoring the kingdom to Israel?'" —Acts. 1:6

How limited is our comprehension of God's word and His plan for restoration of the creation! Even after the disciples had spent the three years of Jesus' ministry with Him, and after His resurrection, they did not comprehend the restoration God had planned for them and for Israel. It is not merely a measure of how far we have fallen. It is a measure of the greatness and glory of God. How exceedingly abundant is His grace beyond anything we ask or think (Eph. 3:20)!

Much-Afraid (and we, through her eyes) begin to catch glimpses of God's plan to empower us to love; not merely a plan to remove us from the pull of the world or the power of the enemy, but to become participating, vigorous members of the body of Christ to overcome it. When we obtain the High Places of Much-Afraid's quest with the Shepherd, we will have the power to give ourselves in love, just as water does!

The same theme is splashed out in the color of the flowers and the songs of the birds, which with all the rest of the creation is lavished on mankind; gifts of unspeakable love! How could we doubt His love for us? Yet we do, and it is God's plan to restore us both to this perfect knowledge and likeness to Him, our Creator. "Thanks be to God for His indescribable gift" (II Cor. 9:15)!

Much-Afraid speaks for all of us, "I never knew before, that the Valley is such a beautiful place and so full of song." The Shepherd immediately relates this beauty and joy "planted in the heart of all created things" with the Love that has been recently planted in her heart.

QUESTIONS AND PRAYER: List some things you recognize as full of beauty and joy in God's message of love to you. Then attempt to express your response to the love He has placed in your heart, through Christ._____

_____

_____

_____

_____

you forgotten that two days ago I planted the seed of Love in your heart? Already it has begun to make you hear and see things which you did not notice before.

"As Love grows in you, Much-Afraid, you will come to understand many things which you never dreamed of before. You will develop the gift of understanding many 'unknown tongues' and you will learn to speak Love's own language too, but first you must learn to spell out the alphabet of Love and to develop hinds' feet. Both these things you will learn on the journey to the High Places, and now here we are at the river, and over on the other side the foothills of the mountains begin. There we shall find your two guides waiting for you."

It was strange and wonderful indeed, thought Much-Afraid, that they had reached the river so quickly and were already approaching the mountains. Upheld by the Shepherd's hand and supported by His strength, she had really forgotten her lameness and had been unconscious of either tiredness or weakness. Oh, if only He would take her the whole way to the mountain places, instead of giving her over to the care of other guides.

When she thought of this, she said to Him imploringly, "Will You not take me all the way? When I am with You I am strong and I am sure no one else but You can get me up to the High Places."

He looked at her most kindly, but answered quietly, "Much-Afraid, I could do what you wish. I could carry you all the way to the High Places Myself, instead of leaving you to climb there. But if I did, you would never be able to develop hinds' feet, and become My companion and go where I go. If you will climb to the heights this once with the companions I have chosen for you, even though it may seem a very long and in some places a very difficult journey, I promise you that you will develop hinds' feet.

"Afterwards you will be able to go with Me, 'leaping on the mountains,' and be able to make the ascent and the descent in the twinkling of an eye.

70

Walk!

READ: Hind's Feet... facing page & **I Corinthians 12:12–31**

"For which is easier, to say, "Your sins are forgiven,"
or to say, "Rise, and walk"? —Matthew 9:5

"..it is appointed for men to die once, and after this comes judgment."
—Hebrews 9:27

Children always prefer to be carried when tired, do they not? When young, the slightest "out of breathness", heat or difficulty will make us want to be carried rather than do the work ourselves. Would you agree this seems to be a general characteristic of all "children"?

Much-Afraid is instructed that she will develop understanding of many different "unknown tongues" while growing in her journey and the Love planted by the Shepherd in her heart. The message is consistent with scripture; Love surpasses every gift and must grow in us until "the perfect comes" (I Cor. 13:10). It is developed through 'walking', from the gift of 'seed' that has been placed there in Christ and by Christ.

It is likely that as Much-Afraid grows in her gifts of understanding the languages of love, and in her own capacity to love that she will also be left as unappreciated as the streams and flowers in what she gives. In many instances her joy will be shared only with God. This is a message for us, especially a message for men, who are to bear the likeness of Christ with their wives. We are to "see the results and be satisfied" (Isa. 53:11), but this is much later, and there will be anguish of soul and loneliness on the way.

Do you ask for an easier way, asking God to "carry" you? Remember the Shepherd's response, "I could carry you all the way to the High Places Myself", but "if I did you would never be able to develop Hinds' feet and become my companion and go where I go." Also, remember Christ's answer regarding the paralytic, "Which is easier...?" He has done the most difficult work of forgiving sin and now asks us to pick up our pallet and "walk". Our life is the only opportunity for this journey.

QUESTIONS AND PRAYER: How may this text be applied to keeping faith, building character, fulfilling responsibilities, building value, etc. of yourself and your family in Christ?_____

_____

_____

_____

_____

Moreover, if I carry you up to the High Places now, with only a tiny seed of Love in your heart, you will not be able to live in the Kingdom of Love. You will have to stay outside on places not so high, still within reach of your enemies."

"Some of them, you know, can visit the lowest parts of the mountain. I have no doubt that you will meet them as you make the ascent. That is why I have most carefully chosen for you two of the very best and strongest guides. I assure you, however, that never for a moment shall I be beyond your reach or call for help, even when you cannot see Me. It is just as though I shall be present with you all the time, even though invisible. And you have My faithful promise that this journey which you are now to make will be the means of developing your hinds' feet."

"You will give me a new name when I get to the top?" quavered poor Much-Afraid, who all of a sudden seemed to have become deaf to the music around her and to be full of fears and forebodings again.

"Yes, certainly. When the flower of Love is ready to bloom in your heart, you will be loved in return and will receive a new name," replied the Shepherd.

Much-Afraid paused on the bridge and looked back over the way they had come. The Valley looked very green and peaceful, while the mountains to whose foot they had come towered above them like gigantic and threatening ramparts. Far away in the distance she could see the trees growing around the village of Much-Trembling, and with a sudden pang she pictured the Shepherd's helpers going about their happy work, the flocks wandering over the pastures and the peaceful little white cottage in which she had lived.

As these scenes rose before her, tears began to prick in her eyes and the thorn pricked in her heart, but almost at once she turned to the Shepherd and said thankfully, "I will trust You and do whatever You want."

Renewing Trust

READ: Hind's Feet... facing page & **Luke 18:1–8**

"And without faith it is impossible to please Him, for he who comes to God must believe that He is, and that He is a rewarder of those who seek Him." —Hebrews 11:6

"To him who overcomes, to him I will give some of the hidden manna, and I will give him a white stone, and a new name written on the stone which no one knows but he who receives it." —Revelation 2:17

Much-Afraid learns that her walk to the High Places must necessarily confront some of her enemies who still have access to its lower reaches, thus reflecting that perhaps the Shepherd's plan for her growth uses her enemies as part of her training. The Shepherd reiterates her need for guides and His carefully having chosen two of the "best and strongest". Who might they be?

The Shepherd repeats His promises to Much-Afraid; this journey is the means of her developing hinds' feet. Upon coaxing, He also confirms His prior promise that when the flower of Love is ready to bloom in her heart, she will be loved in return and given a new name.

Like Much-Afraid we need reassurance that God and His promises are true; that we can personally depend upon Him and them. Yet the LORD is looking for something from us, too, isn't He? Yes! He is looking for our faith. God says that faith is based upon hearing His word (Rom.10:17). God gives us His word when we seek it and uses it to build our faith. On this mighty stone of faith in God and His character, He builds the church. The issue of the ages is still, "When the Son of Man comes, will He find faith on the earth" (Lu.18:8)?

Our heroine looks back. Perhaps a bit like Israel when leaving Egypt, she gazes longingly at the familiar surroundings, but doesn't yield to the pangs. She turns away from the "world" she has known and recommits to the Shepherd with words He wants to hear from each of us, "I will trust You and do whatever You want."

QUESTIONS AND PRAYER: What reassurances have you asked God for lately?

_____

_____

Have you sought Him in the faithful reading of His word? Is your exercise of faith pleasing to you?_____

_____

Then, as she looked up in His face, He smiled most sweetly and said something He had never said before, "You have one real beauty, Much-Afraid, you have such trustful eyes. Trust is one of the most beautiful things in the world. When I look at the trust in your eyes I find you more beautiful to look upon than many a lovely queen."

In a very short time they were over the bridge, and had come to the foot of the mountains, where the path began the ascent of the lower slopes. Here great boulders were scattered all around, and suddenly Much-Afraid saw the figures of two veiled women seated on one of the rocks at the side of the path. As the Shepherd and she came up that place, the two rose and bowed silently to Him.

"Here are the two guides which I promised," said the Shepherd quietly. "From now on until you are over the steep and difficult places, they will be your companions and helpers."

Much-Afraid looked at them fearfully. Certainly they were tall and appeared to be very strong, but why were they veiled? For what reason did they hide their faces? The longer and closer she looked at them, the more she began to dread them. They were so silent, so strong, and so mysterious. Why did they not speak? Why give her no friendly word of greeting?

"Who are they?" she whispered to the Shepherd. "Will You tell me their names, and why don't they speak to me? Are they dumb?"

"No, they are not dumb," said the Shepherd very quietly, "but they speak a new language, Much-Afraid, a dialect of the mountains which you have not yet learned. But as you travel with them, little by little, you will learn to understand their words.

"They are good teachers; indeed, I have few better. As for their names, I will tell you them in your own language, and later you will learn what they are called

Value of Trust

READ: Hind's Feet... facing page & **Matthew 8:1–10**

"I am my beloved's and my beloved is mine." —Song of Solomon 6:3

"You are as beautiful as Tirzah, my darling, as lovely as Jerusalem, as awesome as an army with banners. Turn your eyes away from me, for they have confused me;...." —Song of Solomon 6:4–5

Doesn't it seem marvelous that the centurion caused Jesus to "marvel" at his faith? We should marvel that such a thing causes God to marvel! This is the attribute upon which God places highest value in our lives and upon earth. Anything we can do to enable Him to build this in us is worth the price. He will be trustworthy to do it (I Thess.5:24)!

The succession of verses above from Song of Solomon also serve to confirm and emphasize the dialogue between Much-Afraid and the Shepherd. The first verse is from the bride, declaring as clear as can be said her utter confidence of her relationship with her bridegroom. It is a declaration of faith. The response of the bridegroom, representing Jesus, which immediately follows states poetically the dazzling beauty he sees in his bride, specifically in her eyes, upon hearing such words.

So the Shepherd tells Much-Afraid of how she dazzles Him with the beauty in her trustful eyes, the windows of her soul., describing trust as one of the most beautiful things in the world.

Much-Afraid is now led nearby to meet her two silent, strong and mysterious guides. She dreads them. Do you know who they are? Do you already recognize them as your companions in your walk with Christ? Though silent, they are not dumb. They speak in yet a "new language" skill which will be given to Much-Afraid. She is about to hear their names in her own language, but is promised that later she will learn what they are called in their own tongue.

QUESTIONS AND PRAYER: Do you think in terms of whether an action you take will please God? Does this extend to whether it will delight Him? How can you get on with letting Him build your faith and His pleasure in you? What can you do to increase the trust of your wife or girl friends in you? _____

_____

_____

_____

in their own tongue. "This," said He, motioning toward the first of the silent figures, "is named Sorrow. And the other is her twin sister, Suffering."

Poor Much-Afraid! Her cheeks blanched and she began to tremble from head to foot. She felt so like fainting that she clung to the Shepherd for support.

"I can't go with them," she gasped. "I can't! I can't! O my Lord Shepherd, why do You do this to me? How can I travel in their company? It is more than I can bear. You tell me that the mountain way itself is so steep and difficult that I cannot climb it alone. Then why, oh why, must You make Sorrow and Suffering my companions? Couldn't You have given Joy and Peace to go with me, to strengthen me and encourage me and help me on the difficult way? I never thought You would do this to me!" And she burst into tears.

A strange look passed over the Shepherd's face as he listened to this outburst, then looking at the veiled figures as he spoke, he answered very gently, "Joy and Peace. Are those the companions you would choose for yourself? You remember your promise, to accept the helpers that I would give, because you believed that I would choose the very best possible guides for you. Will you trust Me, Much-Afraid? Will you go with them, or do you wish to turn back to the Valley, and to all your Fearing relatives, to Craven Fear himself?"

Much-Afraid shuddered. The choice seemed terrible. Fear she knew only too well, but Sorrow and Suffering had always seemed to her the two most terrifying things which she could encounter. How could she go with them and abandon herself to their power and control? It was impossible. Then she looked at the Shepherd and suddenly knew she could not doubt Him, could not possibly turn back from following Him; that if she were unfit and unable to love anyone else in the world, yet in her trembling, miserable little heart, she did love Him. Even if He asked the impossible, she could not refuse.

Unwelcome Companions

READ: Hind's Feet... facing page & John 6:61–71

"And when the day came, He called His disciples to Him; and chose
twelve of them, whom He also named as apostles." —Luke 6:13

"Now therefore, I pray Thee, if I have found favor in Thy sight, let me know
Thy ways, that I may know Thee, so that I may find favor in Thy sight.
Consider too, that this nation is Thy people." —Exodus 33:13

Our heroine's two chosen companions, Sorrow and Suffering, are finally introduced. Much-Afraid trembles at their prospects and is confronted again with whether or not to still trust the Shepherd. How many times do we all say to our LORD who rescues us from death, "Why do You do this to me?" It is a child's familiar complaining refrain. We have an awesome God!

It is evident from scripture that God chooses our companions even as He chooses us. We have a choice to follow Him and embrace these companions, or not. When we disobey, God's patience and propitiating power over sin still apply to the "broken glass" of our sin we give to Him. Still, how much less pain might be involved if we could come quickly to the solution that Much-Afraid attains?

She looks *at* the Shepherd! What was impossible becomes possible while looking upon Him, because she can't doubt Him. If everything else in the world fails, He will not fail. She chooses to walk His way. Consequently she will learn His ways, just as Moses did.

Note that Moses, in His request to learn God's ways, opened His request with, "if I have found favor". Then he stated his purpose; the purpose of knowing God, to "find favor" with God. God had already given favor to Moses, as to Much-Afraid and as to us. But all human hearts turn to Christ more and more for fulfillment as we learn His ways and know Him more.

Her response to the possibility of turning back is the same as Peter's, "Oh, LORD, to whom shall we go? You have words of eternal life."

QUESTIONS AND PRAYER: How have you told God recently that you really want to know His ways and know Him more? Do you know if God granted Moses' request? (Hint: See Psalm 103:7)_____

_____

_____

She looked at Him piteously, then said, "Do I wish to turn back? O Shepherd, to whom should I go? In all the world I have no one but You. Help me to follow You, even though it seems impossible. Help me to trust You as much as I long to love You."

As He heard these words the Shepherd suddenly lifted His head and laughed— a laugh full of exultation and triumph and delight. It echoed round the rocky walls of the little canyon in which they stood until for a moment or two it seemed as though the whole mountain range was laughing with Him. The echoes bounded higher and higher, leaping from rock to rock, and from crag to crag, up to the highest summits, until it seemed as though the last faint echoes of it were running into heaven itself.

When the last note had faded into silence, His voice said very softly, "Thou art all fair, my love; there is no spot in thee" (Cant. 4:7). Then He added, "Fear not, Much-Afraid, only believe. I promise that you shall not be put to shame. Go with Sorrow and Suffering, and if you cannot welcome them now, when you come to the difficult places where you cannot manage alone, put your hands in theirs confidently and they will take you exactly where I want you to go."

Much-Afraid stood quite still, looking up into His face, which now had such a happy, exultant look, the look of one who above all things else delights in saving and delivering. In her heart the words of a hymn, written by another of the Shepherd's followers, began to run through her mind and she started to sing softly and sweetly:

> *Let Sorrow do its work, send grief and pain;*
> *Sweet are Thy messengers, sweet their refrain.*
> *If they but work in me, more love, O Christ, to Thee,*
> *More love to Thee, more love to Thee.*

"Others have gone this way before me," she thought, "and they could even sing about it afterwards. Will He who is so strong and gentle be less faithful and

The Exultant Warrior

READ: Hind's Feet... facing page & **Song of Solomon 4:1–7**

"And Jesus said to him, 'If you can!' All things are possible to Him who believes." Immediately the boy's father cried out and began saying, "I do believe; help me in my unbelief." —Mark 9:23–24

"The LORD your God is in your midst, a victorious warrior. He will exult over you with joy, He will be quiet in His love, He will rejoice over with you with shouts of joy." —Zephaniah 3:17

In resolving the crucial question of whether or not she can still follow the Shepherd, Much-Afraid blurts out essentially the same words as the father in Mark, chapter 9, "Help me in my unbelief!" This causes the Shepherd to laugh with shouts of exultant joy and to speak of how fair she is, with "no spot or blemish" (Eph. 5:27, Song 4:7).

It is good to see that Jesus is truly a warrior who has fought successfully His battle over death in wooing His bride. He has the heart just as described in Zephaniah. He has defeated the dragon. He is the lover of His bride and exults over every responsive love that we give Him. What woman does not want to be loved this way? What man does not respond this way to winning His true love, for whom He has died?

In the last reading, we had introduction to the idea of walking in "His way". Much-Afraid meditates over this a bit more now while looking upon the face of the Shepherd. She thinks, "Others have gone this way before me," who could even "sing about it afterwards." It is evident that the LORD is a LORD who delivers His followers and delights to do so. This is the function, joy and life-style of the Bridegroom!

Essentially, Much-Afraid is recognizing that there is an unknown "this way". She doesn't know exactly what it is, because God's ways remain hidden until we have trusted Him and walked with Him. Her insights come just after resolving the chief issue confronting her.

QUESTIONS AND PRAYER: What are your experiences in which Sorrow and Suffering have drawn you into greater love for your Savior? For others? _____

_____

_____

_____

_____

_____

gracious to me, weak and cowardly though I am, when it is so obvious that the thing He delights in most of all is to deliver His followers from all their fears and to take them to the High Places?" With this came the thought that the sooner she went with these new guides, the sooner she would reach those glorious High Places.

She stepped forward, looking at the two veiled figures, and said with a courage which she had never felt before, "I will go with you. Please lead the way," for even then she could not bring herself to put out her hands to grasp theirs.

The Shepherd laughed again and then said clearly, "My Peace I leave with you. My Joy be fulfilled in you. Remember that I pledge myself to bring you to the High Places at the top of these mountains and that you shall not be put to shame and now 'till the day break and the shadows flee away, I will be like a roe or a young hart on the mountains" (Cant. 2:17).

Then before Much-Afraid could realize what was happening, He had leaped on to a great rock at the side of the path and from there to another and to yet another, swifter almost than her eyes could follow His movements. He was leaping up the mountains, springing from height to height, going on before them until in a moment or two He was lost to sight.

When they could see him no longer, Much-Afraid and her two new companions began to ascend the foothills. It would have been a curious sight, had there been anyone to watch, as Much-Afraid started on her journey, limping toward the High Places, shrinking as far as possible from the two veiled figures beside her, pretending not to see their proffered hands. But there was no one there to see, for if there is one thing more certain than another, it is that the development of hinds' feet is a secret process, demanding that there should be no onlookers.

Commencing to Learn His Ways

READ: Hind's Feet... facing page & **Habakkuk 3:6, 3:13–18**

"Oh, the depth of the riches both of the wisdom and knowledge of God!
How unsearchable are His judgments and unfathomable His ways!" —Romans 11:33

"He made known His ways to Moses..." —Psalm 103:7

Habakkuk had a perplexing issue of faith in which it seemed to him God was being unjust in judging Israel so stringently while letting brutal, pagan Chaldea slay other nations without any adverse consequence. He is told prophetically that they will come as a tool of God's judgment against Israel. At the end, despite his inability to comprehend these things, he resolves that He will trust God, waiting "quietly for the day of distress", and he closes in powerful, joyful praise!

The Shepherd repeats to Much-Afraid a key promise; his pledge that "you shall not be put to shame." This is the promise of Isaiah 28:16–18 for all those who put their trust in the "costly cornerstone" God has provided. He leaves her with His peace, His joy and this pledge to bring her to the High Places, then leaps upward "like a roe or a young hart on the mountains."

There is a great deal of 'aloneness' in walking with God, as can be seen by reading Habakkuk and the other prophets. Seldom does the walk of a believer include intimate sharing of the "way" God has chosen for us to develop our faith. Although we touch many others and are to carry the burdens of others (Gal. 6:2) to fulfill the law of Christ, we are also told we shall "bear our own load" (Gal. 6:5).

Much-Afraid starts out with Sorrow and Suffering, limping and pretending she doesn't notice them extending their hands to her. How appropriate that we should read ahead to see the conclusion to which Habakkuk arrived in his final words of praise to God, "The Lord GOD is my strength, and He has made my feet like hinds' feet, and makes me walk on my high places" (Hab.3:19).

QUESTIONS AND PRAYER: How do God's personal expressions of His care and provision for you (and your loved ones) apply to you today? How are you trusting Him today and for your future?_____

_____

_____

_____

CHAPTER 4

Encounter with Pride

From the very beginning the way up the mountains proved to be steeper than anything Much-Afraid had supposed herself capable of tackling, and it was not very long before she was forced to seek the help of her companions. Each time she shrinkingly took hold of the hand of either Sorrow or Suffering a pang went through her, but once their hands were grasped she found they had amazing strength, and seemed able to pull and even lift her upwards and over places which she would have considered utterly impossible to reach. Indeed, without their aid they would have been impossible, even for a strong and sure-footed person.

It was not very long, too, before she began to realize how much she needed their help in another way, for it was not only the steepness of the climb and her own lameness and weakness which made the journey difficult. To her surprise and distress she found there were enemies to meet on the way who would certainly have succeeded in making her turn back had she been alone.

To explain this we must now go back to the Valley of Humiliation and see what was happening there. Great was the wrath and consternation of the whole Fearing clan when it was discovered that Much-Afraid had made her escape from the Valley and had actually gone off to the mountains in the company of the Shepherd they so much hated. So long as she had been just ugly, crippled, and miserable little Much-Afraid, her relatives had cared nothing about her. Now they found it quite intolerable that of them all she alone should be singled

Overview of Sorrow and Suffering

READ: Hind's Feet... facing page & **I Peter 4:7–19**

"If it be so, our God whom we serve is able to deliver us from the furnace of blazing
fire; and He will deliver us out of your hand, O king. But even if he does not,
let it be known to you, O king, that we are not going to serve your gods
or worship the golden image that you have set up." —Daniel 3:17–18

Author Hurnard introduces this chapter with an overview of the amazing strength of
Sorrow and Suffering to lift upwards over places considered "impossible, even for a strong
and sure-footed person." She also provides a synopsis of the wrathful responses of Much-
Afraid's relatives to her having gone off with the Great Shepherd, whom they so much
hate. We should consider again just how obscure sorrow and suffering really are to those
who are not undergoing their processes.

For example, how do we consider the sufferings of Daniel when we read his great book
in the Bible? Do we tend to magnify God's deliverance of him from the lions' den without
considering his emotions and feelings that led to that confrontation with faith? How was
God's greatness on his behalf enabled? Certainly it was through weakness, sorrow and
suffering to which we cannot relate. The same is true of Shadrach, Meshach and Abednego and their visit to the fiery furnace. They were "dead" before God showed His greatness on their behalf. But it is difficult for us to see their sorrow and suffering.

Many unbelievers accuse Christians of being close-minded or make other accusations
of ignorance or egotism. The book of I Peter emphases that such trials of sorrow and suffering are normal and produce value in the believer beyond measure. As long as faith in the
true and living God is no threat to lies of unbelief, even a believer can be tolerated. But real
faith in Christ is a threat to all unbelief. This is where God prevails in His children.

**QUESTIONS AND PRAYER: How do you think the spirits of Much-Afraid's rela-
tives correspond to those of your friends or relatives? How would you pray for
breaking their strongholds of unbelief?** _____

_____

_____

_____

_____

_____

_____

out in this way and be taken to live on the High Places. Perhaps she would be given service in the palace of the great King Himself.

Who was Much-Afraid that this should happen to her while the rest of the family drudged away in the Valley of Humiliation? It was not that they wanted to go to the mountains themselves, far be it, but it was intolerable that Much-Afraid should do so.

So it happened that instead of being a little nobody in the eyes of her relatives, Much-Afraid had suddenly become the central figure in their interest and thought. Not only was her own immediate circle of Fearing relatives concerned about the matter but all of her more distant connections as well. Indeed, the whole population of the Valley, apart from the King's own servants, were angered by her departure, and determined that by some means she must be brought back and the hated Shepherd be robbed of His success in filching her from them.

A great consultation went on between all the more influential relatives, and ways and means discussed by which she could be captured most effectively and be brought back to the Valley as a permanent slave. Finally, it was agreed that some-one must be sent after her as quickly as possible in order to force her to return. But they could not conceal from themselves that force might prove impossible, as apparently she had put herself under the protection of the Great Shepherd. Some means, then, would have to be found to beguile her into leaving Him of her own free will. How could this be accomplished?

In the end it was unanimously decided to send a distant connection of the family named Pride. The choice fell on him for several reasons. First, he was not only very strong and powerful but was also a handsome young man, and when he chose, could be extremely attractive. It was emphasized that if other means proved unsuccessful he was to feel no scruples against exerting all his powers of fascina-tion in order to coax Much-Afraid away from the Shepherd.

Reactions of Unbelief

READ: Hind's Feet... facing page & I Corinthians 2:6–16

"......It was necessary that the word of God should be spoken to you first;
since you repudiate it, and judge yourselves unworthy of eternal life,
behold, we are turning to the Gentiles." —Acts 13:46

"For the wisdom of the world is foolishness before God. For it is written,
"He is the one who catches the wise in their craftiness." —I Corinthians 2:19

We recognize that Much-Afraid's relatives are actually enemy spirits that inhabit the earth, deceiving and captivating humans in lies which keep them from knowing salvation in Jesus Christ. They portray aspects of vicious hatred, intolerance, and jealousy upon discovering that Much-Afraid has left with the Shepherd for the High Places. They don't want to go themselves, but nevertheless hate her. No! They actually hate the Shepherd for "filching her from them," thus identifying their nature as hateful enemies of God.

The Bible explains that God's strategy is actually to humiliate human wisdom with His own plan of salvation, which makes no sense to the human mind or the "pride of life" (I John 2:16). God's strategy removes all value from human works and counts only faith in Him and His work on our behalf as having any value. It is all founded on love; God's work on our behalf regardless of merit. Any idea that portrays men as having to "work" their works of righteousness so that God can cleanse them is a lie. Our approval is founded solely upon the love and merit of Jesus and His substitution for us as a sacrifice for sin. This is a bitter pill for the kingdom of Satan and causes many to repudiate Christ.

Pride is now introduced as one who will attempt to seduce Much-Afraid into voluntarily returning to the Valley of Humiliation and her relatives. How will Pride accomplish this? How can he make himself appear to be so attractive? What are his powers of fascination and deception?

QUESTIONS AND PRAYER: If you could give warning to Much-Afraid right now, what would it be to help her recognize Pride? How might this apply to yourself?_____

_____

_____

_____

_____

Besides, it was a well-known fact that the young man was by nature far too proud to admit defeat or lack of success in any undertaking, and that there would be no giving up on his part until he accomplished his purpose. As everybody knew, to confess defeat and return without Much-Afraid would be the last thing possible to Pride, so when he consented to undertake the task it was felt that the matter was as good as settled.

Much-Afraid and her two companions therefore had only been a few days upon their journey and had made but slow though steady progress, when one morning on turning a corner of the rocky pathway, Pride was seen striding toward them. She was certainly surprised and discomfited at this unexpected apparition, but not unduly alarmed. This cousin had always so disdained and ignored her very existence that at first it never occurred to her that he would even speak to her, but expected to see him pass by in the same haughty manner as usual.

Pride himself, who had been skulking and spying for several hours before he showed himself, was on his part delighted to find that though Much-Afraid seemed to be traveling in the care of two strong companions, yet the Shepherd Himself apparently was not with her. He approached her therefore quite confidently but with a most unusual affability of manner, and to Much-Afraid's great surprise stopped when they met, and greeted her.

"Well, Cousin Much-Afraid, here you are at last. I have had such ado to catch up with you."

"How do you do, Cousin Pride?" said that poor little simpleton. Much-Afraid, of course, ought to have known better than to greet, much less to stop and talk with one of her own relatives from the Valley. But it is rather pleasant, after being snubbed and ignored for years, suddenly to be greeted as an equal. Besides this, her curiosity was awakened. Of course, had it been awful and detestable Craven, nothing would have induced her to stop and speak with him.

The Appeal of Pride

READ: Hind's Feet... facing page & **Proverbs 4:23–27**

"How blessed is the man who has made the LORD his trust, and has not turned to the proud, nor to those who lapse into falsehood." —Psalm 40:4

"Do not enter the path of wicked men." —Proverbs 4:14

God has told us we are to watch over our hearts and look straight ahead, diverting neither to the right nor to the left. Yet how easily deceived we are. How easy it is to recognize Much-Afraid's thoughts in response to the attention Pride gives her, even to being recognized by someone who had previously disdained her! Certainly these thoughts have also been our own. Yes, it certainly is "rather pleasant, after being snubbed and ignored for years, suddenly to be greeted as an equal."

We see Much-Afraid's motivation for acceptance by others. We also see her curiosity. How difficult it is to put these things down! We also observe that there is deception working in her regarding with whom she's dealing. She thinks, of course, she would have paid no attention to her relative Craven, but is willing to entertain conversation with Pride.

Do we understand what it is to "entertain"? It means to "keep the interest of and give pleasure to", to "give hospitality", or to "preserve and maintain". When priorities are such that we are willing to occupy our thoughts and conversation to "entertaining" spirits which war on our souls, we are doing the same thing as a good host in a home would do; that is, we make these spirits to feel "at home". What we should actually be doing is "destroying speculations and every lofty thing that exalts itself against the knowledge of God and taking every thought captive to the obedience of Christ" (II Cor. 10:5).

Is it a wonder that "the gate is small and the way is narrow that leads to life, and few are those who find it" (Matt. 7:14)? Remember, it is the responsibility of our Shepherd to guide us as He does Much-Afraid. We are not on our own!

QUESTIONS AND PRAYER: How conscious are you of enemy spirits you "entertain"? Identify, write them down and renounce them in the name of Jesus Christ._____

_____

_____

_____

_____

"Much-Afraid," said Pride seriously, actually taking her hand in a kindly and friendly manner (it so happened that at that place the path was not quite so steep and she had freed her hands from those of both Sorrow and Suffering), "I have made this journey on purpose to try to help you. I do beg you to allow me to do so and to listen very attentively and seriously."

"My dear cousin, you must give up this extraordinary journey and come back with me to the Valley. You don't realize the true position in which you have put yourself, nor the dreadful future before you. The One Who has persuaded you to start this improper journey (Pride could not bring himself even to mention the Shepherd by name) is well known to have seduced other helpless victims in this same way."

"Do you know what will happen to you, Much-Afraid, if you persist in going forward? All these fair promises He has made about bringing you into His Kingdom and making you live happily ever afterward will prove false. When He gets you up to the wild, desolate parts of the mountains, He will abandon you altogether, and you will be put to lasting shame."

Poor Much-Afraid tried to pull her hand away, for now she began to understand the meaning of his presence there and his bitter hatred of the Shepherd, but as she struggled to free her hand, he only grasped it tighter. She had to learn that once Pride is listened to, struggle as one may, it is the hardest thing in the world to throw him off. She hated the things that he said, but with her hand grasped in his they had the power to sound horribly plausible and true.

Did she not often find herself in her heart of hearts thrusting back the same idea and possibility which Pride was suggesting to her? Even if the Shepherd did not abandon her (and that she could not believe), might it not be that He Who did allow Sorrow and Suffering to be her companions, would also allow her (for her soul's good, of course) to be put to shame before all her relatives and connections? Was she not

Ridiculing the Bride's Vision

READ: Hind's Feet... facing page & Luke 23:35–37

"And I saw heaven opened; and behold, a white horse, and He who sat upon it is
called Faithful and True; and in righteousness He judges and wages war."
—Revelation 19:11

"As a result of the anguish of His soul, He will see the results and be satisfied."
—Isaiah 53:11

There is a vision for the bride and another for the bridegroom. Though different, both
lead to a common result; marriage to each other. The vision of the bride is the vision of
Much-Afraid and all young girls; a knight in shining armor on a white horse who will come
for her, proving his love for her by risking his life to set her free. He will fight and be
victorious over the dragon that keeps her prisoner. She will marry him, pour out her life
upon him, reproduce children in his likeness and live "happily ever after".

Do you recognize this vision as the vision of the gospel? It is given to girls, but not to
boys. Boys have an embryonic vision of the Bridegroom, and sense a destiny to do something great with their lives, but until they are perfected in giving their life up for a girl,
cannot bear the full vision of the Bridegroom, who is Jesus Christ. The vision of the Bridegroom is to give up His life for His bride; "....who for the joy set before Him endured the
cross, despising the shame, and has sat down at the right hand of the throne of God"
(Heb. 12:3).

Both Bride and Bridegroom face ridicule. All who identify with Jesus Christ will face it,
even as He did and promised to all that follow Him (John 15:19–21).

Much-Afraid now faces ridicule of her vision for the Kingdom of Love by her relative
Pride. In the midst of this, however, she begins to discern mistakes she made in entertaining Pride in the first place. Because she would not grasp Sorrow and Suffering, she became
susceptible to Pride's false claims.

QUESTIONS AND PRAYER: How may the Bridegroom's vision apply to your
life? The Bride's vision? What of the lesson of embracing Sorrow and Suffering in
building the character of Christ in your life? _____

_____

_____

_____

almost certainly exposing herself to ridicule? Who could know what the Shepherd might allow her to go through (for her ultimate good, perhaps, but quite unbearable to contemplate).

It is a terrible thing to let Pride take one by the hand, Much-Afraid suddenly discovered; his suggestions are so frightfully strong, and through the contact of touch he can press them home with almost irresistible force.

"Come back, Much-Afraid," he urged vehemently. "Give it up before it is too late. In your heart of hearts you know that what I am saying is true and that you will be put to shame before everybody. Give it up while there is still time. Is a merely fictitious promise of living on the High Places worth the cost you are asked to pay for it? What is it that you seek there in that mythological Kingdom above?"

Entirely against her will, and simply because he seemed to have her at his mercy, Much-Afraid let the words be dragged out of her. "I am seeking the Kingdom of Love," she said faintly.

"I thought as much," sneered Pride. "Seeking your heart's desire, eh?" And now, Much-Afraid, have a little pride, ask yourself honestly, are you not so ugly and deformed that nobody even in the Valley really loves you? That is the brutal truth. Then how much less will you be welcome in the Kingdom of Love, where they say nothing but unblemished beauty and perfection is admitted? Can you really expect to find what you are seeking; no, I tell you again that you feel this yourself and you know it. Then be honest at least and give it up. Turn back with me before it is too late."

Poor Much-Afraid! The urge to turn back seemed almost irresistible, but at that moment when she stood held in the clutch of Pride, feeling as though every word he spoke was the hideous truth, she had an inner vision of the face of the Shepherd. She remembered the look with which He had promised her, "I pledge myself to bring you there, and that you shall not be put to shame." Then it was as though she

An Exercise with Pride

READ: Hind's Feet... facing page & I Corinthians 9:24–27

"But the Spirit explicitly says that in later times some will fall away from the faith, paying attention to deceitful spirits and doctrines of demons by means of the hypocrisy of liars seared in their own conscience as with a branding iron." —I Timothy 4:1–2

"And because lawlessness is increased, most people's love will grow cold. But the one who endures to the end is he who shall be saved." —Matthew 24:12–13

Paul likened the exercise of discipline and training over his body as an athletic contest in which he buffeted his body to keep it disciplined. God is also pictured as a tutor and disciplinarian (Galatians 3, Hebrews 12) leading us to faith and discipleship in Christ. Poor Much-Afraid is now being exercised by God under powers that she cannot comprehend. Nor can the enemy, Pride, really comprehend that he is being unwittingly used as an instrument for the training of the Shepherd's beloved. All things are working for good in Much-Afraid's life, according to promise (Rom.8:28).

Yet it is important to recognize that apostasy (falling away) is very much a characteristic common to discipleship in Christ and is prophesied for the end times to a high degree. In fact, Jesus said that *MOST people's love will grow cold*, because of the increase of lawlessness. Hence, it is important to grasp that Much-Afraid is still drawn by a love of the Shepherd that has not grown cold and that she is being given discernment of her situation.

She discovers suddenly the terrible mistake of letting Pride take her by the hand and the power of his force through direct contact. Now, though, supernatural intervention gives her a vision of the Shepherd's face and His promise, "I promise myself (note: by His own name) to bring you there, and that *you shall not be put to shame.*" It opens the door for her deliverance.

QUESTIONS AND PRAYER: How would you rate the warmth of your love for Christ when being tempted? Would you submit it to Him as a matter for His Lordship? How will it fare in the future during times of lawlessness?_____

_____

_____

_____

_____

_____

heard Him again, repeating softly, as though looking at some radiant vision in the distance:

> *Behold, thou art fair, my love; thou hast dove's eyes.*
> *Thou art all fair, my love; there is no spot in thee.*

Before Pride could realize what was happening, Much-Afraid uttered a desperate cry for help and was calling up the mountain. "Come to me, Shepherd! Come quickly! Make no tarrying, O my Lord."

There was a sound of loose rattling stones and of a prodigious leap, and the next moment the Shepherd was on the path beside them, His face terrible to look at, His Shepherd's staff raised high above His head. Only one blow fell, and then Pride dropped the hand he had been grasping so tightly and made off down the path and round the corner, slipping and stumbling on the stones as he went, and was out of sight in a moment.

"Much-Afraid" said the Shepherd, in a tone of gentle but firm rebuke, "why did you let Pride come up to you and take your hand? If you had been holding the hands of your two helpers this could never have happened."

For the first time, Much-Afraid of her own free will held out both hands to her two companions, and they grasped her strongly, but never before had their hold upon her been so full of pain, so bitter with sorrow.

She learned in this way the first important lesson on her journey upward, that if one stops to parlay with Pride and listens to his poisonous suggestions and, above all, if he is allowed to lay his grasp upon any part of one, Sorrow becomes unspeakably more unbearable afterwards and anguish of heart has bitterness added to it. Moreover, for a while she limped more painfully than ever she had since leaving the Valley. Pride had trodden on her feet at the moment she called for help and left them more lame and sore than ever.

Call Upon the Lord

READ: Hind's Feet... facing page & **Romans** 10:8–13

"Behold the LORD's hand is not so short that it cannot save;
neither is his ear so dull that it cannot hear." —Isaiah 59:1

".....increasing knowledge results in increasing pain." —Ecclesiastes 1:18

The LORD disciplines those whom He loves, but is always near. In time of need He is immediately at hand upon call of His beloved. To those who have faith to call upon His name, He will always save, and sometimes discipline also almost in the same breath.

Much-Afraid calls upon the Shepherd with the aid of the vision she has been given and with the remembrance of His lovely words of her beauty as He sees her and loves her. He immediately sends the enemy reeling and gently rebukes her. But the reader senses that she really is learning.

The scriptures do not portray a clear relationship between choosing sorrow and suffering on the one hand or pride on the other, as in this portrait of Much-Afraid. However, they do clearly identify pride and humility as opposing each other regarding the grace of God (Prov.3:34, Ps. 138:6, Matt. 23:12, Jas. 4:6, I Pet. 5:5). Sorrow and suffering are means by which we may be humbled, exposed in our weakness and made dependent upon the LORD, from whom we would otherwise too easily turn away. "Grasping their hands" is the allegorical call to recognize Sorrow and Suffering as our friends, not enemies. While in their fellowship, it is very difficult for us to be deceived and embraced by the deceptive "friends" offered by the evil one.

With Much-Afraid's lesson comes knowledge; with the knowledge comes deeper pain and anguish in her sorrow. Also, the effect of sin causes her crippling "deformity" to be, for a while, even more debilitating than it was before. This has been true of all sin since Eve was deceived.

QUESTIONS AND PRAYER: When Eve was deceived, do you think she (i.e., women) became more susceptible to deception? Do you have "weak" areas where your susceptibility to sin is high? What is your protection?_____

_____

_____

_____

CHAPTER 6

Detour Through the Desert

After meeting Pride, Much-Afraid and her companions went on their way, but she was obliged to hobble painfully and could go but slowly. However, she accepted the assistance of her two guides with far greater willingness than before, and gradually the effects of the encounter wore off and she was able to make better progress.

Then one day the path turned a corner, and to her amazement and consternation she saw a great plain spread out beneath them. As far as the eye could see there seemed to be nothing but desert, and endless expanse of sand dunes, with not a tree in sight. The only objects breaking the monotony of the desert were strange, towering pyramids, rising above the sand dunes, hoary with age and grimly desolate. To the horror of Much-Afraid her two guides prepared to take the steep path downward.

She stopped dead and said to them, "We mustn't go down there. The Shepherd has called me to the High Places. We must find some path which goes up, but certainly not down there." But they made signs to her that she was to follow them down the steep pathway to the desert below.

Much-Afraid looked to left and right, but though it seemed incredible, there was no way possible by which they could continue to climb upward. The hill they were on ended abruptly at this precipice, and the rocky cliffs towered above them in every direction straight as walls with no possible foothold.

Desert

READ: Hind's Feet... facing page & **Exodus 13:17–22**

"They said, 'Can God prepare a table in the wilderness?'" —Psalm 78:19

"We are afflicted in every way, but not crushed; perplexed, but not despairing; persecuted, but not forsaken; struck down, but not destroyed."
—II Corinthians 4:8–9

Why is it that, just as we think we are beginning to "get the hang of it" in our walk with the LORD, He seems to give us a new twist in the trail that dismays and confuses us? Isn't it just like a school teacher or music or athletic coach to confront us with some new need for learning when we have mastered the last one? Yes! Sometimes the demand to learn can be a shock! Sometimes the difference between "perplexity" and despair is a very fine line. But God has promised over and over that He will not forsake us and has proven it to us, as well. So we should not despair regardless of our consternation and perplexity!

The text testifies that Much-Afraid's will (willingness) has increased. She is now more purposed and able to follow the way and making better progress, when "the way" suddenly turns down into the desert!

Much-Afraid is convinced there has been a mistake. This descent into the desert could not possibly be the correct way to the High Places, could it?! Deserts are desolate, dry, hot, without life. They are monotonous and are quite the opposite to the High Places of mountains and their lovely flowers, trees, streams and cool breezes. So its obvious there has, indeed, been a mistake, but the mistake is with Much-Afraid and her understanding. Her human understanding is not capable of comprehending God's plans and methods, which have their own purposes and always accomplish them (Isa.55:9–12).

She looks for a "way of escape", but there is none. She is confronted with circumstances that overwhelm her senses and her reasoning.

QUESTIONS AND PRAYER: In circumstances which overwhelm your reasoning and senses with amazement, consternation and dismay, how do you react? What is a correct response for you and Much-Afraid?_____

_____

_____

_____

_____

_____

"I can't go down there," panted Much-Afraid, sick with shock and fear. "He can never mean that—never!" He called me up to the High Places, and this is an absolute contradiction of all that He promised.

She then lifted up her voice and called desperately, "Shepherd, come to me. Oh, I need You. Come and help me."

In a moment He was there, standing beside her.

"Shepherd," she said despairingly, "I can't understand this. The guides you gave me say that we must go down there into that desert, turning right away from the High Places altogether. You don't mean that, do You? You can't contradict Yourself. Tell them we are not to go there, and show us another way. Make a way for us, Shepherd, as You promised."

He looked at her and answered very gently, "That is the path, Much-Afraid, and you are to go down there."

"Oh, no," she cried. "You can't mean it. You said if I would trust You, You would bring me to the High Places, and that path leads right away from them. It contradicts all that You promised."

"No," said the Shepherd, "it is not contradiction, only postponement for the best to become possible."

Much-Afraid felt as though He had stabbed her to the heart. "You mean," she said incredulously, "You really mean that I am to follow that path down and down into that wilderness and then over that desert, away from the mountains indefinitely? Why" (and there was a sob of anguish in her voice) "it may be months, even years, before that path leads back to the mountains again. O Shepherd, do You mean it is indefinite postponement?"

He bowed His head silently, and Much-Afraid sank on her knees at His feet, almost overwhelmed. He was leading her away from her heart's desire altogether and gave no promise at all as to when He would bring her back. As she looked out over what seemed an

I Can't, Lord

READ: Hind's Feet... facing page & **Genesis 4:1–14**

"And Jesus said to him, "'If you can!' All things
are possible to him who believes." —Mark 9:23

"I can do all things through Him who strengthens me." —Philippians 4:13

In this passage, notice how many times Much-Afraid uses the words, "I can't!", or, "You can't". She is utterly convinced that she knows her capabilities, the LORD's intentions and what is "right" for her. She uses absolutes in nearly all of her phrases and even uses the words "absolute contradiction of all that He promised" as one of her reasonings. Does this sound familiar to your ears?

Well, who is right? Much-Afraid or the Shepherd? You know, of course, but how quickly do you retreat from these sorts of remonstrations with the LORD when you are dismayed by where He is leading you? If you are like me, you are as much afraid as Much-Afraid, but need to get over it quickly.

Much-Afraid gets one thing right immediately, though. She calls on the LORD, at once. Not bad! Can we say as much? She looks for direct confirmation from Him regarding what her circumstances seem to be saying. This is a good example for us. But then again, after He confirms it, she begins to argue with Him, just as Moses did, using a variety of reasons to explain to God that He is mistaken or there is a better way. Eventually, God may let us have our own way, but it is always to our loss.

After the Shepherd confirms the pathway for her, she argues some more but the LORD becomes silent. Is this also a familiar truth; that after God gives us reasonable direction and confirmation, He falls silent and waits for our obedience or denial, based on our love—or not?

In this case, Much-Afraid further scrutinizes the horizon for some sign of hope. There is nothing for her eyes to see to suggest that this direction will ever bring her to the High Places. She has only the word of the Shepherd.

QUESTIONS AND PRAYER: What confidence do you have in Paul's confession in Philippians 4:13 (above), applied to your own life? Have you circumstances where you could apply it now?_____

_____

_____

endless desert, the only path she could see led farther and farther away from the High Places, and it was all desert.

Then He answered very quietly, "Much-Afraid, do you love Me enough to accept the postponement and the apparent contradiction of the promise, and to go down there with Me into the desert?"

She was still crouching at His feet, sobbing as if her heart would break, but now she looked up through her tears, caught His hand in hers, and said, trembling, "I do love You, You know that I love You. Oh, forgive me because I can't help my tears. I will go down with You into the wilderness, right away from the promise, if You really wish it. Even if You cannot tell me why it has to be, I will go with You, for You know I do love You, and You have the right to choose for me anything that You please."

It was very early morning, and high above them, hanging in the sky over the silent expanse of desert, was a young crescent moon and the morning star shining like a brilliant jewel close beside it. There Much-Afraid built her first altar on the mountains, a little pile of broken rocks, and then, with the Shepherd standing close beside her, she laid down on the altar her trembling, rebelling will. A little spurt of flame came from somewhere, and in an instant nothing but a heap of ashes was lying on the altar. That is to say, she thought at first there were only ashes, but the Shepherd told her to look closer, and there among the ashes she saw a little stone of some kind, a dark-colored common-looking pebble.

"Pick it up and take it with you," said the Shepherd gently, "as a memorial of this altar which you built, and all that it stands for."

Much-Afraid took the stone out of the ashes, scarcely looking at it and feeling that to her life's end she would never need a reminder of that altar, for how could she ever forget it or the anguish of that first surrender, but she dropped the pebble into a little purse or bag which the Shepherd gave her and put it away carefully.

Do You Love Me?

READ: Hind's Feet... facing page & John 14:15–24

"...The wages of a hired man are not to remain with you all night until morning."
—Leviticus 19:13

"I, Jesus, have sent My angel to testify to you these things for the churches. I am the root and the offspring of David, the bright morning star." —Revelation 22:16

Once I became a believer, it became a bit of a mystery to me as to why more skeptics don't respond to the promise of John 14:21, in which Jesus promises He will reveal Himself to those who obey His commandments out of love. What a wonderful challenge! Perhaps it is because love must be in the heart in the first place and that is impossible if a glimpse of Christ's beauty or a commitment to Him has not already occurred.

Much-Afraid makes a beautiful confession of her love for Christ and gives Him the right to direct her anywhere He chooses with no further explanations or visible evidence. It is similar to commitments of Abraham, Moses, David and others in scripture. The passages following this commitment are full of scriptural imagery.

Christ is characterized in His return to earth by the "bright morning star". This is a powerful star visible before the sun rises. It gives weaker light than the sun but powerful promise of the coming sun. The Levitical Law also stipulates that workers are to see their wages before the sun rises. This imagery and law may relate to the return of Christ actually taking place during the waning hours of darkness just before sunrise.

In the ashes of her sacrifice of will, a little stone appears. In the limited light preceding the sunrise, it appears "dark-colored, common-looking". But the Shepherd tells her to "pick it up" and take it with her; a memorial to her altar and sacrifice for Him. What is the stone and His purpose in having her take it? Does this speak to your spirit?

QUESTIONS AND PRAYER: Does this stone represent anything in your walk with Christ? What are some scriptures from which the author might be taking this? _____

_____

_____

What such sacrifices (of will) are there in your walk with the LORD Jesus Christ?

_____

_____

_____

Then they began the descent into the desert, and at the first step Much-Afraid felt a thrill of the sweetest joy and comfort surge through her, for she found that the Shepherd Himself was going down with them. She would not have Sorrow and Suffering as her only companions, but He was there too. As she started down the path He began a song which Much-Afraid had not heard before, and it sounded so sweet and comforting that her pain began to melt away. It was as though the song suggested to her a part at least of the reason for this strange postponement of all her hopes. This is the song He sang:

The Closed Garden

A garden closed art thou, my love,
Where none thy fruits can taste,
A spring shut up, a fountain sealed,
An orchard run to waste.

Awake, north wind! and come, thou south!
Blow on my garden fair,
That all the spices may flow out
As perfume on the air.

(Cant. 4:12–16)

They reached the desert surprisingly quickly, because, although the path was very steep indeed, Much-Afraid was leaning on the Shepherd, and did not feel her weakness at all. By the evening of that same day they were down on the pale sand dunes and walking toward some huts built in the shadow of one of the great pyramids, where they were to rest that night. At sunset, when the sky burned fiery red over the western rim of the desert, the Shepherd led Much-Afraid away from the huts, to the foot of the pyramid. "Much-Afraid," He said, "all of My servants on their way to the High Places have had to make this detour through the desert. It is called 'The furnace of Egypt, and a horror of great darkness' (Gen. 15:13,17).

Grace

READ: Hind's Feet... facing page & **Genesis 37**

"For though the LORD is exalted, yet He regards the lowly;
but the haughty He knows from afar." —Psalms 138:6

"But He gives a greater grace. Therefore it says, "God is opposed
to the proud, but gives grace to the humble." —James 4:6

Being humbled to obedience to God always brings wonderful enabling grace and fellowship with the LORD that creates a hunger for yet more obedience and grace. Hannah Hurnard portrays this by the visible company of the Shepherd with Much-Afraid following her sacrifice, together with her emotions of "thrill and comfort", the song sung by the Shepherd and its message. She finds that the trip to the desert is surprisingly easy despite being very steep. Following this, the Shepherd begins to explain and give her more understanding, illustrating that understanding always follows obedience instead of the other way round, (as we would naturally prefer.)

One of the chief attributes of grace is that it *enables* us to do God's will. Probably no other person has recorded such understanding of this aspect of God's grace than St. Paul. Paul knew that it only took a moment for God's grace to overcome his hardened, murderous heart, his brilliant educated mind, legalistic commitment to the law of Moses and zealous desire to destroy the church of Jesus Christ. In only a split second, his will disappeared into the will of God on the road to Damascus.

It is important to note, too, that God is not limited in His power to give grace, since He promises that the "outpouring of a spirit of grace and supplication" upon Judah will cause the whole nation to mourn and come to "Him whom they have pierced" in a single day (Zechariah 12:7–14). This is powerful grace!!!

Perhaps it is because of this personal understanding that Paul invokes God's grace in prayer at the beginning and end of all his letters, as well as referring to it more than any other Bible author.

QUESTIONS AND PRAYER: Have you experienced "enabling" in God's grace to you to keep His will? When you hold pride? How do you consciously extend grace to others or is it done unconsciously?_____

_____

_____

_____

Here they have learned many things which otherwise they would have known nothing about.

"Abraham was the first of my servants to come this way, and this pyramid was hoary with age when he first looked upon it. Then came Joseph, with tears and anguish of heart, and looked upon it too and learned the lesson of the furnace of fire. Since that time an endless succession of My people have come this way. They came to learn the secret of royalty, and now you are here, Much-Afraid. You, too, are in the line of succession. It is a great privilege, and if you will, you also may learn the lesson of the furnace and of the great darkness just as surely as did those before you. Those who come down to the furnace go on their way afterwards as royal men and women, princes and princesses of the Royal Line."

Much-Afraid looked up at the towering pyramid, now shadowy and black against the sunset sky, and desolate as it looked in the waste of desert, yet it seemed to her to be one of the most majestic objects she had ever seen.

Then all of a sudden the desert was full of people, an endless procession of them. There was Abraham himself and Sarah his wife, those first lonely exiles in a strange land; there was Joseph, the betrayed and wounded brother who had been sold into slavery, who when he wept for his father's tent, saw only the alien pyramid. Then one after another she saw a great host which no man could number stretching across the desert in an endless line. The last one in the line held out a hand which she took, and there she was in the great chain herself. Words came to her ears also, and she heard them quite plainly.

"Fear not, Much-Afraid, to go down into Egypt; for I will there make of thee a great nation; I will go down with thee into Egypt; and I will also surely bring thee up again" (Gen. 46:3).

After this they went back to the huts to rest that night. In the morning the Shepherd called Much-Afraid again and led her away, but this time He opened a

Egypt

READ: Hind's Feet... facing page & **Genesis 39**

"Now there was a famine in the land; so Abram went down to Egypt to sojourn there, for the famine was severe in the land." —Genesis 12:10

"Now a new king arose over Egypt, who did not know Joseph, and he said to his people, "Behold, the people of the sons of Israel are more and mightier than we." —Exodus 1:8–9

Famine is frequently recorded as a tool in the development of God's righteousness in men and women of the Bible. Abram (later Abraham) was the first of many who were sent to "Egypt" to find relief. In the allegory of Much-Afraid, this is described as a place of refining and disciplining of individuals and the entire family of Israel. Although pagan and mutually repugnant to the Hebrews (Genesis 43:32), Egypt was used by God to shape the vessels He wanted to make of His chosen people.

As we will read in the next few studies, God first used Egypt to make a righteous vessel out of young Joseph, the eleventh son of Judah. The preceding sons had become "basket cases" of incest, murder, adultery, betrayal, and lying insubordination to their father. So, God first prepared Joseph as an instrument of righteousness then used Him on the remaining brothers to produce repentance, change and rescue from famine. This process enabled Israel to become a great nation that outnumbered their hosts of Egypt. Satan used this fear to attempt to enslave and destroy Israel, but God used it instead as an instrument to prepare a nation for His greater glory (Exodus 1 through 14).

The analogy of the desert as a refining fire, a furnace, is used to draw an image of how natural men are transformed into "royalty"; the likeness of Christ (Rom.8:29) and to draw Much-Afraid (and us!) into embracing the refining process. How much better to grasp the fire in faith rather than to go through kicking and screaming in opposition to God!

QUESTIONS AND PRAYER: What testimony have you heard of a man who has been through God's "refining fire"?_____

_____

What changes did it produce in him?_____

_____

Does he regret it?_____

Under what (if any) circumstances could you choose this for yourself?_____

_____

little door in the wall of the pyramid and took her inside. There was a passage which led to the center, and from there a spiral staircase went up to the floors above.

But the Shepherd opened another door leading out of the central chamber on the ground floor and they entered a very large room which looked like a granary. There were great piles of grain everywhere except in the middle. There on the open space men were threshing the different kinds of grain in many different ways and then grinding them to powder, some coarse and some finer. At one side were some women sitting on the ground with hollow smooth stones before them, grinding the very best of the wheat into the finest possible powder.

Watching them for a while, Much-Afraid saw how the grains were first beaten and bruised until they crumbled to pieces, but still the grinding and beating process continued, until at last the powder was fine enough to be used for baking the best wheat bread.

"See," said the Shepherd gently, "how various are the methods used for grinding the different varieties of grain, according to their special use and purpose." Then He quoted, "Dill is not threshed with a threshing instrument, neither is a cart wheel turned about upon the cumin; but dill is beaten out with a staff, and the cumin with a rod. Bread corn is bruised, but no one crushes it forever; neither is it broken with the wheel of a cart nor bruised with horsemen driving over it" (Isa. 28:17,28).

As Much-Afraid watched the women pounding the bread corn with their heavy stones she noticed how long the process took before the fine white powder was finished and ready for use. Then she heard the Shepherd saying, "I bring My people into Egypt that they, too, may be threshed and ground into the finest powder and may become bread corn for the use of others. But remember, though bread corn is bruised, no one threshes it forever; only until the bruised and broken grain is ready for its highest use. This also cometh forth from the Lord of Hosts, which is wonderful in counsel and excellent in working" (v. 29).

Grinding and Refining

READ: Hind's Feet... facing page & **Genesis 40**

"And His winnowing fork is in His hand, and He will thoroughly clean His threshing floor; and He will gather His wheat into the barn, but He will burn up the chaff with unquenchable fire." —Matthew 3:12

"I am the living bread that came down out of heaven; if any one eats of this bread, he shall live forever; and the bread also which I shall give for the life of the world is My flesh." —John 6:51

The Shepherd leads Much-Afraid to a scene in which she is shown the refining processes for different types of grains. The reading for today also defines the refining process through which God brought Joseph to mature manhood as an accountable and Godly man, something his father had not been able to accomplish with his ten preceding sons. As such a man Joseph could be entrusted by God with the wisdom required to deal rightly with his brothers when they later showed up to buy grain! Joseph became a grain threshing expert!

These refining processes have the grain beaten and broken in order to be brought to a condition in which they can serve an ordained purpose. The purpose for grain is to be eaten. It is nurture for life. Jesus used this likeness to describe His purpose for coming to earth (John 6:51). Later, in John 12:24–25, Jesus gave the larger truth that a grain of wheat must fall into the earth and die if it is not to remain by itself alone, but reproduce much fruit. This is our path also if we are to be shaped into His likeness. It requires we submit to a process resembling somewhat that chosen for Joseph, but which is special and unique for each of us.

It is usually easy to observe others who are being "threshed". Let us not forget, if we belong to God, that it is we who are being threshed and refined.

QUESTIONS AND PRAYER: Please identify some areas in which you have been threshed and refined. _____

_____

_____

What other partially hidden areas do you consider are still not addressed by God in your life?_____

_____

_____

After this the Shepherd took her back to the central chamber and they ascended the spiral staircase, twisting up and up into the darkness above. There, on the next floor, they came to another and smaller room, in the center of which stood a great wheel, flat, like a table. Beside it stood a potter who wrought a work on the wheel. As he spun the wheel he fashioned his clay into many beautiful shapes and objects. The material was cut and kneaded and shaped as he saw fit, but always the clay lay still upon the wheel, submitting to his every touch, perfectly, unresisting.

As they watched, the Shepherd said, "In Egypt, too, I fashion My fairest and finest vessels and bring forth instruments for My work, according as I see fit" (Jer. 18). Then he smiled and added, "Cannot I do with you, Much-Afraid, as this potter? Behold, as the clay is in the hand of the potter so are you in My hand" (Jer. 18:6).

Last of all He took her up the stairway to the highest floor. There they found a room with a furnace in which gold was being smelted and refined of all its dross. Also in the furnace were rough pieces of stone and rock containing crystals. These were put in the great heat of the oven and left for a time. On being taken out, behold, they were glorious jewels, flashing as though they had received the fire into their very hearts. As Much-Afraid stood beside the Shepherd, looking shrinkingly into the fire, He said the loveliest thing of all.

"O thou afflicted, tossed with tempest, and not comforted, behold, I will lay thy stones with fair colors, and lay thy foundations with sapphires. And I will make thy windows of agates, and thy gates of carbuncles, and all thy borders of pleasant stones" (Isa. 54:11). Then He added, "My rarest and choicest jewels and My finest gold are those who have been refined in the furnace of Egypt," and He sang one verse of a little song:

> *I'll turn My hands upon thy heart,*
> *And purge away thy dross,*
> *I will refine thee in My fire*
> *Remake thee at My cross.*

Preparing a Vessel

READ: Hind's Feet... facing page & **Genesis 41**

"...Shall the potter be considered as equal with the clay, that what is made should say to its maker, 'He did not make me'?" —Isaiah 29:16

"Woe to the one who quarrels with his Maker—an earthenware vessel among the vessels of earth! Will the clay say to the potter, 'What are you doing?'" —Isaiah 45:9

Before clay is placed on the potter's wheel it goes through a refinement process in which it is softened with water and impurities drawn from it by the fingers of the potter. Sand and vegetable matter that would prevent the clay from becoming uniformly soft and pliable are pulled out, one-by-one! Imagine you are that clay trying to hang to your impurities!

After that, there is careful working in of just the right amount of "living water" to bring the clay to life. Then it is slammed onto the potter's wheel (that it may properly stick to the wheel), then worked and reshaped some more into a shape that is pleasing to the potter. Imagine that you are the clay looking forward for the conclusion of all this "messing around" with your life! Do you think you would like to be off the potter's wheel? What a surprise is in store for you!

After coming off the wheel, the pot is placed in a furnace. It is fired several times. The finest china is fired many times, until the clay becomes transformed into a new material that is very tough and able to pass light through it! But this is not the finished process, either.

Following the firing of a resilient and translucent piece of china, it is then glazed and decorated, all by fire. How like our heavenly Father to illustrate to us the process by which we become made as He is!

Can you guess what the last decoration is to be placed upon the finest china? It is the gold! It must be fired at exactly the right temperature that only a master craftsman knows. If too hot, the gold will turn dark. If insufficiently hot, the gold will remain soft and too easily rub off the masterpiece!

QUESTIONS AND PRAYER: What kind of vessel do you desire to be? Can you honestly ask for and embrace a complete work in you by the Master?_____

_____

_____

They stayed at the huts in the desert for several days, and Much-Afraid learned many things which she had never heard before.

One thing, however, made a special impression upon her. In all that great desert, there was not a single green thing growing, neither tree nor flower nor plant save here and there a patch of straggly gray cacti.

On the last morning she was walking near the tents and huts of the desert dwellers, when in a lonely corner behind a wall she came upon a little golden-yellow flower, growing all alone. An old pipe was connected with a water tank. In the pipe was one tiny hole through which came an occasional drop of water. Where the drops fell one by one, there grew the little golden flower, though where the seed had come from, Much-Afraid could not imagine, for there were no birds anywhere and no other growing things.

She stopped over the lonely, lovely golden face, lifted up so hopefully and so bravely to the feeble drip, and cried out softly, "What is your name, little flower, for I never saw one like you before."

The tiny plant answered at once in a tone as golden as itself, "Behold me! My name is Acceptance-with-Joy."

Much-Afraid thought of the things which she had seen in the pyramid: the threshing-floor and the whirring wheel and the fiery furnace. Somehow the answer of the little golden flower which grew all alone in the waste of the desert stole into her heart and echoed there faintly but sweetly, filling her with comfort. She said to herself, "He has brought me here when I did not want to come for His own purpose. I, too, will look up into His face and say, 'Behold me! I am thy little handmaiden, Acceptance-with-Joy.'" Then she stooped down and picked up a pebble which was lying in the sand beside the flower and put it in the purse with the first altar stone.

Radiant Joy

READ: Hind's Feet... facing page & **Jeremiah 31:10–14**

"Count it all joy, my brethren, when you
encounter various trials." —James 1:2

"And Mary said, 'Behold, the bond-slave of the LORD; be it done to me
according to your word.' And the angel departed from her." —Luke 1:38

A small flower flourishes in a desolate waste, having been placed there by some providential guidance—in the only place where there is a meager, seemingly accidental source of dripping water! Are we like that?

In golden tones the golden flower speaks to Much-Afraid's heart, "Behold Me! My name is Acceptance-with-Joy," thereby imparting a valuable lesson to her which is ours to gain also. Scripture teaches that accepting the will of God is a joyful occasion followed by joyful blessings. Recall the virgin Mary's acceptance of her announced pregnancy with Jesus.

Mary didn't stew over what Joseph (or her parents and friends) would think about her virgin pregnancy. This was a formidable problem that would have been impossible for her to work out. It was God's problem to work that out and He did. The Bible doesn't record Joseph's emotions upon his visitation by the angel, but it does record that He wanted to do what was right and was given information to enable him to do so (Matt. 1:18–21). We should infer that by the time of arrival of the joyful wise men after Christ's birth, Joseph was exceedingly joyful, too.

If we let circumstances dictate, it will be difficult to find joy during time of trial. But if we recognize that trials are for the purpose of producing beauty in us and glory to God, then we have occasion to be thankful for God's painstaking hand being placed upon us. As recorded in today's text in Jeremiah, we may be "radiant in the bounty of the LORD ......and our life like a watered garden."

QUESTIONS AND PRAYER: Have you ever made a study of joy from the Bible? Perhaps a brief study of God's promises and purposes would be helpful in embracing James 1:2 in your life. _____

_____

_____

_____

_____

CHAPTER 7

On the Shores of Loneliness

After they walked together through the burning desert sands, one day, quite unexpectedly, a path crossed the main track which they were following. "This," said the Shepherd quietly, "is the path which you are now to follow." So they turned westward with the High Places right behind their backs and came in a little while to the end of the desert. They found themselves on the shore of a great sea.

"It is now time for Me to leave you, Much-Afraid," He said, "and return to the mountains. Remember, even though you seem to be farther away than ever from the High Places and from Me, there is really no distance at all separating us. I can cross the desert sands as swiftly as I can leap from the High Places to the valleys, and whenever you call for Me, I shall come. This is the word I now leave with you. Believe it and practice it with joy. My sheep hear My voice and they follow Me."

"Whenever you are willing to obey Me, Much-Afraid, and to follow the path of My choice, you will always be able to hear and recognize My voice, and when you hear it you must always obey. Remember also that it is always safe to obey My voice, even if it seems to call you to paths which look impossible or even crazy." On saying this He blessed her and went from them, leaping and bounding over the desert toward the High Places, which were now actually right behind her.

Much-Afraid and her two companions walked along the shores of the great sea for many days, and at first it seemed to her that up till then she had never known real loneliness.

To Purpose Obedience

READ: Hind's Feet... facing page & **Matthew 7:24–27**

"If any man is willing to do His will, he shall know of the teaching,
whether it is of God, or whether I speak from Myself." —John 7:17

"...he goes before them, and the sheep follow him
because they know his voice." —John 10:4

The English language no longer carries the true meaning of "willing" as it is expressed in John 7:17, above. The correct meaning is one of purpose (rather than passive submission or being coerced into obedience) and is better captured in the original Greek language or even Martin Luther's translation into German, where the translation reads, "Wenn jemand will......" (i.e., "If anyone wills....") and goes on to explain that knowledge of God's teaching or direction will come to anyone who "wills" to fulfill this condition.

Jesus explained the application of this principle in the parable of the men who build their houses on different foundations. The great difference between the two men is not whether they heard the word of God. It is *whether or not they did* the words of God.

This idea of purposing and *committing to do* is the key to seeing the fulfillment of this promise in our lives. God promises that if we are purposed to do His will, He will certainly let us know, with absolute reliability, what His will is. We will not have to worry about how He tells us or confirms it; the obligation is upon Him to accomplish this. But this is not a promise for the passive, double-minded man or one who loathes doing the will of God. It is for those who are purposed to obey, whatever that requires, and to trust God for the results. It is an exciting way to live!

The Shepherd summarizes this teaching to Much-Afraid, the necessity and safety of obeying His voice and departs from Much-Afraid's sight.

QUESTIONS AND PRAYER: What is your background of obedience to authority? To your father? To your boss? To God?_____
_____

What kind of seed do you think this will reproduce in your children and others you love?_____
_____

What scripture could you cite as an authority for your opinion on this?_____
_____

The green valley where all her friends and she had lived was far away behind her. Even the mountains were out of sight, and there seemed to be nothing in the whole wide world but the endless sandy desert on one side and the endless sea moaning drearily on the other. Nothing grew there, neither tree nor shrub nor even grass, but the shores were scattered with broken driftwood and with great tangled masses of brown and shriveled seaweed. Nothing lived in the whole region save the sea gulls wheeling and crying overhead and the crabs scuttling across the sand into their burrows. At intervals, too, an icy wind came shrilling across the billows, stabbing sharp as a knife.

In those days Much-Afraid never let go of the hands of her two companions, and it was amazing how swiftly they helped her along. Stranger still, perhaps, was the way in which Much-Afraid walked, swifter and more upright than ever before, and with scarcely a limp, for something had happened in the wilderness which had left a mark upon her for the rest of her life. It was an inner and secret mark, and no one would have noticed any difference outwardly, but all the same, a deep inner change had taken place which indicated a new stage in her life.

She had been down into Egypt and had looked upon the grinding-stones, the wheel, and the furnace, and knew that they symbolized an experience which she herself must pass through. Somehow, incredible as it was, she, Much-Afraid, had been enabled to accept the knowledge and to acquiesce in it, and she knew within herself that with that acceptance a gulf had opened between herself and her past life, even between her past self; a gulf which could never again be closed.

She could look back across it to the green valley between the mountains and see herself there with the Shepherd's workers, feeding her little flock, cringing before her relatives and going to the pool morning and evening to keep tryst with the Shepherd. But it was looking at somebody else altogether,

Separation

READ: Hind's Feet... facing page & **Hebrews 11:6–16**

"Therefore, come out from their midst and be separate,"
says the Lord. ...." —II Corinthians 6:17

"But you will not go out in haste, nor will you go as fugitives;
for the LORD will go before you, and the God of Israel
will be your rear guard." —Isaiah 52:12

Much-Afraid finds herself in geography designed to emphasize her desolation and separation from the past. There is nothing quite as emphatic as the beach between ocean and desert to give emphasis to the vastness of sand and water, its desolation, loneliness and monotony of sound and scenery that Much-Afraid now sees.

The desolation gives Much-Afraid opportunity to see what a separation has been made in her life between the present and her past. What a contrast between all aspects of her present surroundings and the green valley where she had lived! She can't go back. As the scenery is different, she realizes she is also a different person than the one that left the valley. Like Noah, Abraham, Sarah, Joseph, Israel and many before her, she is becoming accustomed to "being different"; an alien in a strange land, now no longer a stranger to loneliness.

She also realizes that in the clasp of Sorrow and Suffering, she is now walking swiftly with scarcely a limp and that, along with this, she carries an inner mark that makes her different on the inside.

Her perspectives all suddenly seem to adjust. She can identify and marvel over the place where she accepted that she would go through this difficult process to be made different; establishing that she can never go back or be the same again. She is agreeable to it.

This is real separation and aloneness; separation from the past, its desires and relationships; separation from the world and even the person we once were, and being content over it all in our LORD (I Tim. 6:6).

QUESTIONS AND PRAYER: Where do you stand regarding your identity with being separated from the desires and "places" of your past?_____

_____

Do you see yourself as a stranger and alien in the world? What are the things that tend to hold you to the past?_____

and she said to herself, "I was that woman, but am not that woman now."

She did not understand how it happened, but what the Shepherd had said had come to pass in herself, for those who go down into the furnace of Egypt and find there the flower of Acceptance come up changed and with the stamp of royalty upon them. It is true that Much-Afraid did not feel at all royal, and certainly did not as yet look it. Nevertheless, she had been stamped with the mark, and would never be the same again.

Therefore, though she went with Sorrow and Suffering day after day along the shores of the great sea of Loneliness, she did not go cringingly or complainingly. Indeed, gradually an impossible thing seemed to be happening. A new kind of joy was springing up in her heart, and she began to find herself noticing beauties in the landscape of which until then she had been quite unconscious.

Her heart often thrilled with an inner ecstasy when she caught sight of the sun shining on the wings of the wheeling sea gulls, making them gleam as dazzlingly white as the snow on the peaks of the far-off High Places. Even their wild, mournful cries and the moanings of the water stirred in her a sorrow which was strangely beautiful. She had the feeling that somehow, in the very far-off places, perhaps even in far-off ages, there would be a meaning found to all sorrow and an answer too fair and wonderful to be as yet understood.

Often, too, she found herself laughing aloud as she watched the antics of the funny little scuttling crabs. When the sun shone brightly, as it did at times, even the grey, dreary sea was transformed into a thing of surpassing beauty, with the light gleaming on the curving green breakers and the foaming spray and the horizon blue as a midnight sky. When the sun thus shone on the wild wastes of water it seemed as though all their sorrows had been swallowed up in joy, and then she would whisper to herself, "When He hath tried me,

Beauty in Loneliness

READ: Hind's Feet... facing page & **Genesis** 17:1–19, 18:1–15

"And indeed if they had been thinking of that country from which they went out, they would have had opportunity to return." —Hebrews 11:15

"He was despised and forsaken of men, a man of sorrows, and acquainted with grief; and like one from whom men hide their face, He was despised, and we did not esteem him." —Isaiah 53:3

Scriptures that we didn't appreciate before meeting Christ take on entirely new perspective after we realize and accept God's love through Him. One of these areas is in realizing the beauty of lives lived in loneliness while following God.

The lonely trials of Noah, Abraham, Sarah, Jacob, Joseph, etc. and the other saints were inherent with their walk with God, in which their trust in Him enabled them to stand apart from the world. In the process, God revealed His glory to them and through them, to us.

Much-Afraid has become less "cringing and complaining", noticing beauties in the landscape she had not noticed before. Light, the wings of sea-gulls, the sounds of their cries and the moaning of the water stir in her a "strangely beautiful sorrow". We can see her situation and understand. We can see into the lives of the saints and begin to comprehend, perhaps glimpsing also with Much-Afraid that there is a surpassing meaning to be found in sorrow that we cannot yet understand.

But even this vicarious identification with the saints of the Bible is possible only if we have some personal knowledge of what loneliness is, through our own personal experience. If we are not willing to stand alone, then perhaps loneliness resulting from not getting our own way (a by-product of sin and selfishness) will introduce the sorrow and suffering we need to grasp God and His ways.

QUESTIONS AND PRAYER: Do you have kids? How do they tolerate being separated from their friends? Pray for wisdom, watch and see how God deals with them. But be sure that you are planting the right seed in your own life._____

_____
_____
_____
_____
_____

I shall come forth as gold. Weeping may endure for a night, but joy cometh in the morning."

One day they came to a place on the shore where there were high cliffs and great rocks scattered about. In this place they were to rest for a time, and while there Much-Afraid wandered off by herself. After climbing the cliff she found herself looking down into a lonely little cove completely enclosed on three sides by the cliffs and with nothing in it but driftwood and stranded seaweed. The chief impression it made upon her was its emptiness. It seemed to lie there like an empty heart, watching and longing for the far-off tide, which had receded to such a distance that it could never again return.

When, however, drawn by an urge to revisit the lonely cove, Much-Afraid went back to the same spot some hours later, all was changed. The waves were now rushing forward with the strength of a high tide urging them onward. Looking over the edge of the cliff, she saw that the cove which had been so empty was now filled to the brim. Great waves, roaring and laughing together, were pouring themselves through the narrow inlet and were leaping against the sides, irresistibly taking possession of every empty niche and crevice.

On seeing this transformation, she knelt down on the edge of the cliff and built her third altar. "O my Lord," she cried, "I thank Thee for leading me here. Behold me, here I am, empty as was this little cove, but waiting Thy time to be filled to the brim with the flood-tide of Love." Then she picked up a little piece of quartz and crystal which was lying on the rocky cliff and dropped it beside the other memorial stones in the little bag which she carried with her.

It was only a short time after the building of that new altar that her enemies were all upon her again. Far away in the Valley of Humiliation, her relatives had been awaiting the return of Pride with his victim, but as time passed and he did not return and Much-Afraid did not reappear it became obvious

Seeing and Understanding

READ: Hind's Feet... facing page & **Proverbs 2:1–5**

"For His anger is but for a moment, His favor is for a lifetime. Weeping may last for the night, but a shout of joy comes in the morning." —Psalm 30:5

"My (Wisdom's) fruit is better than gold, even pure gold, and my yield than choicest silver." —Proverbs 8:19

Probably there is no gift of the spiritual life that should be so coveted by the saints of God as the ability to "see"; to gain wisdom and discernment regarding what God is doing, the meaning of things and how to apply this in harmony with God's purposes. Solomon sought this more than any other gift and it was granted by God (II Chr.1:10–12). We are told that God's people die for lack of knowledge (Hosea 4:6) and that we should seek to prophecy more than any other gift (I Cor.14:1). Prophetic knowledge and discernment is one of the most effectual for edifying (building up) the body of Christ in love (I Cor.14:3–6, 12, 24–26).

Now Much-Afraid is experiencing this gift. Through her eyes we see the prophetic application of the "lesson of the tides" revealed to her. Many poetic words and phrases reveal the great extent of this gift in author Hurnard as she not only describes the lesson, but the "filling" to the brim of the previously dry cove, the "roaring and laughing" of the water as it rushes into the inlet and the characteristic of water to fill every empty niche and crevice.

Count the ways this lesson is being manifested here!! We have Much-Afraid observing it in the inlet and cove while God fulfills it in her life, then through her eyes and mind recognizing it! This is as seen through the eyes of author Hurnard on behalf of the LORD, Who taught it to her that He could communicate it to us!

Much-Afraid picks up another pebble to commemorate the lesson and drops it into her little bag.

QUESTIONS AND PRAYER: How does this lesson fit in your "little bag"? Have you passed through desert emptiness to "filling to the brim"? How might this experience touch others through you?_____

_____
_____
_____
_____

that he must have been unsuccessful in his undertaking and was too proud to admit it. They decided that reinforcements must be sent as soon as possible, before Much-Afraid could reach the really High Places and be altogether beyond their reach.

Spies were sent out, who met Pride and brought back word that Much-Afraid was nowhere on the mountains but was far away on the shores of the Sea of Loneliness. She was going in quite a different direction from the mountains altogether. This was unexpectedly delightful and encouraging news, and quickly suggested to them the best reinforcements to be sent to the help of Pride. There was complete unanimity in deciding that Resentment, Bitterness, and Self-Pity should hurry off at once to assist in bringing back Much-Afraid to her eagerly-awaiting relatives.

Off they went to the shores of Loneliness, and Much-Afraid now had to endure a time of really dreadful assaults. It is true that her enemies soon discovered that this was not the same Much-Afraid with whom they had to deal. They could never get within close reach, because she kept so near to Sorrow and Suffering and accepted their assistance so much more willingly than before. However, they kept appearing before her, shouting out their horrid suggestions and mocking her until it really seemed that wherever she went one or another popped up (there were so many hiding-places for them among the rocks) and hurled their darts at her.

"I told you so," Pride would shout viciously. "Where are you now, you little fool? Up on the High Places? Not much! Do you know that everyone in the Valley of Humiliation knows about this and is laughing at you? Seeking your heart's desire, eh, and left abandoned by Him (just as I warned you) on the shores of Loneliness. Why didn't you listen to me, you little fool?"

Then Resentment would raise his head over another rock. He was extremely ugly to look at, but his was a horribly fascinating ugliness. Sometimes Much-

Rejecting "Familiar" Spirits

READ: Hind's Feet... facing page & **Galatians 5:16–26**

"See to it that no one comes short of the grace of God; that no root of bitterness springing up causes trouble, and by it many be defiled." —Hebrews 12:15

"There is nothing outside the man which going into him can defile him; but the things which proceed out of the man are what defile the man." —Mark 7:15

How easily we should smile at recognizing our familiar tormentors. Yes! We have wasted precious time in the past with Resentment, Bitterness and Self Pity. How long did it take us to begin to recognize and deal with them? How long before we stopped entertaining them and began resisting them by the word of God? Also, how well do we do when we are not in the comfort of our devotional time with the LORD, but on the battlefront of life?

Although these spirits are not literally the spirits of the dead denounced in the Bible (Lev. 19:31, 20:6, 27, Deut.18:11), they are demonic and do lead to death. We are not to "host" and entertain them. But governing the flesh in which they preside requires the power of the Holy Spirit.

We are told to walk in the Spirit and not in the flesh, so that we may produce the fruit of the Spirit. The two are directly opposed to each other so that both may not be satisfied at the same time. "Now the LORD is the Spirit; and where the Spirit of the LORD is, there is liberty" (II Cor. 3:17).

By grasping Sorrow and Suffering, Much-Afraid now has some capacity to keep these demons away. But there remains a horrible fascination with Resentment. Is this like us? Does it seem that Resentment is a small pebble in our mouth that we enjoy sucking despite its giving no nourishment or drink at all? Yes! Resentment only lies to those who entertain it.

QUESTIONS AND PRAYER: Have you ever cleansed your life of resentment of those who have hurt you? Do you know that resentment leads to bitterness, which defiles you ? Draw up a prayerful list of all such people and forgive them in Jesus' divine name, closing all accounts in heaven and on earth (Matt. 5:44, 18 I Cor.13:5)._____

_____

_____

_____

Afraid could hardly turn her eyes away when he stared at her boldly and shouted, "You know, Much-Afraid, you act like a blind idiot. Who is this Shepherd you follow? What sort of a person is He to demand everything you have and take everything you offer and give nothing in return but suffering and sorrow and ridicule and shame? Why do you let Him treat you like this? Stand up for yourself and demand that He fulfill His promise and take you at once to the High Places. If not, tell Him that you feel absolved from all necessity to follow Him any longer."

Bitterness would then break in with his sneering voice, "The more you yield to Him, the more He will demand from you. He is cruel to you, and takes advantage of your devotion. All He has demanded from you so far is nothing to what He will demand if you persist in following Him. He lets His followers, yes, even women and children, go to concentration camps and torture chambers and hideous deaths of all kinds. Could you bear that, you little whiner? Then you'd better pull out and leave Him before He demands the uttermost sacrifice of all. Sooner or later, He'll put you on a cross of some sort and abandon you to it."

Self-Pity would chime in next, and in some dreadful way he was almost worse than any of the others. He talked so softly and in such a pitying tone that Much-Afraid would feel weak all over.

"Poor little Much-Afraid," he would whisper. "It is too bad, you know. You really are so devoted, and you have refused Him nothing, absolutely nothing; that this is the cruel way in which He treats you. Can you really believe when He acts toward you like this that He loves you and has your real good at heart? How can that be possible?"

"You have every right to feel sorry for yourself. Even if you are perfectly willing to suffer for His sake, at least other people ought to know about it and pity you instead of misunderstanding and ridiculing as they do. It really seems as though the One you follow takes delight in making you suffer and leaving you

Variations on Truth

READ: Hind's Feet... facing page & **Matthew 4:1–11**

"For all that is in the world, the lust of the flesh and the lust
of the eyes and the boastful pride of life, is not from the
Father, but is from the world." —I John 2:16

"You are of your father the devil, and you want to do the desires of your father.
He was a murderer from the beginning, and does not stand in the truth,
because there is no truth in him. Whenever he speaks a lie, he speaks
from his own nature; for he is a liar, and the truth is not in him." – John 8:44

Much-Afraid is given a monologue by her four tempters. Actually, we might question as to whether it could be a bit of a dialogue because we cannot see the extent to which she is actually "entertaining" their allegations or to which they are speaking her thoughts. At any rate we are given a good view of how subtly Satan can distort the truth.

Resentment's distortions are similar to those given in Jesus' wilderness temptation, such as "demanding" (i.e., testing) God to fulfill His promises and temptation to proceed without the "necessity" to follow God's way. We see Bitterness characterize God as "demanding" things from Much-Afraid. He uses the word "demand" repeatedly to falsely portray the Shepherd. He also attempts to raise the fear of the cross in a form that appears repelling rather than attractive. (True, for Satan it is repelling and death dealing!)

Self Pity is the most insidious, playing to Much-Afraid's devotion and sacrifice and portraying them as a "works" basis to expect more from the Shepherd. Without better *reward*, Self Pity argues that the Shepherd must not truly love her. He then moves on to "rights"; the need for others to know of her works in order to sympathize with her. How familiar all this is. It is the same strategy as the one used on Eve and on us; lying about God's character as though He would withhold any good thing from us.

QUESTIONS AND PRAYER: Does putting these appeals to death on the cross through your flesh seem attractive to you? Too hard?_____

_____

_____

Consider Romans 6 and pray/agree with God to banish Bitterness, Resentment and Self Pity through obedient faith in Christ._____

_____

_____

to be misunderstood, for every time you yield to Him He thinks up some new way of wounding and bruising you."

That last remark of Self-Pity's was a mistake, because the word "bruising" suddenly reminded Much-Afraid of what the Shepherd had said when they stood together on the threshing floor in the pyramid. "Bread corn is bruised," He had said, "but no one threshes it forever, only till it is ready to be made bread for others. This also cometh forth from the Lord of Hosts who is wonderful in counsel and excellent in working (Isa. 28:28,29).

When she thought of this, to Self-Pity's dismayed astonishment, Much-Afraid actually picked up a piece of rock and hurled it at him, and as he said afterwards to the other three in an aggrieved tone of voice, "If I hadn't ducked and bolted like a hare it could have laid me out altogether, the little vixen!"

But it is exhausting to be assaulted day after day with suggestions like these, and while Sorrow and Suffering were holding her hands, naturally Much-Afraid could not cover her ears, so her enemies were really able to give her a dreadful time. At last, things came to a crisis.

One day when her companions actually seemed to be sleeping for a little while, Much-Afraid unwarily wandered off alone. Not this time to her favorite spot looking down into the little cove, but in a new direction, and she came to a place where the cliffs jutted out into the sea, forming a very narrow peninsula, which ended in a sheer precipice.

When she reached the end of this promontory she stood looking out over the endless expanse of sea, and suddenly found to her horror all four of her enemies approaching and closing in on her. That already she was becoming a different person was then quite apparent, for instead of nearly fainting with fright at their approach, although she did look very pale and frightened, she actually seized a stone in each hand and, putting her back against a great rock, prepared to resist

Resist the Devil

READ: Hind's Feet... facing page & I John 2:18–3:3

"Submit therefore to God. Resist the devil and he will flee from you."
—James 4:7

"But resist him, firm in your faith, knowing that the same
experiences of suffering are being accomplished by your
brethren who are in the world." —I Peter 5:9

If there has been any doubt regarding the extent to which Much-Afraid might have been "entertaining" the enemy, it is removed at this point. There seems to be a dependable trait of Satan's fallen nature that he will over-play his hand. He really does not comprehend God's nature or promises because of His hatred of God. As a result, he makes mistakes which alert us and enable God to open our eyes. This now happens with Much-Afraid when she is suddenly reminded of the words of the Shepherd regarding "bruising". She immediately goes into combat mode, picking up a rock and throwing it at the enemy! Wow! Our heroine is beginning to develop some spiritual muscle!

One day, Sorrow and Suffering seem to be sleeping for a little while, as a result of which Much-Afraid unwarily wanders off alone. What does this mean? She goes in a "new direction" with no companionship and suddenly finds herself in trouble; isolated and cut-off by her four enemies who have been stalking her. What will happen? We know that this time she is prepared to resist them. Will she attempt it on her own strength? Or will she call upon the LORD?

We should be strengthening our own walk with the Shepherd as we gain more identity with Much-Afraid and her understanding of God's wonderful beauty, reliability and strength on our behalf. Who else loves us with such irresistible love or has lavished such an inheritance upon us (Ephesians 1)? Only the LORD, our God, who has moved heaven and earth that we might be saved and know Him as He is!

QUESTIONS AND PRAYER: Do you feel you are a "warrior" in your faith?_____
_____
Do you use your weapons of warfare (Eph. 6:11–18) on behalf of the saints?_____
_____
What self-analysis could you share with other people with whom you fellowship?
_____
With the LORD?_____

them to the limit of her strength. Fortunately the place was too narrow for all four to approach together, but Pride put himself in front of the others and stepped toward her holding a strong cudgel.

"You can put down those stones, Much-Afraid," said he savagely. "There are four of us here, and we mean to do as we please with you now that you are in our power. You shall not only listen to us but shall go with us."

Much-Afraid lifted her face toward the seemingly empty sky, and with all her strength called out, "Come to my deliverance and make no tarrying, O my Lord."

To the horror of the four ruffians, there was the Shepherd Himself, leaping toward them along the narrow promontory more terrible than a great mountain stag with thrusting horns. Resentment, Bitterness, and Self-Pity managed to hurl themselves flat on the ground and edge away as He bounded toward the place where Pride was just seizing hold of Much-Afraid. Catching him by the shoulders, the Shepherd spun him around, lifted him in the air, where he uttered a loud, despairing shriek, and then dropped him over the edge of the cliff into the sea.

"O Shepherd," gasped Much-Afraid, shaking with relief and hope, "thank You. Do You think Pride is really dead at last?"

"No," said the Shepherd, "it is most unlikely." He glanced over the cliff as He spoke, and caught sight of Pride swimming like a fish toward the shore, and added, "There he goes, but he has had a fall today which he will not forget, and I fancy he will limp for some time to come. As for the other three, they have made off into some hiding place, and are not likely to trouble you again in the same way now that they realize that I am within call."

"Shepherd," asked Much-Afraid earnestly, "tell me why I nearly got into Pride's clutches again, and why Resentment, Bitterness and Self-Pity have been able to

Escape!

READ: Hind's Feet... facing page & **Psalm 34**

"He will fulfill the desire of those who fear Him; He will
also hear their cry and will save them." —Psalm 145:19

"Search me O God, and know my heart; try me and know my anxious thoughts; and
see if there be any hurtful way in me, and lead me in the everlasting way."
—Psalm 139:23–24

Pride doesn't have a clue regarding Much-Afraid's willingness to resist. He thinks she will play his game according to his rules and steps toward her holding a strong cudgel. He speaks lying words of doom to her telling her she is in the power of these evil relatives and that she will "go with them".

Now we have our answer to the prior lesson! Much-Afraid is prepared to fight but does not misunderstand that she should accomplish it on her own strength. She calls upon the LORD, who makes short work of Pride.

There are interesting aspects to the discussion which follows. Much-Afraid character-izes her hope that Pride has been done in by inquiring as to whether he is really "dead". The Shepherd, however, does not reply according to her hope and characterization. Instead, Pride is referred to as injured and having a memory. He also mentions that the other three relatives are not likely to trouble Much-Afraid "in the same way" in the future. He makes it clear that this is not final victory! Possibly they will return again to be used in Much-Afraid's training.

Finally, perhaps most interesting and important for application to our own lives, is Much-Afraid's next response. She wants to know "why?" and gets into the question of "What needs fixing in me?" Her attitude is similar to that of David, who in Psalm 139 asked to be personally searched for any unclean or wicked way and to be led in the everlasting way.

QUESTIONS AND PRAYER: Please recall your most recent "trap" and "escape" from the enemy and outline its basic lies of temptation or intimidation; then how you found the aid of the LORD. Now review with Him the weakness and possible mistakes on your part that led to this difficulty._____

_____
_____
_____

pester me for so long in this dreadful way. I did not call You before, because they never dared to come close to me or to make a real attack, but they have been lurking around all the time and making their horrible suggestions, and I couldn't get away from them. Why was it?"

"I think," said the Shepherd gently, "that lately the way seemed a little easier and the sun shone, and you came to a place where you could rest. You forgot for a while that you were My little handmaiden Acceptance-with-Joy and were beginning to tell yourself it really was time that I led you back to the mountains and up to the High Places. When you wear this weed of impatience in your heart instead of the flower Acceptance-with-Joy, you will always find your enemies get an advantage over you."

Much-Afraid blushed. She knew how right He was in His diagnosis. It had been easier to accept the hard path and to be patient when the sea was grey and dull than now when the sun shone and everything else around looked bright and happy and satisfied. She put her hand in the Shepherd's and said sorrowfully, "You are quite right. I have been thinking that You are allowing me to follow this path too long and that You were forgetting Your promise." Then she added, looking steadfastly into His face, "But I do tell You now with all my heart that You are my Shepherd Whose voice I love to hear and obey, and that it is my joy to follow You. You choose, my Lord, and I will obey."

The Shepherd stooped down and picked up a stone which was lying beside her feet and said smilingly, "Put this in your bag with the other stones as a memorial of this day when for the first time you saw Pride toppled over before you, and of your promise that you will wait patiently until I give you your heart's desire."

Discerning Impatience

READ: Hind's Feet... facing page & I Peter 2:11–20

"....Patience of spirit is better than haughtiness of spirit." —Ecclesiastes 7:8

"...do not lead us into temptation, but deliver us from evil..." —Matthew 6:13

In response to her inquiry regarding why her relatives were able to come close enough to make a real attack against her, Much-Afraid is told by the Shepherd that she had been developing a "weed of impatience" in her heart. She had forgotten that she was as the little flower "Acceptance-with-Joy; (that stood in glory in the desert in the nurture of the dripping water!)

I became convicted of this problem one day in my own devotions, having become impatient in my work and prayers (with some hurting men whose wives had left them!) If I am to serve the LORD effectively, I must accept the work He has given me and trust Him for results. But, as you can see, joy is not something related to the circumstances themselves and I *am not* compelled to be joyful. No! It is the fact that the LORD is LORD indeed, of all that is placed in His care that gives me joy. Nothing in His care escapes His perfection and beauty! I rejoice because I know this. I know Him and I know His work is perfect. Praise God!

Impatience is referred to as a "weed". Weeds grow rapidly, reproduce and choke out the choice plants of the garden. Why should we nurture it? Patience, on the other hand, is identified as a fruit of the Spirit (Gal. 5:22).

If you have ever attempted to teach a young boy to tie his shoes or learn to play baseball, you can personally identify with the fact that he will be patient when things are really new and difficult. It is when he begins to make progress that he begins to become impatient with instruction!

QUESTIONS AND PRAYER: How may this text be applied to building Godly character in yourself and your family? Is there a weed of impatience in your garden?_____

_____

_____

_____

_____

_____

CHAPTER 8

On the Old Sea Wall

A few days had passed after the victory over Pride, and Much-Afraid and her companions were continuing their journey along the shore of the great sea. One morning the path unexpectedly turned inland again and they found themselves facing back over the desert in the direction of the mountains, although, of course, they were too far away to be visible. With a thrill of indescribable joy Much-Afraid saw that at last the path did actually run straight toward the east and that it would lead them back to the High Places.

She dropped the hands of her two guides in order to clap her own, and gave a little skip of joy. No matter how great the distance between them and the mountains, now at last they were to go in the right direction. All three started back across the desert, but Much-Afraid could not wait for her guides, and actually ran on ahead as though she had never been lame at all.

Suddenly the path took another turn at right angles and went straight before her as far as she could see, not toward the mountains at all, but southward again to where far ahead the desert seemed to end in some sort of hill country. Much-Afraid stood quite still, dumb with dismay and shock. Then she began to tremble all over. It could not be possible, no, it couldn't, that yet again the Shepherd was saying "No," and turning her right away from the High Places.

"Hope deferred maketh the heart sick," said the wise man of long ago, and how truly he spoke! Now she had been skipping and running so excitedly along the path toward the

Safeguarding Hope

READ: Hind's Feet... facing page & **Genesis 11:27–12:8**

"Hope deferred makes the heart sick, but desire fulfilled is a tree of life.
The one who despises the word will be in debt to it, but the one who fears
the commandment will be rewarded." —Proverbs 13:12–13

"For in hope we have been saved, but hope that is seen is not hope;
for why does one also hope for what he sees?" —Romans 8:24

There are many things for which we hope, but do not yet see. Abraham (perhaps his father, Terah, also) was directed to the land of Canaan. He spent years in the land of Ur waiting and travelling deserts. Abraham went from one crisis to the next, only seldom seeing his hopes fulfilled while building his altars. But eventually his hopes were fulfilled. A view of how God safeguards our hope through frequent "death" is helpful.

The Proverb that speaks of the grief of deferred hope is followed by another which warns of disobedience and gives promise with regard to obedience. Learning to trust and obey God is the chief pilgrimage upon which Much-Afraid, Abraham and we walk! Hopes are fulfilled in our learning of the love of God through this process.

Note that Abraham, despite instructions to "leave his relatives", took Lot with him anyway. This later led to big difficulties in Abraham's life (which God used for good, anyway!). Also, after successfully completing his desert travels, arriving in Canaan and building his altar, Abraham soon "bailed out" and went off to Egypt when a famine hit. His lack of trust and obedience got him into a terrible scrape there when he gave his wife to Pharaoh to attempt to save his own life!

This is typical. We sincerely hope for the promises of God, but tend to think that this can only be confirmed through the sight of our earthly eyes. With this in mind, we are not surprised to see Much-Afraid's reaction to her "change of direction" after her hope has been stirred up.

QUESTIONS AND PRAYER: What overall perspective do you think Much-Afraid has of her journey? How do you rate your perspective? Your family's? Can you think of a way to improve your perspectives?_____

_____

_____

_____

_____

mountains that she had left Sorrow and Suffering quite behind, and while they were catching up with her she was standing quite alone at the place where the path turned away from the mountains.

Up from behind a sand dune close beside her rose the form of her enemy Bitterness. He did not come any nearer, having learned a little more prudence, and was not going to make her call for the Shepherd if he could avoid it, but simply stood and looked at her and laughed and laughed again, the bitterest sound that Much-Afraid had heard in all her life.

Then he said, as venomously as a viper, "Why don't you laugh too, you little fool? You knew this would happen." There he stood, uttering those awful bursts of laughter until it seemed that the whole desert was filled with the echoes of his mockery. Sorrow and her sister came up to Much-Afraid and stood by her side quite silently, and for a little while everything was swallowed up in pain and "a horror of great darkness." A sudden swirling wind shrieked over the desert and raised a storm of dust and sand which blinded them.

In the silence which succeeded the storm Much-Afraid heard her voice, low and trembling, but quite distinct, saying, "My Lord, what dost Thou want to say to me? Speak—for Thy servant heareth."

Next moment the Shepherd was standing beside her. "Be of good cheer," He said, "It is I, be not afraid. Build Me another altar and lay down your whole will as a burnt offering."

Obediently Much-Afraid raised a little heap of sand and loose stones, which was all that she could find in the desert, and again laid down her will and said with tears (for Sorrow had stepped forward and knelt beside her), "I delight to do Thy will, O my God."

From somewhere, though they could not see the source, there came a spurt of flame which consumed the offering and left a little heap of ashes on the altar.

Bitterness

READ: Hind's Feet... facing page & **Hebrews 12:1–17**

"I delight to do Thy will, O my God; Thy Law is within my heart." —Psalm 40:8

"...for it is God who is at work in you, both to will and
to work for His good pleasure." —Philippians 2:13

The poetry of this scene is very powerful. Sorrow and Suffering are "left behind". While they are catching up, Much-Afraid is exposed to venomous attacks of Bitterness. When Sorrow and Suffering do catch up with her she is swallowed up in pain and a "horror" or darkness. A storm of dust and sand blind them. Does this describe our own series of reactions to hope and disappointment? Do sorrow and suffering bring us to Much-Afraid's response? In the silence that follows the storm, she quietly calls out to the LORD. He who is called Faithful appears and speaks to her, "Be of good cheer!"

Bitterness is a destroying spirit. We see in the scriptures above (from Hebrews) that it is rooted in the defiling disappointments of immorality, temporal values or unforgiveness. The claims of our flesh for "satisfaction" and of our eyes and ears to "need" the world's things cause bitter disappointment when we do not get them. Our reaction to injustice against our "rights" produces probably the deepest bitterness of all. They all "deprive" us, embitter us and defile us.

Over and over, we see that the issue with Much-Afraid is always with her will. Each sacrifice is a laying down of her will. It is her will that is becoming more and more quickly submitted to the Shepherd as she is softened and shaped in His hand. It is the same with us. I am sometimes surprised at exposure of an aspect of my own will that is not submitted to God; therefore generating such powerful demands of its own regarding "my rights" or "my needs". I greatly sympathize with Much-Afraid, don't you? But let us not sympathize with our own flesh.

QUESTIONS AND PRAYER: Can we agree together that we desire our wills to be compliant to the will of the Shepherd? Let us ask Him to hasten the work of shaping us into His likeness and expect an answer when we consciously claim, "I desire to do Thy will, O my God." _____

_____

_____

_____

_____

Then came the Shepherd's voice. "This further delay is not unto death, but for the glory of God; that the Son of God may be glorified."

Another gust of wind sprang up and whirled the ashes away in every direction, and the only thing remaining on the altar was a rough, ordinary-looking stone which Much-Afraid picked up and put into the bag with the others. Then she rose to her feet, turned her face away from the mountains, and they all started southward. The Shepherd went with them for a little way so that Resentment and Self-Pity, who were hiding close at hand awaiting an opportunity to attack, lay flat behind the sand dunes and were not seen at that time at all.

Presently they reached a place where the sea, which they had left behind when they turned inland, came sweeping into the desert, forming a great estuary. A strong tide was surging into it, filling it completely with swiftly-flowing waters. However, a stone causeway with many arches had been built across the estuary, and an earthen ramp led up to it. The Shepherd led Much-Afraid to the foot of the ramp and told her to follow this path across the sea. Once more He repeated with great emphasis the words which He had spoken beside the altar, then departed.

Much-Afraid, followed by her two companions, scrambled up the ramp and found themselves on top of the old sea wall. From the height on which they now stood they could look back over the desert. On one side was the sea, and on the other, so blurred with distance that they could not be sure if they really saw it, was a haze which might be part of the mountains, or was it only wishful thinking?

Then, looking ahead they saw that the causeway would indeed bring them across the estuary into a different kind of country altogether, a well-wooded land of hills and valleys with cottages and farmsteads among orchards and fields. The sun was shining brilliantly, and up there on the wall they could feel the full force

Delay and Glory

READ: Hind's Feet... facing page & **John 11:1–45**

"They will find gladness and joy, and sorrow and sighing will flee away."
—Isaiah 35:10

"And His disciples asked Him, saying, 'Rabbi, who sinned, this man or his parents,
that he should be born blind?' Jesus answered, 'It was neither that this man sinned,
nor his parents; but it was in order that the works of God might be displayed in
him.'" —John 9:2–3

Perhaps the reader has noticed by now that the "relatives" of Much-Afraid "lay flat" on the ground when the Shepherd appears. I think author Hurnard is expressing that the enemy cannot stand in His presence. They are driven away as fleeing shadows before the LORD's glory. This pattern occurs again and, like many things she and we do not understand at first, Much-Afraid takes up another stone from her sacrifice.

Jesus' disciples probably did not grasp what He meant with the statement, "this sickness is not unto death, but for the glory of God". They were certainly confused after Jesus told them Lazarus was dead. Had Jesus gone earlier, and in the Father's will, He could have healed Lazarus from illness. But He instead delayed and raised Him from the dead. Which is eternally more to the glory of God? Which would you rather be involved in as a witness or as a minister of faith?

Much-Afraid is told that the delay of her objective has the same ramifications. Her delay is for the glory of God. The path now leads her up onto a causeway upon which only one thing changes. It is her "height" above the ground; i.e., her viewpoint. What a tremendous analogy!

With this minor change in her viewpoint, other things also change! She is given a different perspective. Might this relate to seeing the glory of God?

Much-Afraid now sees things differently. Even the distant mountains seem to appear. She sees she is going into a different kind of country altogether.

QUESTIONS AND PRAYER: How could a different early perspective have helped Lazarus' relatives and the disciples? How was their perspective after Lazarus was raised? _____

_____

_____

_____

of the great wind which was urging and lashing the rushing waves to flow swifter and swifter. It reminded Much-Afraid of a pack of hounds, urged on by the huntsmen, following one another, leaping and surging and roaring beneath the causeway and then flowing forward far inland, brimming the shores of the estuary.

Somehow the roar of the wind and the surge of the waters seemed to get into her blood and coarse through her being like a glorious wine of life. The wind whipped her cheeks and tore at her hair and clothes and nearly toppled her over, but she stood there, shouting at the top of her voice, though the wind seized the sound of it and carried it off, drowned in a deafening roar of its own. What Much-Afraid was shouting up there on the old sea wall was this:

"And now shall mine head be lifted up above mine enemies round about; therefore I will sing praises unto the Lord; yea I will offer the sacrifice of joy and will praise the Name of the Lord" (Psa. 27:6).

As she sang she thought of herself, "It must be really dreadful to be the Shepherd's enemies. Always, always to find themselves frustrated. Always, always to have their prey snatched away. How simply maddening it must be to see even the silliest little weaklings set up out of reach on the High Places and made to triumph over all their enemies. It must be unbearable."

While still on the causeway she picked up another stone as the Shepherd had taught her, this time as a memorial of His victory in making her triumph over her enemies, and dropped it into the little bag of treasured memories. So they made their way across the causeway and down the ramp on the other side and immediately found themselves in a wood.

The change in scene after their long journey through the desert was wonderful. A long-deferred spring was just loosening everything from the grip of winter, and all the trees were bursting into fairest green and the buds were swelling. In between the trees were glades of bluebells and wild anemones,

Perspective

READ: Hind's Feet... facing page & **Daniel 2**

"Then Joshua the son of Nun sent two men as spies secretly from Shittim, saying, Go, view the land, especially Jericho.' So they went and came into the house of a harlot whose name was Rahab, and lodged there."—Joshua 2:1

Would you agree that the Bible is full of visions, dreams and interpretations of those dreams and visions? Yes! There are dozens of them. Some of them are as routine as "spying out the land" under Joshua; others are as complex as the entire book of Revelation. One, given to Paul, was given without permitting him to speak of it. Daniel had many, some of which seem well understood (such as chapter two, above) and others less well understood. Nearly all of the prophets had such visions.

The verse from Joshua may appear to be mundane regarding the land that was to be "viewed", but notice who is mentioned. It is the first mention of Rahab, the harlot of Jericho. This is the woman who became justified by faith in the God of Israel, married the Israelite Salmon and gave birth to one of the most Godly men of the Bible, Boaz! She later shows up in the New Testament as having been placed in the direct lineage of Jesus Christ! Is this some additional perspective, or what?!!!!

From the causeway, Much-Afraid is caught up in images of the life and power that is in water, one of the central theme's of Hurnard's writing. She has us actually "seeing" this in her own and Much-Afraid's eyes.

With her new perspective, Much-Afraid begins to praise the LORD, using the appropriate words of the Psalmist, David, that her head and viewpoint "has been lifted up". From that perspective her head also begins to entertain new thoughts. "What a dreadful plight to be the Shepherd's enemies". She sees the frustrating, maddening ramifications of opposing Him, as even the "silliest weaklings" are made to triumph in Him.

QUESTIONS AND PRAYER: Have you thought about how frustrated your tormenting enemies must be in opposing the Lamb of God's victory in you? Would you write this out and share this new perspective with someone?_____

_____

_____

_____

_____

_____

and violets and primroses grew in clumps along the mossy banks. Birds sang and called to one another and rustled about, busily absorbed in nest-building.

Much-Afraid told herself that never before had she realized what the awakening from the death of winter was like. Perhaps it had needed the desert wastes to open her eyes to all this beauty, but she walked through the wood, almost forgetting for a little that Sorrow and her sister also walked with her.

Everywhere she looked it seemed that the unfurling green on the trees and the nesting birds and the leaping squirrels and blossoming flowers were all saying the same thing, greeting one another in their own special language with a sort of ecstasy and calling cheerfully, "You see, the winter has gone at last. The delay was not unto death but for the glory of God. Never was there a fairer spring than this."

At the same time Much-Afraid herself was conscious of a wonderful stirring in her own heart, as though something were springing up and breaking into new life there too. The feeling was so sweet, yet so mixed with pain that she hardly knew which predominated. She thought of the seed of Love which the Shepherd had planted in her heart, and half-afraid and half-eager, she looked to see if it had really taken root and was springing up. She saw a mass of leaves, and at the end of the stem a little swelling which might almost prove to be a bud.

As Much-Afraid looked at it another stab went through her heart, for she remembered the words of the Shepherd that when the plant of Love was ready to bloom she would be loved in return and would receive a new name up there on the High Places. But here she was, still far away from them, indeed farther than ever before, and with apparently no possibility of going there for a long time to come. How could the Shepherd's promise prove true? When she thought of that her tears fell again.

Green and Tender Shoots

READ: Hind's Feet... facing page & Isaiah 35

"The flowers have already appeared in the land; the time has arrived for pruning the vines, and the voice of the turtledove has been heard in the land." —Song of Solomon 2:12

"For He grew up before Him like a tender shoot and like a root out of parched ground." —Isaiah 53:2

As Much-Afraid enters the springtime of her new area of walk she witnesses the "springtime" of her heart, where new life is springing forth. The awakening of the land from the death of winter and opening of her eyes to all this beauty is a reflection of what is happening to her. It amplifies and shows us the truth about us as we let Christ plant His seed in our hearts and reproduce it. He is the One first likened to a "tender shoot" that arose out of dead and "parched ground".

She looks at her heart and discovers that there are indeed leaves appearing and a stem upon the end of which is a slight swelling that might prove to be a bud. As she remembers the promise of when this bud will bloom, she considers her circumstances and how far away the Kingdom of Love seems. Can it all be true? She again begins to weep.

The power of the vision of a future with a Bridegroom needs to be tenderly remembered by men on behalf of their wives and daughters. Theirs is a much more powerful vision than men's, applying to life on earth as well as in heaven, and is easily ruined in this perverted world. A woman was chosen by God to express this allegory in such powerful words and pictures. Girls long for a man whose character and strength give them a true picture of God, as portrayed for Much-Afraid in the Shepherd. Men should draw women to God, not give them a perverted picture, nor destroy a vision that may look "far away" even under the best of circumstances.

QUESTIONS AND PRAYER: Do brides (wife, daughters and possibly sisters under our care) see in us a true picture of Christ and the promises for their lives? Are they drawn to God by our attitudes and actions? What changes could we make to improve their view of God? (A possible example: How we resolve conflicts?)_____

_____

_____

_____

_____

You may think that Much-Afraid was altogether too much given to shedding tears, but remember that she had Sorrow for a companion and teacher. There is this to be added, that her tears were all in secret, for no one but her enemies knew about this strange journey on which she had set out. The heart knoweth its own sorrow and there are times when, like David, it is comforting to think that our tears are put in a bottle and not one of them forgotten by the One who leads us in paths of sorrow.

But she did not weep for long, for almost at once she caught sight of something else, a gleam of gold. Looking closer, what should she see but an exact replica of the little golden flower which she had found growing near the pyramids in the desert. Somehow it had been transplanted and was actually growing in her own heart. Much-Afraid gave a cry of delight, and the tiny golden thing nodded and said in its little golden voice, "Behold me, here I am, growing in your heart, 'Acceptance-with-Joy.'"

Much-Afraid smiled and answered, "Why, yes, of course, I was forgetting," and she knelt down there in the wood, put a pile of stones together and laid sticks on them. As you have noticed, altars are built of whatever materials lie close at hand at the time. Then she hesitated. What should she lay on the altar this time? She looked at the tiny swelling on the plant of Love which might be a bud and again might not, then she leaned forward, placed her heart on the altar and said, "Behold me, here I am; Thy little handmaiden Acceptance-with-Joy and all that is in my heart is Thine."

This time, though there came a flame of fire and burned up the sticks, the bud was still on the stem of the plant. Perhaps, thought Much-Afraid, because it was too small to offer. But nevertheless something lovely had happened. It was as though a spark from the flame had entered her heart and was still glowing there, warm and radiant. On the altar among the ashes was yet another stone for her to pick up and put with the rest, so now there were six stones of remembrance lying

Seed-in-Kind (Joy in the Heart)

READ: Hind's Feet... facing page & **Matthew 13:1–23**

"Then God said, "Let the earth sprout vegetation, plants yielding
seed, and fruit trees bearing fruit after their kind, with their seed in
them, on the earth"; and it was so." —Genesis 1:11

"These things I have spoken to you that My joy may be in
you, and that your joy may be made full." —John 15:11

God wasted little time in revealing His plan for reproduction in the Bible. In the eleventh verse He laid it all out. Everything reproduces according to its own seed. It is no different with the Seed of Woman, the son of God (Gen. 3:15). When He is truly planted in the womb of our heart, He reproduces Himself.

The parable of the Sower makes it clear that the word of God comes to our heart (Matt.13:19), takes root, grows and reproduces according to the conditions it finds there. Our heart is a replica of a woman's womb and a garden all at the same time!

Much-Afraid finds to her surprise that there is an "exact replica" of the little desert flower 'Acceptance-with-Joy' in her heart. In the context of her tears and the quotation about our bottled tears (Ps. 56:8), one wonders if the drops of her tears are related in the same way to the flower's growth. How the earth transforms and reproduces seed-in-kind is a mystery; "first the blade, then the head, then the mature grain in the head," but "how" we ourselves "do not know" (Mark 4:26–29). God knows and wants us to desire to be in the likeness of His wonderful, awesome Son.

Incredibly, rather than coveting the plant and bud that God has grown in her heart, Much-Afraid offers it all back to Him again. I think I would want to keep it, don't you? God keeps it untouched by fire. Much-Afraid has grown quite a bit during her pilgrimage through the desert and is now giving us lessons on mature discipleship!

QUESTIONS AND PRAYER: Have you taken the Whole Seed, the Son of God, into your heart? Are you confident you are "fertile soil", as sold out as Much-Afraid is? Is everything in your heart yet given to Christ? What rights does God have to take it all away?_____

_____

_____

_____

_____

in the bag she carried. Going on their way, in a very short time they came to the edge of the wood and she uttered a cry of joy, for Who should be standing there, waiting to meet them, but the Shepherd Himself. She ran toward Him as though she had wings on her feet.

"Oh, welcome, welcome, a thousand times welcome!" cried Much-Afraid, tingling with joy from head to foot. "I am afraid there is nothing much in the garden of my heart as yet, Shepherd, but all that there is, is Yours to do with as You please."

"I have come to bring you a message," said the Shepherd. "You are to be ready, Much-Afraid, for something new. This is the message, 'Now shalt thou see what I will do'" (Ex. 6:1)

The color leaped into her cheeks, and a shock of joy went through her, for she remembered the plant in her heart, and the promise that when it was ready to bloom she would be up on the High Places and ready to enter the Kingdom of Love.

"O Shepherd," she exclaimed, almost breathless with the thought. "Do You mean that I am really to go to the High Places at last? Really—at last?"

She thought He nodded, but He did not answer at once, but stood looking at her with an expression she did not quite understand.

"Do you mean it?" she repeated, catching His hand and looking up at Him with almost incredulous joy. "Do you mean You soon will be taking me to the High Places?"

This time He answered, "Yes," and added with a strange smile, "now shalt thou see what I will do."

Joy in Everything

READ: Hind's Feet... facing page & **Luke 1:5–44**

"He who has the bride is the bridegroom; but the friend of the bridegroom, who stands and hears him, rejoices greatly because of the bridegroom's voice. And so this joy of mine has been made full." —John 3:29

"For you will go out with joy, and be led forth with peace; the mountains and the hills will break forth into shouts of joy before you, and all the trees of the field will clap their hands." —Isaiah 55:12

John the Baptist opened and closed his life with joy. The scripture opening this devotion records his leap in the womb of his mother, Elizabeth, when he heard the voice of the Savior's mother, Mary. Near the close of his life he was rejoicing in the voice of the Bridegroom calling His bride to Him. Yet, in Christ, we are all more blessed than John (Luke 7:28).

The close of this chapter is filled with joy. Four times it is described in Much-Afraid; she shouts (cries) with a joy of greeting, she "tingles" with joy, she has a "shock" of joy of remembrance, and she looks at the Shepherd with joy. Rogers and Hammerstein must have had something like this in mind when they wrote, "June Is Busting Out All Over!" Only here we have pure "joy busting out" all over.

Much-Afraid runs "as though she had wings on her feet." Her lameness seems to have totally disappeared. She seems to have no interest in what the "something new" is that the Shepherd is promising. She just wants to get on with her goal of getting to the High Places with Him.

Free women and the bride of Christ are vital and motivated. An unwounded woman will always exhibit joy, openness, transparency, exuberance and freedom. God is building a "free woman" (Galatians 4:22–31). It is hard to discourage or put-off a free woman. Much-Afraid is submitted, but will not be "put-off"!

QUESTIONS AND PRAYER: In what ways are you being ministered "freedom" in Christ (Gal. 5:1–14)? How are you ministering freedom to others and can you see the joy of freedom as a fruit of the Spirit (Gal. 5:22)? Do you see this merely in words or in your spirit?_____

_____

_____

_____

_____

CHAPTER 9

Great Precipice Injury

After that, for a little while Much-Afraid had a song in her heart as she walked among the fields and orchards and the low hills of the country to which they had come. It hardly seemed to matter now that Sorrow and Suffering were still with her because of the hope leaping up in her heart that soon they would cease to be her companions altogether, for when she came to the mountains again and they had helped her up to the High Places she would need them no longer. Neither did it matter that the path they followed still led southward, twisting among the hills and leading through quiet valleys, because she had the Shepherd's own promise that soon it would lead her back to the eastern mountains and to the place of her heart's desire.

After a time the path began sloping upward toward the summits of the hills.

One day they suddenly reached the top of the highest of the hills and just as the sun rose found themselves on a great plateau. They looked eastward toward the golden sunrise, and Much-Afraid burst into a cry of joy and thankfulness. There, at no great distance, on the farthest side of the plateau, were the mountains, quite distinct and rising like a great wall, crowned with ramparts and towers and pinnacles, all of which were glowing rose-red and gold in the sunrise. Never, thought she, had she seen anything so beautiful.

As the sun rose higher and the glow faded from the sky, she saw that the highest peaks were covered with snow, so white and glittering that her eyes were dazzled with their glory. She was looking at the High Places themselves. Best of

142

Hilltop Glory

READ: Hind's Feet... facing page & **Ezekiel 1:1–28**

"Then the glory of the Lord will be revealed, and all flesh will see it together."
—Isaiah 40:5

"...looking for the blessed hope and the appearing of the glory of our great God and Savior, Christ Jesus, who gave Himself for us, that He might redeem us from every lawless deed and purify for Himself a people for His own possession, zealous for good deeds." —Titus 2:13–14

When I was a college student, I used to drive home at the end of the school year from Boston, Massachusetts to Seattle, Washington. Every year we took a different way, but one experience was always gloriously the same. That was the approach to the Rocky Mountains from across the great plains. It was always a great thrill to see the first faint, hazy trace of these majestic mountains from a distance. At first one could not be sure he was actually seeing the mountains. But with each passing hour they would rise up higher and more clearly, until, just before the road would enter the foothills, they could be seen rising like a "great wall". The details of each crag and snow field became "quite distinct". It was incredibly beautiful and thrilling, made more so by the knowledge that I was drawing closer to home!

In lesson #12 we discussed the biblical picture of "mountain-top" experiences. Now we are seeing author Hurnard's own portrait of the same thing—on a hilltop, to be sure, but the application is the same. From the highest of the hills she gets a point-blank view of her goal. The dazzling of her physical senses is a portrait of what we feel effecting our spiritual senses when we actually see the glory of God at such times with Him. It dazzles every aspect of our spirit, soul and body, usually resulting in weeping, worship and giving of thanks.

QUESTIONS AND PRAYER: Recall that this biblical pattern is usually followed by a time of great temptation and trial. How might you apply this today to the keeping of your faith or the faith of your family and friends?_____

_____

_____

What do you anticipate now happening with Much-Afraid?_____

_____

_____

all, the path they were following here turned eastward and led directly toward the mountains.

Much-Afraid fell on her knees on the hilltop, bowed her head and worshipped. It seemed to her at that moment that all the pain and the postponement, all the sorrows and trials of the long journey she had made, were as nothing compared to the glory which shone before her. It seemed to her, too, that even her companions were smiling with her. When she had worshiped and rejoiced she rose to her feet and all three started to cross the plateau. It was amazing how quickly they went, for the path was flat and comparatively smooth, and before they could have believed it possible they found themselves approaching the mountains and were among the slopes and boulders at their very feet.

As they approached, Much-Afraid could not help being struck by the steepness of these slopes, and the nearer they drew, the more like impassable walls the mountains appeared to become. But she told herself that when she was right up to them they would find a valley or gorge, or a pass up which they could proceed, and that she certainly would not mind how steep the way was if only it led upward. In the late afternoon they did come to the top of the lower slopes and to the very foot of the mountains. The path they were following led them right up to the foot of an impassable precipice and there stopped dead.

Much-Afraid stood still and stared. The more she looked, the more stunned she felt. Then she began to tremble and shake all over, for the whole mountain range before her, as far as she could see to left and right, rose up in unbroken walls of rock so high that it made her giddy when she put her head back and tried to look up to the top. The cliffs completely blocked the way before her, yet the path ran right up to them, then stopped. There was no sign of a track in any other direction, and there was no way at all by which the overhanging, terrifying wall of cliff could be ascended. They would have to turn back.

144

Impossible?

READ: Hind's Feet... facing page & **Romans 8:1-18**

"And looking upon them Jesus said to them, "With men this is impossible, but with God all things are possible." —Matthew 19:26

"For nothing will be impossible with God." —Luke 1:37

Much-Afraid has a worship experience on the hilltop while personally realizing the truth of Romans 8:18 in her own life; the trials which brought her there are not worthy of being compared to the glory which shines before her. As in her previous similar experiences, the next few moments of her journey seem to fly by!

But then what she sees begins to stupefy her. One can hear the mind games begin as she begins to think thoughts entirely apart from what she has learned of the Shepherd. The nearer she draws, the more impassable the walls "appear" to become. The word "appear" is a key word of caution for us. But Much-Afraid proceeds with her thoughts on the basis of appearance and begins to describe things in very difficult terms. The path leads up to an "impassable precipice", stops "dead", etc..

Much-Afraid is "stunned", trembles and shakes. She is whipped even before she arrives at what appears to be the end of the path. There is "no way at all" by which the cliff can be ascended. Do you see how her word pictures lead to the only possible conclusion? "They would have to turn back!"

Do you also see how we all tend to attach labels to things we see with our eyes that limit God? Our choice of words, even in our thoughts, can tend to put away God's mighty power on our behalf, with no opportunity for us to apply our faith in Him if we allow circumstances to dictate to us through our earthly eyes and minds —and language!

QUESTIONS AND PRAYER: You have probably had an experience where you felt that finding a solution to some great need or desire was thought to be "impossible"; completely beyond your abilities or expectations. Yet you worked through it with incredible success! List the factors to which you relate your eventual victory._____

_____

How can you apply this to your circumstances today?_____

_____

Just as this overwhelming realization came to her, Suffering caught her hand and pointed to the rocky walls. A hart, followed by a hind, had appeared from among the jumbled rocks around them and were now actually beginning to ascend the precipice.

As the three stood watching, Much-Afraid turned dizzy and faint, for she saw that the hart, which was leading the way, was following what appeared to be a narrow and intensely steep track which went zigzagging across the face of the cliff. In some parts it was only a narrow ledge, in others there appeared to be rough steps, but in certain places she saw that the track apparently broke right off.

Then the hart would leap across the gap and go springing upward, always closely followed by the hind, who set her feet exactly where his had been, and leaped after him, as lightly, as sure-footed, and apparently unafraid as it was possible for any creature to be. So the two of them leaped and sprang with perfect grace and assurance up the face of the precipice and disappeared from sight over the top.

Much-Afraid covered her face with her hands and sank down on a rock with a horror and dread in her heart such as she had never felt before. Then she felt her two companions take her hands in theirs and heard them say, "Do not be afraid, Much-Afraid, this is not a dead end after all, and we shall not have to turn back. There is a way up the face of the precipice. The hart and the hind have shown it to us quite plainly. We shall be able to follow it too and make the ascent."

"Oh, no! No!" Much-Afraid almost shrieked. "That path is utterly impossible. The deer may be able to manage it, but no human being could. I could never get up there. I would fall headlong and be broken in pieces on those awful rocks." She burst into hysterical sobbing, "It's an impossibility, an absolute impossibility. I cannot get to the High Places that way, and so can never get there at all." Her two guides tried to say something more, but she put her hands over her ears and

146

The Way Revealed

READ: Hind's Feet... facing page & **Romans 1:16–20**

"Thus Sarah obeyed Abraham, calling him lord, and
you have become her children if you do what is right without
being frightened by any fear." —I Peter 3:6

"Jesus said to him, 'If I want him to remain until I come,
what is that to you? You follow Me!'" —John 21:22

There are portraits in nature that "show us the truth and the way". One is illustrated by the hart (the male deer) leading the way for the hind (the female). He faces the risks of going first and she follows in his footsteps "without being frightened by any fear." This is the way of the Shepherd who has gone before us, teaching us to follow Him without any fear.

There are applications here also to the husband-wife relationship, too often lost in finger pointing between the two. The man usually focuses on his wife's anxieties and refusal to follow; her desire to control or "lead". The wife usually focuses on her husband's unreliability; her good reasons not to trust him. But, nevertheless, the hart's and hind's way is God's way. The husband must lead, being willing to fall to his death, if necessary, to meet his responsibilities for finding wisdom and to carry out leadership gently and faithfully. The wife finds her protection only in trusting God to work through the one ultimately responsible for the family.

Much-Afraid providentially sees "the way" revealed, but in her response finds herself immobilized by fear; heart-stopping terror that is in complete contrast to the path and message she has seen.

"There is a way", say her companions. "Oh, no! No!" shrieks Much-Afraid. Her words capture her convictions: "I could never..", "impossibility", "I cannot..", "can never", etc.. This is a true portrait of what is in her mind. But it is not from the LORD.

QUESTIONS AND PRAYER: In the prior devotional lesson you were asked to summarize an event which you thought was "impossible", but which you ultimately accomplished in your life. Please review the key elements of this again. What do you think was the single most important key?_____

_____

_____

_____

broke into another clamor of terrified sobs. There was the Shepherd's Much-Afraid, sitting at the foot of the precipice, wringing her hands and shaking with terror, sobbing over and over again, "I can't do it; I can't. I shall never get to the High Places." Nothing less like royalty could be imagined, but far worse was to follow.

As she crouched on the ground, completely exhausted, they heard a crunching sound and a rattling of loose stones, then a voice close beside her.

"Ha, ha! My dear little cousin, we meet again at last! How do you find yourself now, Much-Afraid, in this delightfully pleasant situation?"

She opened her eyes in fresh terror and found herself looking right into the hideous face of Craven Fear himself.

"I thought somehow," he went on with a look of the most horrible gloating. "Yes, I really thought that we could come together again at last. Did you really believe, you poor little fool, that you could escape from me altogether? No, no, Much-Afraid, you are one of the Fearings, and you can't evade the truth, and what is more, you trembling little idiot, you belong to me. I have come to take you back safely and make sure that you don't wander off again."

"I won't go with you," gasped Much-Afraid, too shocked by this awful apparition to have her wits about her. "I absolutely refuse to go with you."

"Well, you can take your choice," sneered Craven. "Take a look at the precipice before you, my dear cousin. Won't you feel lovely up there! Just look where I'm pointing, Much-Afraid. See there, halfway up, where that dizzy little ledge breaks right off and you have to jump across the chasm on to that bit of rock. Just picture yourself jumping that, Much-Afraid, and finding yourself hanging over space, clutching a bit of slippery rock which you can't hold on to another minute. Just imagine those ugly, knife-like rocks at the foot of the precipice, waiting to receive and mangle you to pieces as your strength gives out, and you plunge down on them."

Perceptions of Obstacles

READ: Hind's Feet... facing page & **Numbers 13**

"And you were dead in your trespasses and sins, in which you formerly
walked according to the course of this world, according to the prince of the power
of the air, of the spirit that is now working in the sons of disobedience."
—Ephesians 2:1–2

"But my servant Caleb, because he has had a different spirit and has
followed Me fully, I will bring into the land which he entered, and his
descendants shall take possession of it." —Numbers 14:24

That we live in a world under demonic dominion is made clear in scripture. Just as clear is that this evil is constrained by God and that we have deliverance offered through Jesus Christ and no other way. How we are influenced in our mind and flesh by spiritual forces determines the outcome. We will either see overwhelming, fearful prospects of defeat and death as most of Israel saw the promised land, and turn back, or we will find the resolve to "go ahead" despite the obstacles.

Another man and I were once defeated in climbing a formidable peak in the Cascade Mts. of Washington, when only about 75 feet from the top. We were intimidated by the fearful exposure. We quit and went on with the rest of the party. Two days later, when about to leave the area for the last time, we decided to attempt it again, requiring a long strenuous trek to retrace our steps. On the second try, we succeeded. The key was in deciding to "go back again" despite our earlier intimidation and the considerable extra effort needed.

Caleb and Joshua trusted in God's promise to "give them the land." It was not clear how they could prevail, but they were willing ("purposed") to go in. God honored them and their offspring for their faith.

Much-Afraid now faces Craven Fear as an "apparition', a true description of his spiritual power. He speaks to her in terms of her flesh, appealing to the vessel in which he controls her by vicious words painting a picture of her imminent "mangling" and death.

QUESTIONS AND PRAYER: What are the chief "appeals" of your flesh which immobilize you with fear? Pain? Loss of health? Death? Looks? Money? Reputation? Which is the most fearful? How are you dealing with these fears?_____

_____
_____
_____

"Doesn't it give you a lovely feeling, Much-Afraid? Just take time to picture it. That's only one of many such broken places on the track, and the higher you go, you dear little fool, the farther you will have to fall. Well, take your choice. Either you must go up there, where you know that you can't, but will end in a mangled heap at the bottom, or you must come back and live with me and be my little slave ever afterward." And the rocks and cliffs seemed to echo again with his gloating laughter.

"Much-Afraid," said the two guides, stooping over her and shaking her by the shoulder gently but firmly. "Much-Afraid, you know where your help lies. Call for help."

She clung to them and sobbed again. "I am afraid to call," she gasped. "I am so afraid that if I call Him, He will tell me that I must go that way, that dreadful, dreadful way, and I can't. It's important. I can't face it. Oh, what shall I do? Whatever shall I do?"

Sorrow bent over her and said very gently but urgently, "You must call for Him, Much-Afraid. Call at once."

"If I call Him," shuddered Much-Afraid through chattering teeth, "He will tell me to build an altar, and I can't. This time I can't."

Craven Fear laughed triumphantly and took a step toward her, but her two companions put themselves between him and his victim. Then Suffering looked at Sorrow, who nodded back. In answer to the nod Suffering took a small but very sharp knife which hung at her girdle, and bending over the crouching figure, pricked her. Much-Afraid cried out in anguish, and then, in utter despair at finding herself helpless in the presence of all three, did that which she ought to have done the moment the path brought them to the foot of the precipice. Though now she felt too ashamed to do it, she did so because she was forced by her extremity. She cried out, "O Lord, I am oppressed; undertake for me. My fears have taken hold upon me, and I am ashamed to look up."

Immobilized by Fear

READ: Hind's Feet... facing page & **Genesis 41:53–42:38**

"But speaking the truth in love, we are to grow up in all aspects
into Him, who is the head, even Christ." —Ephesians 4:15

"If I have to boast, I will boast of what pertains
to my weakness." —II Corinthians 11:30

The "claw" of fear is sunk deeply into poor Much-Afraid by her enemy Craven Fear, even as it was also sunk deeply into Jacob. Fear is not inaccurate regarding the track ahead, but its attitudes prevent a response. It speaks maliciously and demeaningly. It "freezes" us.

To Much-Afraid he states that it is her choice, but places the thought "you can't" in her head and gloats that she is in his power as his slave forever. Speaking truth brings bondage if it is not spoken in love. Will she believe the lie, "I can't"?

Her responses are a word study in immobilization. She is incapacitated even to pray, captured by terror. "I am afraid to call." "I am so afraid that if I call Him, He will tell me that I must go that way". "I can't. " "Its impossible." She says, "I'm afraid," and, "I can't," over and over again. Does this sound like us? Does it sound like the person who refuses to commit his life to Christ because he is afraid of being "sent to Africa as a missionary"? God's love must cast out our fear (I John. 4:18)!

A powerful lesson is demonstrated here by Much-Afraid. In complete helplessness and "utter despair" she does what she is forced to do by her helplessness, despite shame of her fear and emotions. She manages a confession of her true condition to the LORD. Did you know that "confession" merely means "agreement"? Much-Afraid makes agreement with the Shepherd regarding her true condition, even including her being ashamed to look up. She is drawn to the LORD in abject weakness, not in strength. This is the truth and is the door to her being set free.

QUESTIONS AND PRAYER: As a separate word study, please read II Corinthians 11, 12 and 13, counting the number of times that Paul cites or "boasts" in his weakness. Compare this with how you "agree" with God in your attitudes of weakness._____

_____

_____

_____

"Why, Much-Afraid." It was the Shepherd's voice close beside her. "What is the matter? Be of good cheer, it is I, be not afraid."

He sounded so cheery and full of strength, and moreover, without a hint of reproach, that Much-Afraid felt as though a strong and exhilarating cordial had been poured into her heart and that a stream of courage and strength was flowing into her from His presence.

She sat up and looked at Him and saw that He was smiling, almost laughing at her. The shame in her eyes met no answering reproach in His, and suddenly she found words echoing in her heart which other trembling souls had spoken. "My Lord is of very tender compassion to them that are afraid." As she looked, thankfulness welled up in her heart and the icy hand of fear which had clutched her broke and melted away and joy burst into bloom. A little song ran through her mind like a trickling stream.

> *My Beloved is the chiefest*
> *Of ten thousand anywhere.*
> *He is altogether lovely*
> *He is altogether fair,*
> *My Beloved is so gentle*
> *And is strong beyond compare.*

"Much-Afraid," said the Shepherd again, "tell Me, what is the matter? Why are you so fearful?"

"It is the way you have chosen for me to go," she whispered. "it looks so dreadful, Shepherd, so impossible. I turn giddy and faint whenever I look at it. The roes and hinds can go there, but they are not limping, crippled, or cowardly like me."

"But, Much-Afraid, what did I promise you in the Valley of Humiliation?" asked the Shepherd with a smile. Much-Afraid looked startled, and the blood rushed

Set Free

READ: Hind's Feet... facing page & **Genesis 43:1–14**

"If there is an angel as mediator for him, one out of a thousand, to remind a man what is right for him, then let him be gracious to him, and say, 'Deliver him from going down to the pit, I have found a ransom.'" —Job 33:23–24

We have been reading again of Jacob, the father of Joseph and Judah, a fearful, deceitful man who reproduced much "bad seed" in his offspring. In the reading today we see how he was delivered from crippling fear and enabled to release his son Benjamin to face the danger of the trip to Egypt. His deliverance is based upon a mighty principle true of the creation and written throughout scripture. It is also the principle that ministered in the Spirit to Job, by the wise young man who had remained silent throughout all the remonstrations of Job's foolish friends! It is the principle of ransom. We are set free by ransom. We are delivered by someone else paying the price in our place. It is justice and mercy in a perfect combination.

When Judah offered himself to become "surety" and to "stand" in the place of responsibility for Benjamin, he "triggered" the enabling power of God in his father Jacob to let Benjamin go and to personally accept the consequences. It was the key to responding to Pharaoh's (Joseph's) demands and placed the sons of Jacob into the discipline Joseph intended, to make them responsible for their sins. It was the key to ransoming Jacob's entire family from famine, fear and evil threatening to destroy them all!

There is a principle of "ownership" associated with ransom. We have been purchased for a price (Acts 20:28, I Cor.6:20, 7:23). Why? <u>Because we are loved</u>! Because we are valuable and worth the price. We belong to the One who has proved we are precious, by exchanging His life for ours. Therefore, our value is set far beyond measure.

Much-Afraid turns to the Redeemer who set her free!

QUESTIONS AND PRAYER: When one gives his life for another, do you think it brings the two closer together? _____

_____

How does it get closer? What happens to the relationship? In which of your relationships can this possibly be seen? _____

_____

In which relationships should it be seen?_____

_____

into her cheeks and ebbed again, leaving them as white as before. "You said," she began and broke off and then began again. "O Shepherd, You said You would make my feet like hinds' feet and set me upon mine High Places."

"Well," He answered cheerily, "the only way to develop hinds' feet is to go by the paths which the hinds use—like this one."

Much-Afraid trembled and looked at Him shamefacedly, "I don't think—I want—hinds' feet, if it means I have to go on a path like that," she said slowly and painfully.

The Shepherd was a very surprising person. Instead of looking either disappointed or disapproving, He actually laughed again. "Oh, yes you do," He said cheerfully. "I know you better than you know yourself, Much-Afraid. You want it very much indeed, and I promise you these hinds' feet. Indeed, I have brought you on purpose to this back side of the desert, where the mountains are particularly steep and where there are no paths but the tracks of the deer and of the mountain goats for you to follow, that the promise may be fulfilled. What did I say to you the last time that we met?"

"You said, 'Now shalt thou see what I will do,'" she answered, and then, looking at Him reproachfully, added, "But I never dreamed You would do anything like this! Lead me to an impassable precipice up which nothing can go but deer and goats, when I'm no more like a deer or a goat than is a jellyfish. It's too—it's too—" she fumbled for words, and then burst out laughing. "Why, it's preposterously absurd! It's crazy! Whatever will You do next?"

The Shepherd laughed too. "I love doing preposterous things," He replied. "Why, I don't know anything more exhilarating and delightful than turning weakness into strength, and fear into faith, and that which has been marred into perfection. If there is one thing more than another which I should enjoy doing at

"Preposterous" Truth

READ: Hind's Feet... facing page & **Romans 11:22–36**

"Now to Him who is able to do exceedingly abundantly beyond all that we ask or think, according to the power that works within us." —Ephesians 3:20

"But we speak God's wisdom in a mystery, the hidden wisdom, which God predestined before the ages to our glory." —I Corinthians 2:7

Many times in scripture God tells His people that He will "show (or teach) them things"; miracles, power, signs and the "way we should go". He told Jehoshaphat and his people to "stand and see" the salvation of the LORD on their behalf. Always, when God shows Himself, we are confounded and astonished! How can anyone counsel or anticipate the actions of the Holy God who "works all things according to the counsel of His will" (Eph.1:11)? It is foolishness to think otherwise, yet we often do that, don't we?

How natural and humorous the conversation flows. "How else would you expect to gain hinds' feet, except to go by the paths they use?" It does seem sort of obvious, doesn't it? Is that the way we think when we are being asked by God to forgive, extend mercy or "turn the other cheek" to enemies and follow His paths of righteousness? Note: the righteousness of His paths is His, not ours. We must follow His path.

Well, sure, it is easy to see now that Much-Afraid should have expected a surprise; something that would fill her with consternation. I recall times when I've been hesitant due to some "dread" as to how God would answer my prayers of commitment because I was nearly certain He would dismay me! Have you also had this experience?

So we are led from one preposterous, impossible situation to the next by a preposterously wonderful, awesome, humorous, loving and perfectly confident and divine God; not dismayed in the least by our weaknesses. He knows nothing more exhilarating and delightful than turning weaknesses into strength and "jellyfish into mountain goats"!

QUESTIONS AND PRAYER: Let us delight in the LORD's delightful ways. Thank Him for at least one humorous testimony He's given you which show these characteristics in your life._____

_____

_____

_____

_____

this moment it is turning a jellyfish into a mountain goat. That is My special work," He added with the light of a great joy in His face. "Transforming things—to take Much-Afraid, for instance, and to transform her into—" He broke off and then went on laughingly. "Well, we shall see later on what she finds herself transformed into."

It was a really extraordinary scene. In the place where just a little while before all had been fear and despair were the Shepherd and Much-Afraid, sitting on the rocks at the foot of the impassible precipice, laughing together as though at the greatest joke in the world.

"Come now, little jellyfish," said the Shepherd, "do you believe that I can change you into a mountain goat and get you to the top of the precipice?"

"Yes," replied Much-Afraid.

"Will you let Me do it?"

"Yes," she answered, "if You want to do such a crazy and preposterous thing, why certainly You may."

"Do you believe that I will let you be put to shame on the way up?"

Much-Afraid looked at Him and then said something that she had never been willing to say before. "I don't think I mind so very much if You do; only have Your will and way in me, Shepherd. Nothing else matters."

As she spoke, something lovely happened. A double rainbow appeared above the precipice, arching it completely, so that the zigzag path up which the roe and the doe had gone was framed in the glowing colors. It was such a beautiful and extraordinary sight that Much-Afraid gasped with wonder and delight, but there was something else about it which was almost more wonderful. She saw that Sorrow and Suffering, who had drawn aside while the Shepherd spoke to her, were standing one at either side of the path, and where the ends of the rainbow touched the earth, one touched Suffering and the other Sorrow.

Willing to Bear Shame

READ: Hind's Feet... facing page & Hebrews 13:9–13

"...fixing our eyes on Jesus, the author and perfector of faith, who for the joy set before Him endured the cross, despising the shame, and has sat down at the right hand of the throne of God." —Hebrews 12:2

"For if we have become united with Him in the likeness of His death, certainly we shall be also in the likeness of His resurrection." —Romans 6:5

In His confidence and edifying laughter, the Shepherd builds up Much-Afraid. His confidence and perspective become hers. Words that would have been destructive from Craven Fear become an endearing "pet-name" from the Shepherd. "Come now, little jelly-fish......", He says. He asks her a few questions and she gladly embraces "crazy and preposterous things". Then, in this rich fellowship and confidence, she also gladly embraces shame, if He wills that for her, too.

Grace comes through humility (I Pet. 5:5), and nothing is as humbling as shame. When it comes and is dealt with rightly it is wonderfully cleansing. But few embrace it willingly without a fight with the flesh!

Much-Afraid immediately sees a vision in which Sorrow and Suffering are transfigured in a rainbow to such beauty that she is dazzled. In Matthew, chapter 17, James, John and Peter also saw Jesus transfigured, where His face shown like the sun and His garments became as white as light. When Peter leaped to conclusions about what he should do, our Heavenly Father overshadowed them as a bright cloud and admonished them to listen to His Son, Jesus (Matt. 17:1–9).

We can conclude that Much-Afraid is being given a vision of the future transfiguration of Sorrow and Suffering into glorious beings, possibly among her personal companions for eternity, but this does not change her present task to embrace them as they are and obey the Shepherd.

QUESTIONS AND PRAYER: Do you tend to think of God's promises being more powerful in the past or future than at present? Do you recall that He is the God, "I Am"? Can you claim something today from Him to "listen to"? _____

_____

_____

_____

_____

In the shining glory of the rainbow colors, the two veiled figures were so transfigured with beauty that Much-Afraid could only look at them for a moment before being dazzled.

Then she did that which only a short time before had seemed utterly impossible. She knelt down at the foot of the precipice and built an altar and laid on it
her will, her dread, and her shrinking, and when the fire had fallen she found
among the ashes a larger and rougher-looking stone than any of the others, sharp-
edged and dark in color, but otherwise quite ordinary looking.

This she put in her purse and then rose to her feet and waited for the Shepherd to show her what to do. In her heart she was hoping that He would accompany her up the dreadful ascent as He had gone with her down into the desert,
but this He did not do.

Instead, he led her to the foot of the precipice and said, "Now, Much-Afraid,
you have really come at last to the foot of the High Places, and a new stage of the
journey is to begin. There are new lessons for you to learn.

"I must tell you that this precipice to which the path has led you is at the foot
of Mount Injury. The whole mountain range stretches a long way beyond this in
either direction, and everywhere it is as steep or even steeper than here. There are
even more terrible precipices on the sides of Mount Reviling and Mount Hate and
Mount Persecution and others besides, but nowhere is it possible to find a way up
to the High Places and into the Kingdom of Love without surmounting at least
one of them. This is the one which I have chosen for you to ascend.

"On the way here you have been learning the lesson of acceptance-with-joy,
which is the first letter in the alphabet of Love. Now you must learn the B of the
alphabet of Love. You have come to the foot of Mount Injury, and I hope and
expect that on the way up the precipice you will discover what is this next letter
of the alphabet, and that you will learn and practice it as you have the A of Love.

A Guarded Kingdom

READ: Hind's Feet... facing page & **Genesis 3:22–24**

"Enter by the narrow gate; for the gate is wide, and the way is broad that leads to destruction, and many are those who enter by it. For the gate is small and the way is narrow that leads to life, and few are those who find it." —Matthew 7:13–14

Eden is guarded with cherubim stationed at the east, lest man "take also from the tree of life, and eat, and live forever". Yet there is one way from death to life, the keys of which are given to the Son of Man, who administers life according to the will of the Father (John 5:24, 6:44). Much-Afraid now confronts this allegorically in the form of an impassable range of mountains of "terrible precipices", being told that all who would enter the Kingdom of Love, must surmount at least one of the difficult mountains of Reviling, Hate, Persecution, Injury or others similar.

She is also told that she is on a search; a quest for her second lesson in learning the alphabet of Love. The Shepherd "hopes and expects" she will discover it on the way up the precipice, then "learn and practice it." It seems things are slightly more organized for her now; she is on a definite procedural search for discovering and applying secrets to her life. We think of Easter Egg hunts, searches for wild blackberries or nuts, difficult experiments or school examinations. These are only examples of the quest that God really has us about.

What will happen if we work at it? Are there promises? "Seek, and you shall find; knock, and it shall be opened to you" (Matt. 7:7). "He is a rewarder of those who seek Him" (Heb. 11:6). "The effective prayer of a righteous man can accomplish much" (Jas. 5:16). Yes! We are assured that diligence pays off with God, too! Let us pray for a spirit of diligence in seeking God's secrets of the Kingdom of Love.

QUESTIONS AND PRAYER: There is possibly an area in which your father, employer, wife or children have been used by God to call you to discover a "secret of Love" to apply. If so, what is it?_____

_____

_____

How can you correctly respond in this as an actual quest with God?_____

_____

_____

_____

Remember that though you must now meet Injury and surmount it, there is nothing on the way up this terrible-looking precipice nor indeed anything that you
may meet above and beyond it that can do you the slightest harm or hurt if you
will learn and steadfastly practice the second lesson in the Ascent of Love."

When He had said this He put His hands upon her with special solemnity and
gentleness and blessed her. Then He called her companions, who immediately
stepped forward. Next He took a rope from a crevice in the wall of rock, and with
His own hands roped together the three who were to ascend the precipice. Sorrow was in front and Suffering behind, with Much-Afraid in the middle, so that
the two who were so strong and sure-footed went before and after. In this way,
even if Much-Afraid slipped and fell, they would be able to hold her up and support her by the rope.

Lastly, He put His hand to His side and brought out a little bottle of cordial
which He gave to Much-Afraid, telling her to drink a little at once and to make
use of it if ever she felt giddy or faint on the way up. The label on the bottle read,
"Spirit of Grace and Comfort," and when Much-Afraid had taken a drop or two
she felt so revived and strengthened that she was ready to begin the ascent without any feeling of faintness, although there was still a sensation of dread in her
heart.

By this time the evening was well advanced, but being summer there were yet
two or three hours before it would begin to be dark, and the Shepherd charged
them to start at once for, said He, "Although you cannot possibly reach the top
before nightfall, there is a cave farther up the cliff which you cannot see from
here, and there you can rest and spend the night in perfect safety. If you stay
down here at the foot of the precipice your enemies will most certainly steal upon
you and seek to do you harm. However, they will not follow you up this track, and
while you are going up you will be beyond their reach. Though I doubt not," He
added warningly, "that you will meet them again when you have reached the top."

With that He smiled encouragingly upon them and immediately Sorrow put
her foot upon the first step of the narrow little track which zigzagged up the face
of the cliff. Much-Afraid followed next, and then Suffering, and in a moment or
two they were beginning the ascent.

160

Parakletos'—Advocate, Comforter

READ: Hind's Feet... facing page & **John 14:16–31, 15:26–27**

"And do not get drunk with wine, for that is dissipation,
but be filled with the Spirit." —Ephesians 5:18

"The mind of a man plans his way, but the LORD directs his steps."
—Proverbs 16:9

Sorrow and Suffering are revealed now to Much-Afraid as more than companions whose hands can keep her from entertaining the spirits of the Fearing family. By providing a rope and instruction, the Shepherd now instructs more direct support toward helping her on her journey.

He also hands her a little bottle of cordial, representing the Holy Spirit, which scripture advises is to be taken continually as the alternative to being drunk on alcohol. The name is "Spirit of Grace and Comfort". The Greek word used in the Jesus' description of the Spirit's ministry is *Parakletos* ; Advocate or Comforter (Helper, as translated in the NASB). God describes Himself as "the God of all comfort, who comforts us in all our affliction so that we may be able to comfort those who are in any affliction with the comfort with which we ourselves are comforted by God" (II Cor. 1:3–4). A drop or two revives and strengthens Much-Afraid.

Despite the well advanced hour of the evening, the Shepherd directs them to start at once. It is normal to make plans according to what seems prudent, but then to respond to the LORD's redirection of our actual steps. We see now also the close keeping of author Hurnard's allegory to the terms of scripture for "walking", "steps", "the way", "journey", etc., which typify all descriptions of walking by faith throughout the New Testament.

The analogy is made complete when Sorrow complies "immediately" to the Shepherd's charge to them and puts her foot down on the first step of the long climb ahead.

QUESTIONS AND PRAYER: Can you recall the actual day you committed to "walk" with the Holy Spirit as the director of your "steps"? Have you accepted by faith the Holy Spirit as your Comforter? Can you note a date on this also, and if not, invite or renew in writing now the Holy Spirit's authority in you?

_____

_____

_____

_____

CHAPTER 10

Ascent of the Precipice Injury

Once on the track, Much-Afraid discovered to her surprise and deep thankfulness that it was not nearly so appalling in actual fact as it had seemed in anticipation. Steep, difficult, and slippery it certainly was, and also painfully narrow, but the feeling of being securely roped to her strong companions was very reassuring. Also, the cordial of the Spirit of Grace and Comfort which she had just drunk kept her from feeling giddy and faint when she looked over the edge, the thing she had most dreaded. Moreover, for the first half-hour of their ascent the rainbow still shone above them, and though the Shepherd had disappeared from view Much-Afraid had a lovely sense that He was still close beside them.

She did not look down unless obliged to do so, but once quite soon after they had started she had to wait in a little niche in the rock at one of the difficult places while Sorrow felt her way forward and Suffering waited in the rear.

Just then, she looked down, and felt very thankful indeed that the Shepherd had charged them to start the ascent that evening and not spend the night down below. Sitting on the rocks below were all five of her enemies, gazing up at them and grimacing with fury and spite. Indeed, as she looked she was startled to see Self-Pity (who always looked less ugly and dangerous than his companions) stoop down and pick a sharp stone which he flung at her with all his might. Fortunately they were already practically out of reach of stone-throwing, but the

Climbing "Roped"

READ: Hind's Feet... facing page & **Ecclesiastes 4:9–12**

"I will extol Thee, O LORD, for Thou hast lifted me up, and hast not let my enemies rejoice over me." —Psalm 30:1

"Five of you will chase a hundred , and a hundred of you will chase ten thousand, and your enemies will fall before you by the sword." —Leviticus 26:8

There are a number of biblical references to the multiplication of safety, protection or power when people are agreed to "walk together". This includes obtaining multiple witnesses to avoid deception and error (Deut. 19:15, Matt. 18:16, I Tim. 5:19, I Cor. 4:29, etc.), chasing the enemy (Deut. 32:30) and even mountain climbing. "For if either of them falls, the one will lift up his companion. But woe to the one who falls when there is not another to lift him up" (Eccl. 4:10). There is great strength in a group of people working together, and those trained in mountain climbing will recognize these analogies immediately!

The way becomes "painfully narrow" for Much-Afraid, emphasizing the Matthew 7:14 reference to the "narrow way" we studied earlier. She experiences the head clearing effect of her Cordial, which keeps her from feeling "giddy and faint" when she looked over the edge (just the opposite effect one would expect from alcohol.) Then, at an appropriate time, she does look down and thankfully discovers her enemies below her. She makes some interesting observations:

First, she sees distinction between Self Pity and the others. She is beginning to develop discernment and possible ability to distinguish between spirits (I Cor. 12:10). She illustrates growing perspective in her view of her enemy. She also sees she has been "lifted up" above her enemies.. How quickly Sorrow and Suffering have assisted her!

QUESTIONS AND PRAYER: Can you name an enemy spirit (such as anger, sexual lust, lying, fear, etc.) above which you have been raised by the LORD?

_____

_____

Do sorrow and suffering relate to this? Weakness? How does this give you new perspective for prayers of (a) thanksgiving or (b) perspective for other enemies which torment you?_____

_____

jagged piece did hit the cliff just below her, and Much-Afraid was greatly relieved when she felt Sorrow pull gently on the rope to tell her that she now could move forward.

She remembered the Shepherd's warning that she was likely to meet these enemies again when the precipice was surmounted, though how they would get up onto the Mount Injury she did not know; only that there must be some other way which they could use.

So the three of them climbed higher and higher while the shadows thrown by the cliffs lengthened over the plain below and the sun went down in a blaze of glory beyond the desert and the great sea. From the height which they had now reached they could plainly see the western sea, along the shores of which they had traveled for so long.

The track they followed wound up and ever upward, back and forth across the face of the cliff, and though it was crumbling and even broken in some places, Much-Afraid was tremendously relieved to find that nowhere at all was it too difficult, nor even at the spot halfway up the cliff which Craven Fear had so particularly pointed out to her.

On arriving there just as darkness fell, she found that though the path had indeed broken right away, a plank had been laid across the gap and a rope placed through iron rings in the rock face to form a handrail to which she could cling as she walked across the narrow bridge. The hart and the hind, of course, had disdained such unnecessary assistance and had leaped across the chasm, making it look as though there was nothing there. However, even with the handrail to steady her, Much-Afraid was very careful to close her imagination altogether to the picture which Craven Fear had painted. From bitter experience she knew that pictures thrown on the screen of her imagination could seem much more unnerving and terrible than the actual facts.

Disciplining the Mind

READ: Hind's Feet... facing page & II Peter 1

"And do not be conformed to this world, but be transformed by the renewing of your mind, that you may prove what the will of God is, that which is good and acceptable and perfect." —Romans 12:2

"We are destroying speculations and every lofty thing raised up against the knowledge of God, and we are taking every thought captive to the obedience of Christ." —II Corinthians 10:5

Much-Afraid's journey to the High Places reveals her mind now coming under more control of God's Spirit. Sorrow's pull on the rope is welcome relief! She also remembers the Shepherd's warning about meeting her enemies again and meditates over how they would gain access to the higher slopes of Mount Injury. (I wonder, too, don't you? Perhaps we'll soon see!)

But mainly, she is able to keenly see and learn during her ascent, as things she couldn't see from below become apparent; the handrail, the plank and the fixed line in its iron rings; illusions of the deer regarding the difficulty of the track. It is evident that others have been here before her! Now, however, even with the handrail there to steady her, Much-Afraid is very careful to "close her imagination" altogether "to the picture which Craven Fear had painted." From the word of the Shepherd and from "bitter experience" she has learned that her mind can make things seem "much more unnerving and terrible than the actual facts."

As portrayed by Much-Afraid, women tend to be tormented in thoughts of inadequate security. Men tend to be tormented in thoughts of inadequate bodily nurture (sex, food, drink, rest, etc.). Both are "lusts" due to the effects of sin and "soulish" desires (I Cor.3:1–3) and, like the fires of hell, are never satisfied by the world (Prov.27:20). Only Christ can provide healing and godly contentment in such areas.

QUESTIONS AND PRAYER: Do you and/or your wife have conflicting desires in finances, security, eating, drinking or sexual appetites? Other appetites? How do you deal with these as indicators of sinful behavior for which Jesus' blood has authority to remove the curse (Gal. 3:13)?_____

_____

_____

_____

_____

When the plank was crossed safely they discovered themselves to be in an exceedingly narrow gorge quite invisible from below. Directly facing them was the very resting place which the Shepherd had spoken of, a little cave where they were to pass the night.

With a sense of great relief and thankfulness she went inside and looked around. Its situation was such that though she could not look down into the dizzy depths beneath, it was possible to look right out over the plateau and the desert to the far-off sea. The moon had just risen and was shedding a pure silver light over everything, and the first stars appeared like faint flickers in the darkening sky. In the cave itself flat rocks had been placed to form rude seats and a table, and on the ground at one side were piled sheepskins on which they could rest.

Not far from the cave entrance a tiny waterfall trickled down the cliff, and they went to it in turn and refreshed themselves. Then Sorrow and Suffering produced two packages of bread and dried fruits and nuts which the Shepherd had given them at the foot of the ascent. With these they gladly satisfied their hunger, and then, overcome by weariness, they laid themselves down in the cave and fell into dreamless slumber.

Much-Afraid woke with the first light of dawn, and getting up, walked to the entrance of the cave. In the cold light of early morning she could not help telling herself that a scene of utter desolation lay before her. As far as the eye could see was nothing but empty plain and sea, with lowering cliffs above her and jagged rock below. The pleasant wooded country which they had left was out of sight, and in all the vast area upon which she looked she saw not a single tree and scarcely a stunted bush. "How desolate," thought Much-Afraid, "and those rocks beneath look very cruel indeed, as if they were waiting to injure and destroy anything which falls upon them. It seems as though nothing can grow anywhere in all this barren waste."

Refreshment and Rest

READ: Hind's Feet... facing page & **Hebrews 4:1–10**

"Repent therefore and return, that your sins may be
wiped away, in order that times of refreshing may come
from the presence of the LORD." —Acts 3:19

"'Behold, I will stand before you there on the rock at Horeb; and you shall strike
the rock, and water will come out of it, that the people may drink.' And Moses
did so in the sight of the elders of Israel." —Exodus 17:6

God is merciful and full of loving-kindness; very much involved with the rest and re-freshment of His people. Aside from the fact that "rest" is a basic tenet of the creation, marked by the Sabbath, He is also mindful of our frame, "that we are but dust" (Ps. 104:14), and of the effects of sin and separation from Him. He knows we need refreshment and provides for it throughout nature and in Christ.

Hannah Hurnard illustrates her familiarity with the Swiss Alps by her accurate portrait of the spirit of a small sheltered spot part way up the slope, watered by a small waterfall in the midst of a steep, rocky waste. Every provision for food, water and rest is provided. What a cozy spot to spend a night on the cliffs. "Sheepskins" provide a warm bed to cover and rest weary bodies .

Much-Afraid awakes the next morning, refreshed and with a mind given to meditating and observing. She does not appear to be "entertaining" evil, but merely marveling over the harshness of the desolation. She is naturally led by her observations and meditations about how things "seem" to a frame of mind ready for her next major discovery.

QUESTIONS AND PRAYER: God tells us that the messages "clearly seen" in nature leave us "without excuse" regarding His eternal power and divine nature (Rom. 1:20). What activities do you have where you can also spend time alone observing and relating the word of God to nature? Would you consider making a covenant of time to do this with those you love, where God is the center of the activity?_____

_____

_____

With such a covenant, do you think God will reveal further secrets of His creation and nature to you as He did to Hannah Hurnard?_____

_____

Just then she looked up at the cliffs above her head and started with surprise and delight. In a tiny crevice of the rock, where a few drops from the trickling waterfall could occasionally sprinkle it, was a single plant. It had just two or three leaves, and one fragile stem, almost hair-like in its slenderness, grew out at right angles to the wall. On the stem was one flower, blood red in color, which glowed like a lamp or flame of fire in the early rays of the sun.

Much-Afraid stared at it for some moments, noticing the wall which completely imprisoned it, the minute aperture through which it had forced its way to the light, and the barren loneliness of its surroundings. Its roots were clamped around by sheer rock, its leaves scarcely able to press outside the prison home, yet it had insisted on bursting into bloom, and was holding its little face open to the sun and burning like a flame of joy. As she looked up at it Much-Afraid asked, as she had in the desert, "What is your name, little flower, for indeed I never saw another like you."

At that moment the sun touched the blood-red petals so that they shone more vividly than ever, and a little whisper rustled from the leaves.

"My name is 'Bearing-the-Cost,' but some call me 'Forgiveness.'"

Then Much-Afraid recalled the words of the Shepherd, "On the way up the precipice you will discover the next letter in the alphabet of Love. Begin to practice it at once."

She gazed at the little flower and said again, "Why call you that?"

Once more, a little whispering laugh passed through the leaves, and she thought she heard them say, "I was separated from all my companions, exiled from home, carried here and imprisoned in this rock. It was not my choice, but the work of others who, when they had dropped me here, went away and left me to bear the results of what they had done.

Likeness to Joseph

READ: Hind's Feet... facing page & **Psalm 66**

"And Judah said to his brothers, "What profit is it for us to kill our brother and
cover up his blood? Come and let us sell him to the Ishmaelites and not lay
our hands on him; for he is our brother, our own flesh." And his brothers
listened to him." —Genesis 37:26–27

"that I may know Him, and the power of His resurrection and the fellow—
ship of His sufferings, being conformed to His death." —Philippians 3:10

Over a number of lessons we've read the story of Joseph and are now familiar with his
ordeals resulting from his brothers having sold him into slavery. Much-Afraid now meets a
flower which sounds like Joseph. The analogies of this comparison are stunning; at least
five of them in the second paragraph, alone!

The flower has overcome its confines, a rock prison, coming through a "narrow" aperture (way), to the "light", contrasting beautifully to its barren, hostile surroundings. It holds
its face open to the "sun" it sought. How beautiful! All of these are portraits of the children
of God being drawn to the Savior. Its character is "Bearing-the-Cost".

Blood-red petals portray the sacrificial blood made in payment of "Bearing-the-Cost".
For "without shedding of blood, there is no forgiveness" (Heb.9:22). Without Christ, we
have no forgiveness. In conformance with Him, we can forgive anything.

The flower has no misgivings or complaints; all of its circumstances have been used for
the building of Love, the love of the sun, himself. All of the features of its experience are
those of Joseph, who was made into a beautiful man of God by having been taken away
from the spirit of his father and the abominable family into which he was born. Slavery
produced a chaste, wise man able to hear and obey God, serving as an instrument of accountability in his family's salvation. He became the instrument that forged a righteous
Judah.

QUESTIONS AND PRAYER: The flower has pressed its face toward its love, the
sun. Do you see the allegory of this picture? How would you describe the manner
in which you are being drawn toward the "sun"? _____
_____
_____
_____
_____
_____

"I have borne and have not fainted; I have not ceased to love, and Love helped me push through the crack in the rock until I could look right out onto my Love the sun himself. See now! There is nothing whatever between my Love and my heart, nothing around to distract me from him. He shines upon me and makes me to rejoice, and has atoned to me for all that was taken from me and done against me. There is no flower in all the world more blessed or more satisfied than I, for I look up to him as a weaned child and say, 'Whom have I in heaven but Thee, and there is none upon earth that I desire but Thee.'"

Much-Afraid looked at the glowing flame above her head, and a longing which was almost envy leaped into her heart. She knew what she must do. Kneeling on the narrow path beneath the imprisoned flower, she said, "O my Lord, behold me—I am Thy little handmaiden Bearing-the-Cost."

At that moment a fragment of the rock which imprisoned the roots of the flower above her loosened and fell at her feet. She picked it up and put it very gently with the other seven stones in her purse, then returned to the cave. Sorrow and Suffering were waiting for her with a further supply of bread and raisins and nuts, and after they had given thanks and had eaten, they roped themselves together again and continued up the precipice.

After a little while they came to a place which was very steep and slippery. Suddenly Much-Afraid had her first fall and cut herself quite badly on the pieces of jagged rock which had tripped her. It was a good thing she was so securely roped, for a great terror came upon her and she became so giddy and faint that had she not been tied she might have slipped over the edge of the path and been dashed to pieces on the rocks below. As this thought struck her she was so overcome with panic and trembling that all she could do was to crouch against the wall of rock and cry out to her companions that she was fainting and was in terror of falling.

The Sun and The Son

READ: Hind's Feet... facing page & Psalm 19

"But for you who fear My name the sun of righteousness will rise with healing in its wings; and you will go forth and skip about like calves from the stall."
—Malachi 4:2

"...and His face shone like the sun, and His garments became as white as light." —Matthew 17:2

The analogies of the flower "Bearing-the-Cost" are completed by description of its undistracted love and worship for the sun, "himself". He "shines upon me and makes me to rejoice". Then the flower quotes from Psalm 73, identifying the "sun" as the LORD.

The sun is identified in Psalm 19 as being like the "Bridegroom" going forth to spread its light over the earth. In many different scriptural portraits of light and life we gather that the design of the sun of our heavens is merely an astronomical "picture" of the true Sun, the Son of God.

The power of prisons, barrenness and sterility to enable our undistracted focus upon the LORD is stupendous. Away from the world and the flesh; the spirits that war against our souls are diminished when there is no material hope or comfort. Sorrow and suffering become wonderful companions to get our faces directed toward the true source of life.

Much-Afraid resolves to be conformed to the lesson of the flower. As a symbol of a "wall-breaking" that then takes place in her, a rock "loosens" and falls to her feet. She places it in her purse with the others.

Is it no surprise that after this resolution Much-Afraid is injured and sheds blood on the sharp rocks of her path? Notice that these are not superficial scratches and bruises; they are severe cuts that impede her walk. But it is not merely the physical injury that impedes her; mental panic and trembling also break out. She claims "fainting" and is in terror of falling even though she has already seen the reliability of the rope.

QUESTIONS AND PRAYER: How are your attitudes toward sorrow and suffering changing with these studies? Do you feel differently toward the process by which God has chosen for you to be conformed to Christ?_____

_____

_____

_____

_____

Immediately Sorrow, who was in front, tightened the rope, then Suffering came up to her, put her arms around her and said urgently, "Drink some of the cordial which the Shepherd gave you."

Much-Afraid was so faint and frightened that she could only lie in the arms of Suffering and gasp, "I don't know where the bottle is—I can't move even to fumble for it."

Then Suffering herself put her hand into the bosom of the fainting girl, drew out the bottle, and poured a few drops between her lips. After a few moments the color returned to Much-Afraid's cheeks, and the faintness began to pass off, but still she could not move. She took more of the Spirit of Grace and Comfort and began to feel strengthened.

Then Sorrow, who had come back to the place where she was crouching, gently shortened the rope so that Much-Afraid could take her hand and again they started to climb. In the fall, however, Much-Afraid had cut both knees so severely that she could only limp forward very painfully, moaning continually and halting constantly. Her companions were very patient, but progress was so slow that finally it became necessary to make greater speed, or they would not reach the top of the precipice before nightfall, and there was no other cave where they could rest.

At last Suffering stooped over her and asked, "Much-Afraid, what were you doing when you left the cave this morning and went off by yourself?" Much-Afraid gave her a startled look, then said with a painful flush, "I was looking at a flower which I had not seen before, growing in the rock by the waterfall."

"What flower was that?" persisted Suffering very gently.

"It was the flower of Bearing-the-Cost," replied Much-Afraid in a very low voice, "but some call it Forgiveness." For a few moments she was silent, remembering the altar she had built and realizing that she was not practicing this new and difficult letter of the alphabet of Love. Then said she, "I wonder if it would help my knees if we put a few drops of the cordial on them."

Suffering in the Flesh

READ: Hind's Feet... facing page & Revelation 6:1–11

"...'If only we had perished when our brothers perished before the LORD! Why then have you brought the LORD's assembly into this wilderness, for us and our beasts to die here?" —Numbers 20:3–4

"You have not yet resisted to the point of shedding blood in your striving against sin." —Hebrews 12:4

I have observed in myself many times the tendency to magnify and plead for sympathy over my fleshly experiences. Do I think it will bring me relief? Perhaps! In fact, I was usually in the midst of physical distress when, over the years I worked in Boy Scouting, I also had to discern from the pleas and complaints of boys the extent to which they had serious problems. Usually, but not always, they were merely complaining. On a long hike trip, if I did not correctly discern this one way or the other, it could seriously jeopardize either a boy or the group's goals and safety. It was a great teaching discipline for me to minister to both individual needs and group needs while I myself was also hurting.

Much-Afraid receives some ministry of the Spirit through the flask of Cordial, but goes up the trail quite audibly, moaning continually and halting constantly, exactly as thousands of boys and millions of people have done under similar circumstances. Their attitudes, however, if not changed, will eventually drag down the goals and welfare of the whole group; forty years in the desert for Israel, loss of opportunity to come into the promised land for Moses. Now, Much-Afraid's attitude threatens to prevent completing the day's needed goal unless her companions do something.

Suffering gets the job done "at last" by two gentle questions which reveal to Much-Afraid that she has failed to emulate the lesson of "Bearing-the-Cost". In her repentance she also receives an inspiration.

QUESTIONS AND PRAYER: Please identify two areas where you "audible" your suffering to others and allow it to slow your progress._____

_____

Can you see why you do this? What is a solution?_____

_____

Why does inspiration frequently come on the heels of repentance?_____

_____

"Let us try," said Sorrow and Suffering both together. "It is an excellent suggestion."

As they dropped a little of the cordial on both knees, almost at once the bleeding ceased, and the worst of the smart and pain died away. Her legs remained very stiff and she was still obliged to limp quite badly, but they did go forward at a much better pace. By late afternoon they were right at the top of the awful ascent, and found themselves in a forest of young pine trees with moss and blueberries growing on the banks beside the path, and the precipice which had looked so impassable actually behind them. They sat down on one of the mossy banks in the wood to rest, then heard a voice singing quite close at hand.

> *Thou art fair, my dearest love,*
> *There is no spot in thee.*
> *Come with me to the heights above,*
> *Yet fairer visions see.*
> *Up to the mount of Myrrh and thence*
> *Across the hills of Frankincense,*
> *To where the dawn's clear innocence*
> *Bids all the shadows flee.*
>
> *Come with me, O my fairest dear,*
> *With me to Lebanon,*
> *Look from the peaks of grim Shenir,*
> *Amana and Hermon.*
> *The lions have their dens up there—-*
> *The leopards prowl the glens up there,*
> *But from the top the view is clear*
> *Of land yet to be won.*

(Cant. 4:7,8)

There, coming toward them through a clearing in the trees, was the Shepherd Himself.

Spirit Over Flesh

READ: Hind's Feet... facing page & **Galatians 5:16–26**

"Keep watching and praying, that you may not come into temptation;
the spirit is willing, but the flesh is weak." —Mark 14:38

"And being aroused, He rebuked the wind and said to the sea, 'Hush,
be still.' And the wind died down and it became perfectly calm." —Mark 4:39

Through the inspiration given to Much-Afraid and encouragement of her companions, she discovers that the Spirit of Grace and Comfort, the Holy Spirit, has authority over her flesh. It quiets the worst of her pain and enables her to proceed at a more rapid pace. In a pilgrimage with the LORD, we should embrace such power to bring the flesh under discipline.

Galatians and other scripture make it clear that the flesh and the Spirit cannot both have their way at the same time, for they mutually oppose each other. One or the other prevails. We know the flesh will always attempt to destroy or diminish the work of God and his goals for our lives. The Spirit will pursue the goals identified in John 14, 15 and 16 by Jesus.

The result is also illustrated geographically. Much-Afraid rises above elements which threaten her (the precipice and the time limitation) into peaceful, more friendly environs. If she could see the whole lesson at once, she would see that the Spirit enables her to always rise above the elements of her place and time, geography, storms, circumstances, etc.. Christ is in complete control of these things and when we abide in Him, we are truly above all these things. Do you know this is true? How are we so easily diverted into behavior that seems to show we don't believe it? Perhaps it is because we cannot see the whole lesson at once, as we would prefer.

A singing voice sounds close at hand. It is the Shepherd, singing a poem drawn from verses of Song of Solomon. Then beyond the song, we see the Shepherd Himself.

QUESTIONS AND PRAYER: What difference does it make if the Holy Spirit is "President" in you, or merely "resident"?_____

_____

When and how do you confess sin and re-appropriate the Holy Spirit to direct your paths? Do you employ I John 1:9? Colossians 2:6? What else reminds you of Jesus's words and His power over sin through faith in Him?_____

_____

_____

CHAPTER 11

In the Forests of Danger and Tribulation

With what joy they welcomed the Shepherd as He sat down in the midst, and after cheerfully congratulating them on having surmounted the precipice, He laid His hands gently on the wounds which Much-Afraid had received when she fell, and immediately they were healed. Then he began to speak to them about the way which lay ahead.

"You have now to go through the forests which clothe the sides of these mountains almost up to the snowline. The way will be steep, but you will come to resting places here and there. These are the Forests of Danger and Tribulation, and often the pine trees grow so tall and so closely together that the path may seem quite dark. Storms are very frequent up here on these slopes, but keep pressing forward, for remember that nothing can do you any real harm while you are following the path of My will."

It did seem strange that even after safely surmounting so many difficulties and steep places, including the "impassable precipice" just below them, Much-Afraid should remain so like her name. But so it was! No sooner did the Shepherd pronounce the words "danger and tribulation" than she began to shake and tremble all over again.

"The Forests of Danger and Tribulation!" she repeated with a piteous quaver in her voice. "O Shepherd, wherever will You lead me next?"

"To the next stage on the way to the High Places," He answered promptly, smiling at her as nicely as possible.

176

The Way Ahead

READ: Hind's Feet... facing page & **I Peter 3:13–4:19**

"And now I have told you before it comes to pass, that when it comes to pass you may believe." —John 14:29

"These things I have spoken to you, that in Me you may have peace. In the world you have tribulation, but take courage; I have overcome the world." —John 16:33

The Bible devotes considerable portions to informing us of the future, both in general and specific terms; for nations and for individuals. The purpose is to help us, not cause dismay. God wants us to see His words validated along the way in order to substantiate and build our faith. He also wants us to understand and not be overwhelmed by the process of building saints, as "though something unusual was happening" to us. We're being tested and tried by fire to build faith in God. There is only one "work" that we can do that counts and that is to believe in Christ (John 6:29). God presents us with varied opportunity to get it right in many situations.

Danger and Tribulation is the name of the game. As men we might think that poor little Much-Afraid portrays the extreme opposite of women and men; women tending to shrink with fright from every risk, while men boldly look danger in the face! Oh, yes! Men should recall Peter, who was so full of bravado and self-deception, who could be frightened by looking away from Jesus to the storm (Matt. 14:28–30) or by a servant girl into denying Jesus (Mark 14:29–30, John 18:17).

The Shepherd heals Much-Afraid but this does not increase her faith in Him. In a few moments of His sketching out the way ahead, she is reduced to trembling and shaking all over again! As in the Old Testament, miracles do not change people's hearts, but serve instead as another type of "allegory" in which lessons may be taught. Our faith is built upon the word of God and results of exercising it.

QUESTIONS AND PRAYER: Is Jesus your Healer? How do you demonstrate that you believe all circumstances are given to you to enhance your trust in Christ?

_____

Do you agree that trusting Christ is the only work of permanent value which God has given to you to exercise?_____

Do you agree that miracles themselves don't bring lasting change to the human heart?_____

"I wonder if You will ever be able to get me there!" groaned poor foolish little Much-Afraid. "I wonder why You continue to bother with me and don't give up the job altogether. It looks as though I never shall have anything but lame feet, and that even You won't be able to make them like hinds' feet." She looked disconsolately at her feet as she spoke. Certainly at the moment they did look even more crooked than ever.

"I am not a man that I should lie," said the Shepherd gravely. "Look at Me, Much-Afraid. Do you believe that I will deceive you? Have I said, and shall I not do it? Or have I spoken, and shall I not make it good?"

Much-Afraid trembled a little, partly at the tone of His voice and partly because she was still Much-Afraid by nature and was already trying to picture what the Forests of Danger and Tribulation would be like. That always had a disastrous effect upon her, but she answered penitently, "No—I know that You are not a man who would lie to me; I know that You will make good what You have said."

"Then," said the Shepherd, speaking very gently again, "I am going to lead you through danger and tribulation, Much-Afraid, but you need not be the least bit afraid, for I shall be with you. Even if I lead you through the Valley of the Shadow itself you need not fear, for My rod and My staff will comfort you."

Then He added, "Thou shalt not be afraid for the terror by night; nor for the arrow that flieth by day; nor for the pestilence that walketh in darkness; nor for the destruction that wasteth at noonday. Though a thousand fall at thy side, and ten thousand at thy right hand, it shall not come nigh thee ... For I will cover thee with My feathers, and under My wings shalt thou trust" (Psa. 91:4–7). The gentleness of His voice as He said these things was indescribable.

Then Much-Afraid knelt at His feet and built yet another altar and said, "Yea, though I walk through the Valley of the Shadow of Death, I will fear no evil: for

Character Challenge!

READ: Hind's Feet... facing page & **John 16:16–23**

"...on my own behalf I will not boast, except in regard to my weaknesses."
—II Corinthians 12:5

"'Bring the whole tithe into the storehouse, so that there may be food in My house, and test Me now in this.' says the LORD of hosts, 'if I will not open for you the windows of heaven, and pour out for you a blessing until there is no more need.'" —Malachi 3:10

Much-Afraid opens this reading with a mixed bag of observations and attitudes. She appears overwhelmed with her "deformities"; i.e., the consequences of sin and the despicable human heart which she has inherited (Jer.17:9). There is also a possible self-pity in her words, or the readiness to entertain self-pity. She is certainly discouraged and depressed. In this state of mind, her deformities appear worse than ever. Nevertheless, she is certainly speaking eloquently of her weakness! Then God, who "comforts the depressed", speaks through the Shepherd.

Quoting from Numbers 23:19, He challenges her to speak her belief regarding His character. Is He a liar or not? In this scriptural passage, God is actually arguing while He challenges. Note that He presents the same question in four different forms to argue and persuade the case. Quite often in scripture God will speak two forms of His assertion of truth, but seldom four in one verse. God is really challenging us and Much-Afraid by this verse. There is only one answer (we hasten to say when we are challenged!)

On the basis of her profession, He gives her new promises from Psalm 23 and Psalm 91, promises we should have memorized. As Much-Afraid, we should be able at any time to speak them as she does, back to the LORD or to others that need them for building up.

QUESTIONS AND PRAYER: God challenges us forcefully in Deuteronomy 6:1– 9 to memorize His word and have it on our minds and tongues at all times. How do you agree with this and what do you do to display it?_____

_____

_____

Have you undertaken to memorize scripture in order to effectively do it?_____
How do you feel about your recognition and responses to God when He is challenging you?_____

Thou art with me." Then, because she found that even as she spoke her teeth were chattering with fright and her hands had gone quite clammy, she looked up into His face and added, "For Thou art not a man that Thou shouldest lie, nor the Son of man that Thou shouldest repent. Hast Thou said, and shalt Thou not do it? And has Thou spoken and shalt Thou not make it good?"

Then the Shepherd smiled more comfortingly than ever before, laid both hands on her head and said, "Be strong, yea, be strong and fear not." Then He continued, "Much-Afraid, don't ever allow yourself to begin trying to picture what it will be like. Believe Me, when you get to the places which you dread you will find that they are as different as possible from what you have imagined, just as was the case when you were actually ascending the precipice. I must warn you that I see your enemies lurking among the trees ahead, and if you ever let Craven Fear begin painting a picture on the screen of your imagination, you will walk with fear and trembling and agony, where no fear is."

When He had said this, He picked up another stone from the place where she was kneeling, and gave it to her to put with the other memorial stones. Then He went His way, and Much-Afraid and her companions started on the path which led up through the forests.

Almost as soon as they had reached the trees they saw the face of mean, sickly Self-Pity, looking out from behind one of the trunks. He gabbled ever so quickly before he dodged back into hiding, "I say, Much-Afraid, this really is a bit too thick. I mean, whatever will He do next, forcing a poor little lame, frightened creature like yourself to go through dangers which only brave, strong men ought to be expected to face. Really, your Shepherd is almost more of a bully than Craven Fear himself."

Hardly had he stopped before Resentment put his head out and said crossly, "There's absolutely no reason for it either, because there's another perfectly good path which

Obedient Tongue

READ: Hind's Feet... facing page & James 3:1–12

"But I am afraid, lest as the serpent deceived Eve by His
craftiness, your minds should be led astray from the simplicity
and purity of devotion to Christ." —II Corinthians 11:3

"...if you confess with your mouth Jesus as Lord, and believe in your heart
that God raised Him from the dead, you shall be saved." —Romans 10:9

Much-Afraid finds herself suffering physical problems as a result of her fears and "because" of this begins to speak more scripture back to the Shepherd. What a valuable lesson lies in only this simple six-line portrait! Speaking scripture to God ministers to us!

This profound principle ties together the power of God's truth (Heb.4:12), the abundance of the heart (Matt.12:34) and our obedience to bring the tongue into harmony with the heart and the word. It insures the entire person is harmonious with the word of God, with no hidden rebellious spirit. It is the same principle upon which assurance of salvation is made in Romans 10:9.

Much-Afraid sees His smile to be more comforting than ever, then receives his blessing and warnings. He introduces a subject of the next several lessons; guarding our hearts and minds from evil. She is explicitly warned to guard the pictures of her mind in somewhat similar words as the boy of Proverbs 4:23–26 in which he is warned to guard his heart. In the same fashion as Job (Job 31:1), men are warned to guard their eyes, while as we shall see, Much-Afraid is being taught to guard her ears.

Though both men and women see and hear, their doors to fulfillment and temptation are different for each. Men are most greatly fulfilled and tempted through their eyes, while women are so through their ears. By God's design and function of the sexes, both have entirely different needs for protection.

QUESTIONS AND PRAYER: Please review the means by which Eve fell.____

Adam? ____

Consider how you find contentment. Stimulation? Fulfillment? How about your wife, mother, sisters or daughters? What distinctions do you see between what men and women see, hear and think?____

____

____

skirts the forest altogether and brings you right up to the snowline without going anywhere near these unnecessary dangers. Everybody else goes that way, so why shouldn't you? Tell Him you won't go this way, Much-Afraid, and insist on being taken by the usual path. This way is for martyrs only, and you, my dear, don't fit into the picture at all."

Then Craven Fear leered at her for a moment and said contemptuously, "So you think you're going to become a little heroine, do you? And go singing through the Forest of Danger! What will you bet, Much-Afraid, that you won't end up shrieking and screaming like a maniac, maimed for the rest of your life?"

Bitterness was next to speak, and sneered from behind another tree, "He would do this. It's just as I told you. After you have dutifully gone through one terrifying experience He's always got something still worse lying ahead for you."

Then Pride (who was still limping badly and seemed extra venomous as a re-sult) said, "You know, He won't be able to rest content until He has put you to complete shame, because that's the way He produces that precious humility He's so crazy about. He'll humble you to the dust, Much-Afraid, and leave you a grov-eling idiot in front of everyone."

Much-Afraid and her companions walked on without answering and without taking any notice, but as before, Much-Afraid discovered that she limped more painfully whenever she heard what they said. It was really terribly perplexing to know what to do. If she listened, she limped, and if she put her fingers in her ears, she couldn't accept the hands of her two guides, which meant that she stumbled and slipped.

So they stopped for a moment or two and discussed the matter, and then Suffering opened the little First Aid kit hanging at her girdle, took out some cotton and firmly plugged the ears of Much-Afraid. Although this was uncomfortable, it did seem to have the desired effect, at least temporarily, for when the five sulkers saw that they could not

Guarding the Portals

READ: Hind's Feet... facing page & **Proverbs 4:20–27**

"for false Christs and false prophets will arise and will show signs and wonders in order, if possible, to lead the elect astray." – Mark 13:22

"But the Spirit explicitly says that in later times some will fall away from the faith, paying attention to deceitful spirits and doctrines of demons." – I Timothy 4:1

The words "seduce" and "deceive" mean essentially the same thing. In scripture there is no distinction and they are used interchangeably. Possibly the sexual idea associated with "seducing" as used in modern times is related to the idea that illicit "seed" gets planted through believing lies, bearing the same bitter fruit as the lying ideas themselves.

Sensuality or lasciviousness is a fruit of the flesh identified in Galatians 5:19, identifying that susceptibility we have to desiring to satisfy our senses (Prov.27:20, Eccl.6:7). Another danger is that failing to discipline our two chief senses, sight and hearing, can lead to our being seduced through them into believing lies. This is what now confronts Much-Afraid.

The enemies hurl their lies at her and she is not taken in by them, but they definitely hinder her walk. It slows the group. The idea of stopping her ears comes but can't be implemented without loosing grasp of Sorrow and Suffering. So, counsel and wisdom provide the answer of using ear-plugs! The key is "not hearing" what the enemy says. It is related to "tearing down speculations that exalt themselves against the knowledge of God and bringing every thought captive to the obedience of Christ" (II Cor.10:5). To the extent that she can keep her mind stayed on Christ, she is more greatly protected. The Bible indicates that, for women, both reward and fulfillment (Prov.31:10–31) as well as deception (Gen. 3:1–5) come chiefly through their ears.

QUESTIONS AND PRAYER: If you are a man, have you ever deceived a woman with your words? Have you ever repented of this? Have you set up a guard for your soul by giving God sovereignty over your eyes and ears?

_____

If you are a woman, have you ever been injured by a man's deceit? How have you dealt with this in the Lord Jesus Christ? Have you established a guard over your ears?_____

_____

Have you need for repentance from unforgiveness and cleansing from bitterness?

_____

make her hear them they soon tired of bawling at her and left her alone until another opportunity should occur for badgering her again.

At first the forest did not really seem too dreadful. Perhaps it was that up there on the mountains the air was so fresh and strong that it made those who breathed it fresh and strong too. Also, the sun was still shining, and Much-Afraid began to feel a sensation which was completely new to her, a thrill of excitement and, incredible as it seemed, of almost pleasurable adventure.

Here she was, lame Much-Afraid, actually walking through the Forest of Danger and not really minding. This lasted for quite a time until huge black clouds gradually rolled over the sky, and the sun went in. In the distance thunder rolled and the woods became dark and very still. Suddenly a bolt of lightning scorched across the sky, and somewhat ahead of them was a rending crash as a great forest tree fell to the earth, then another and another. Then the storm in all its fury was bursting around them, thunder rolling, lightning sizzling and crackling in every direction until the whole forest seemed to be groaning and shaking and falling about them.

The strangest thing was that though Much-Afraid felt a shuddering thrill go through her at every crash she was not really afraid. That is, she felt neither panic nor desire to run, nor even real dread, for she kept repeating to herself, "Though a thousand shall fall at thy side and ten thousand at thy right hand, it shall not come nigh thee ... For I will cover thee with My feathers, and under My wings shalt thou trust." So throughout the whole storm she was filled with a strange and wonderful peace such as she had never felt before, and walked between her two companions saying to herself, "I shall not die, but live and declare the works of the Lord."

At last the storm began to rumble off into the distance, the crashes died down, and there was a quiet lull. The three women stopped to wring the water out of their clothes and

Confident Women

READ: Hind's Feet... facing page & **Psalm 118:17–24**

"Then the LORD said to Cain, "Why are you angry? And why has
your countenance fallen? If you do well, will not your countenance
be lifted up? And if you do not do well, sin is crouching at the door;
and its desire is for you, but you must master it." —Genesis 4:6–7

"...blessed are those who hear the word of God, and observe it." —Luke 11:28

Protected women and confident women are not necessarily the same. Confidence is based on trust in one's personal well-being. But it's possible to be confident in things that are untrustworthy or to be anxious and fretful, though perfectly protected.

Many women lose trust in men and God and are unable to live free of anxiety because they have been so damaged by broken trust and emotional abuse. Chief cause is sexual immorality. It is possible for women to be healed by discovering they are really greatly loved and valued. Men must repent, but so must women and in the LORD they must administer tearing down of strongholds resulting from these sins (IICor.10:4–5). God is eager to heal them both.

We see Much-Afraid's strongholds yielding to the word of God. She is now "doing rightly" in God's word and will experience good results. She is not basing her responses, as Cain did, upon her feelings. We see her finding "pleasurable adventure" in the storm. Her well-being is not distressed, because she knows she is secure. In the Spirit, she meditates and speaks back the word of God in Psalm 91. It has taken root!

Prior to life-threatening surgery, I also experienced the security of Psalm 91. When later recounting the story and reciting Psalm 91's precious personal words to me, I wept. By her portrait, I feel sure author Hurnard also shared a Psalm 91 experience.

Many men are constantly tormented because their wives show anxiety and insecurity. It tears husbands down because it exposes them as failures; inadequate to provide security. Husband and wife are at war. It is because of past sin and its damage. Men should repent and confess their past sins to God and work for protection, healing and freedom for their wives. Women should learn how to affirm Christ and their husbands. It is their task!

QUESTIONS AND PRAYER: God's word is a powerful two-edged sword, able to do mighty things, including tearing down strongholds. How do you personally root it in your heart, speak it and pray it?_____
To what extent do you have an anxious wife or daughters?_____
To what extent do you either "tear down" or affirm and build up your husband?

_____

hair and try to tidy themselves. As they did this, Craven Fear appeared near them again and yelled at the top of his voice, "I say, Much-Afraid, the storm has only gone round the mountains for a short time. Already it is beginning to approach again and will be worse than before. Make a bolt back down the path as quickly as you can and get away from these dangerous trees before it starts again or you will be killed. There is just time for you to make good your escape."

"Look here," exclaimed Much-Afraid most unexpectedly, water still dripping from her hair and her sodden skirts clinging like wet rags around her legs, "I can't stand that fellow shouting at me any longer. Please help me—both of you," and setting the example, she stooped down, picked up a stone and flung it straight at Craven Fear.

Her two companions actually laughed for the very first time and started hurling a barrage of stones among the trees where the five were lurking. In a moment or two none of their enemies were visible. Then, just ahead of them, through the trees, they saw a log hut which seemed to offer a promise of shelter and protection from the storm, which certainly was again drawing nearer. Hurrying toward the cabin, they found that it stood in a clearing well away from the trees, and when they tried the door latch, to their joy it opened and they thankfully slipped inside. With great presence of mind, Suffering immediately closed the door and bolted it behind them, and none too soon!

The next minute their enemies were banging on the door and shouting, "Hi! I say—open the door and let us in. The storm is starting again. You can't be so inhuman as to shut us outside and leave us to our fate."

Much-Afraid went to the door and shouted through the keyhole the advice they had offered her, "Make a bolt down the path as quickly as you can and get away from these dangerous trees, or you will be killed. You have just time to make good your escape before the storm starts again."

Away With Fear

READ: Hind's Feet... facing page & **Luke 8:15–21**

"For this reason I say to you, do not be anxious for your life, as to what you shall eat, or what you shall drink; nor for your body, as to what you shall put on. Is not life more than food, and the body than clothing?" —Matthew 6:25

"Behold, I stand at the door and knock; if any one hears My voice and opens the door, I will come in to him, and will dine with him, and he with Me." —Revelation 3:20

Having exercised the words of Psalms 91 and 118 in her spirit, Much-Afraid now has unexpected opportunity. She is still under empowerment of the Holy Spirit when Craven Fear puts in an appearance and gets his head "shot off". The three women drive off the bully by throwing rocks at him!

How do you observe the transforming relationship that is taking place with Sorrow and Suffering? Do you agree that Much-Afraid is now beginning to exercise polite Lordship in a close relationship with them? Notice their responses to Much-Afraid's request for "help" in driving off the enemy. It brings laughter for the "very first time". Yes! Away with fear!

In the face of the storm, they find a cabin and take refuge. With great "presence of mind", Suffering closes the door and bolts it behind them. What does this signify? God likens the heart to a house with a door, with Him at the door and we controlling it. Perhaps suffering does remove fear. Can a dead man be tempted or fear death? Can a man who is suffering fear suffering? In embracing suffering, even death may lose its power!

The picture drawn is that, as the Shepherd instructed on page 6, the "household" has been taken captive by Much-Afraid and her companions and is no longer an entertainment center for the Fearing family. Temptation to let them in is recognized, renounced and put away. Away with Fear!

QUESTIONS AND PRAYER: On a scale of 1–10, how would you assess your progress in putting away fear or other enemy relatives you identified in lesson #4? _____
Do you feel that, since then, you can recognize and renounce them more easily? If so, why? _____

_____
What requests would you now make of Christ?_____

_____

There was a sound of muttering curses outside, then of hurrying feet fading away into the distance, and it seemed as though this time the advice was being acted upon. Back rolled the storm, fiercer and more terrible than before, but they were safely sheltered in the hut out of range of the crashing trees, and their shelter proved perfectly weatherproof, for not a drop came through the roof.

They found in the room a supply of firewood stacked beside a small kitchen range with a kettle and some saucepans on it. While Suffering busied herself lighting the fire, Sorrow held the kettle under a spout outside the window and filled it with rain water. Much-Afraid went to a cupboard on the wall to see if it would yield any treasure. Sure enough, there was crockery on the shelves and a supply of tinned foods, as well as a big tin of unleavened biscuits.

So in a very little time, while the storm still furiously raged and rattled outside, there they were, sitting around a crackling fire, warming themselves and drying their sopping garments while they drank comforting hot cocoa and satisfied their hunger. Though the uproar of the tempest without was almost deafening and the hut shuddered and shook in every blast, yet inside was nothing but peace and thanksgiving and cheerful contentment.

Much-Afraid found herself thinking with astonished awe that it was really the happiest and the most peaceful experience during the whole of her journey up till that time. As they lay down on the mattresses which they discovered piled in another part of the hut, she repeated again to herself very softly: "He has covered me with His feathers, and under His wings I do trust."

The storm continued with great violence for two or three days, but while it lasted the three travelers rested quietly in the shelter of the hut, going outside only during the brief lulls to gather wood. This they dried in the oven to replenish the stock they were using, so that others, following on behind,

Protection From Storm

READ: Hind's Feet... facing page & **Matthew 7:21–27**

"And there shall be a shelter to give shade from the heat by day, and refuge and protection from the storm and the rain." —Isaiah 4:6

"And He said to them, 'Where is your faith?' And they were fearful and amazed, saying to one another, 'Who then is this, that He commands even the winds and the water, and they obey Him?'" —Luke 8:25

Notably, the Old Testament has many uses of the word "storm", but the New Testament does not. A storm occurs only once and is used in parable only once. Jesus Christ is clearly identified as the only safe foundation and true source of safety in storms. The matter is then left; i.e., resolved. Storms are resolved. Jesus resolves all storms. We are to look to the man who "stilled the waters" and no longer look at storms.

After solving a storm, Jesus asks just one question; the concern God is always asking, *"Where is your faith?"* Why is God so concerned with this? He provides our protection, but then where is our knowledge of God? The conviction of His character, love, and purpose reflected in such astonishing protection seems to dissipate so quickly in the face of the world. But it is His plan to overcome the world and the flesh by this knowledge. He has done it in His own flesh and is doing it now through ours. By this means the surpassing glory of God can be revealed to a skeptical, doubting world. Faith in God enables the fulfillment of His promises; the revelation of His certain upholding of His precepts! How wonderful when Salvation will shine to the ends of the earth (Is. 49:6, 62:11)!

Much-Afraid discovers warmth, utensils, food, water, security and comfort in the cabin. She enjoys at leisure while still relating to the scriptures being fulfilled in her life. She attends to replacing dry wood; a key feature of security provided on the way for those "following on behind" to the High Places.

QUESTIONS AND PRAYER: What are you doing to help provide a safer way for those following you? _____

_____

_____

How do you minister security to your family? Friends? What is your greatest interference in doing this?_____

_____

_____

might not be left without fuel. There seemed to be a good store of tinned foods and unleavened biscuits and they supposed that some of the Shepherd's servants must visit the hut from time to time with a new supply.

During those quiet days in the midst of the raging tempest Much-Afraid came to know her two companions in a new way and also to understand more of the mountain dialect which they spoke. In some strange way she began to feel that they were becoming real friends, and not just attendants whom the Shepherd had commanded to go with her as guides and helpers. She found, too, that now she was accepting their companionship in this way she seemed more alive than ever before to beauty and delight in the world around her.

It seemed as though her senses had been quickened in some extraordinary way, enabling her to enjoy every little detail of her life; so that although her companions actually were Sorrow and Suffering, she often felt an almost inexplicable joy and pleasure at the same time. This would happen when she looked at the bright, crackling flames in the log fire, or listened to the sound of lashing rain overhead emphasizing the safety and peace within the hut, or when she saw through the window the tossing trees waving their arms against a background of scurrying clouds or lightning-rent sky. Or again, very early before daybreak, when she saw the morning star shining serenely through a rift in the clouds or heard the clear, jubilant note of a bird during a lull in the storm.

All these things seemed to be speaking to her in the mountain dialect, and to her growing astonishment, she found it an incredibly beautiful language, so that sometimes her eyes filled with tears of pure joy and her heart seemed so full of ecstasy that she could hardly bear it.

One morning when the storm was rattling and raging through the forest louder than ever, she noticed Sorrow sitting by the fire singing quietly to herself, the words, of course,

"Seeing" More Clearly

READ: Hind's Feet... facing page & **John 1:44–51**

"Thou hast turned my mourning into gladness; Thou hast loosed my
sackcloth and girded me with gladness." —Psalm 30:11

"Now faith is the assurance of things hoped for, the
conviction of things not seen." —Hebrews 11:1

During the time of her sojourn in the cabin, Much-Afraid has time to rest and allow God's Spirit to lead her in a different sort of "journey". She is led to observation of herself and her surroundings. She makes "discovery" of things, her senses and her companions, Sorrow and Suffering. It is sort of a Sabbath "rest", giving her deeper enjoyment of God.

She now recognizes that Sorrow and Suffering bring something "inexplicable" in the way of joy and pleasure. Possibly we may accept this on limited faith, because of more limited experience and knowledge of God's word than we will someday have. She appears to be close to "embracing" their companionship at a new level. She experiences the contrast of the tempest outside the cabin and her peace and safety within.

Nathaniel was impressed with Jesus' having "seen" him under the fig tree, and immediately declared that He was the Son of God. But Jesus told him that he had hardly begun to "see"; that in the future he would "see the heavens opened and the angels of God ascending and descending upon the Son of Man." Things we once thought we "saw" are also later shown to be only limited views of the true unseen world. Also, things which we thought to be against us continually turn out to be blessings instead, by an intellect, wisdom and power we can barely comprehend, except in terms of a mighty God who loves us.

Believers are on a journey where ears once stopped and eyes once blind are being continually opened to new understanding about the unseen world; the wonderful character of divine God working in our favor through the Savior of the world, Jesus Christ.

QUESTIONS AND PRAYER: How do you provide for times of rest, "seeing" your surroundings and enjoyment of God in your life? _____

_____

_____

What other purposes do you see for use of rest, as well?_____

_____

_____

_____

being in the mountain dialect, which Much-Afraid was learning to understand. This is the best translation that I can give, but you will realize that the original was much more beautiful and full of forest sounds and music.

How lovely and how nimble are thy feet,
O prince's daughter!
They flash and sparkle and can run more fleet
Than running water.
On all the mountains there is no gazelle,
No roe or hind,
Can overtake thee nor can leap as well—-
But lag behind.

(Cant. 7:1)

"Why, Sorrow," Exclaimed Much-Afraid, "I didn't know that you could sing, nor even that you knew any songs."

Sorrow answered quietly, "Neither did I, but on the way up here through the forest I found the words and tune coming into my head just as I am singing them now."

"I like it," said Much-Afraid. "It makes me think of the time when I shall have hinds' feet myself, and so it is comforting and the tune is so nice and springy. It makes me want to jump." She laughed at the thought of her crooked feet being able to jump, then coaxed, "Teach me the song—please do."

So Sorrow sang it over several times until Much-Afraid knew it perfectly and went about the hut humming it to herself, trying to picture what it would be like to be a gazelle leaping on the mountains, and able to jump from crag to crag, just as the Shepherd did. When the day came for her to receive her hinds' feet, she would be able to follow Him wherever He went. The picture was so lovely she could hardly wait for it to come true.

192

Affirming Vision

READ: Hind's Feet... facing page & Jeremiah 31:27–34

"The lamp of the body is the eye; if therefore your eye is clear,
your whole body will be full of light." —Matthew 6:22

"You will only look on with your eyes and see the recompense of the wicked."
—Psalm 91:8

Much-Afraid overhears a song that she likes. It is an affirmation of her vision; the freedom and beauty of movement of hinds' feet for herself. What she actually hears is a view through the eyes of the one who loves her, shaped for her ear. He is expressing what He sees, even as Solomon was expressing his love for his bride and Christ for His (John 3:29). This poetic form is expressed in an allegory of wild life; one form expressed by Christ for us relating to nature. But there are other forms of this same expression possible for other ears, as we shall see.

Jeremiah's New Covenant vision is also powerfully affirming; one of many expressed in the Old Testament. How can it fail to lift up believers of the Old Testament? Yet, many neither hear nor believe it (Rom.10:14). Perhaps it is not yet rightly shaped for their ear!

Is sorrow a sort of "lens" by which longings of the heart are amplified and focused? To me certain music seems to amplify sorrow and bring out unusual pathos and longing. Have you observed this, too? Sorrow replies to Much-Afraid's surprise; she is also being transformed. This is her first song.

Much-Afraid laughs at the thought of her crooked feet able to jump. Many times already her feet have appeared to be almost straight and her walk unimpeded. She seems to be unaware that the dream is already coming true; not deferred until some far off day in the future. Still, the vision of the Shepherd worded just for her ears gives her a fitting completion to her rest during the storms. She has been affirmed and renewed through meditation and fellowship with her companions.

QUESTIONS AND PRAYER: You will soon be asked to tailor words which "fit" your wife's ears, or daughters, too, if you have them. If this is difficult, ask God to show you how He sees them._____

_____

_____

_____

_____

CHAPTER 12

In the Mist

At last the storm gradually died down, the clamor on the mountains ceased, and it was time to resume the journey. However, the weather had broken completely, and though the storm itself was over, thick mist and cloud remained, shrouding everything on the heights.

When they started the mist was so thick that they could see only the trees on either side of the narrow path, and even they looked ghostly and unreal. The rest of the forest was simply swallowed up and entirely lost to sight, veiled in a cold and clammy white curtain. The ground was dreadfully muddy and slippery, and although the path did not climb nearly so steeply as before, after some hours Much-Afraid found to her amazement that she was missing the rolling thunder of the storm and even the sickening crash of the trees as the lightening splintered them.

She began to realize that, cowardly though she was, there was something in her which responded with a surge of excitement to the tests and difficulties of the way better than to easier and duller circumstances. It was true that fear sent a dreadful shuddering thrill through her, but nevertheless it was a thrill, and she found herself realizing with astonishment that even the dizzy precipice had been more to her liking than this dreary plodding on and on through the bewildering mist. In some way the dangers of the storm had stimulated her; now there was nothing but tameness, just a trudge, trudge forward, day after day, able to see nothing except for white, clinging mist which hung about the mountains without a gleam of sunshine breaking through.

In Mist

READ: Hind's Feet... facing page & **Luke 12:35–40**

"Do not boast about tomorrow, for you do not know
what a day may bring forth." —Proverbs 27:1

"Yet you do not know what your life will be like tomorrow. You are just a
vapor that appears for a little while and then vanishes away." —James 4:14

Hannah Hurnard was a missionary to Israel who presumably gained her perceptions of the deserts and ocean shores previously described, from the eastern regions of the Mediterranean. When possible, she took her furloughs in the Swiss Alps and it was there that she received her original inspirations for *Hinds' Feet in High Places*. One of her frequent tests was the occurrence of clouds and fog in the Alps which would keep her from seeing the mountains, streams and flowers she loved to view. Such a mist sets the stage for this scene and its effects upon people not able to "see".

One effect is to interfere with visual gratification or updating of a sense of progress. Things previously visible become invisible. We know they exist, but can gradually become frustrated by being unable to enjoy them, to update ourselves on where we are in relationships or progress toward goals. Enough dreary plodding with no reward can become monotonous. Life becomes dull when there is no contrast, color, achievement, excitement and newness. Expectations can become dulled. We are much like children or animals, needing gratification to induce us to obey or keep going.

Much-Afraid introduces another aspect of contrast to the life she has begun to enjoy —the excitement of adventures in risky living following the Shepherd. Now life has become dull by contrast. We've all had such periods and still do. Now is a good time to review their effects. Do we become bored? Can boredom more likely lead to impatience or to slackness? How do we behave when we become impatient? Where is the LORD at such times?

QUESTIONS AND PRAYER: Please make a short self-evaluation of your own answers to the above questions. _____

_____

Which direction do you tend to go when you are taken into the "mist"? What results are produced?_____

_____

_____

At last she burst out impatiently, "Will this dull dreary mist never lift, I wonder?" And would you believe it! A voice she knew all too well immediately answered from beyond the trees.

"No, it won't," replied Resentment. "Moreover you might just as well know now that this is going to continue for no one knows how long. Higher up the mountains the mist hangs thicker and thicker still. That's all you can expect for the rest of the journey."

Much-Afraid pretended not to hear, but the voice went on again almost at once.

"Have you noticed, Much-Afraid, that the path which you are following isn't going up the mountain at all, but is almost level? You've missed the upward way, and you are just going round and round the mountain in circles."

Much-Afraid had not exactly noticed this fact, but now she could not help realizing that it was true. They were not climbing at all, but simply moving along the mountainside with constant ups and downs, and the downs seemed to be getting more frequent. Could it be possible that they were really gradually descending the mountain instead of going up? In the bewildering mist one simply could not see anything, and she found she had lost all sense of direction. On asking her companions what they thought about it they answered rather shortly (because, of course, she ought not to have listened to any suggestion from Resentment) that they were on the path which the Shepherd had pointed out, and would certainly not allow anyone to persuade them to leave it.

"But," persisted Much-Afraid petulantly, "don't you think that we may have missed the way in this mist? The Shepherd said the path led upward, and as you see, this one doesn't. It runs along the side of the mountain. There may easily have been a more direct way up which we didn't notice in the mist."

Their only answer was that they knew better than to listen to any suggestion made by Resentment.

Impatience — Uncertainty

READ: Hind's Feet... facing page & **Numbers 20:13**

"Be patient, therefore, brethren, until the coming of the Lord. Behold,
the farmer waits for the precious produce of the soil, being patient about it,
until it gets the early and late rains." —James 5:7

"...But if when you do what is right and suffer for it you patiently
endure it, this finds favor with God." —I Peter 2:20

Do you feel badly for Moses to read of how God disciplined him when he became impatient with the unruly and ungrateful mob He was required to lead in the wilderness? "And from everyone who has been given much shall much be required" (Luke 12:48). It seems so much to demand of a man described as the humblest man who ever lived, but God was teaching him patience and we are to learn from it. The lesson for Moses was that impatience dishonors our holy God.

We see that Much-Afraid's reaction to the drudgery of walking in the mist is impatience. It immediately leads to temptation from Resentment and new training. She pretends not to hear, but begins to entertain the voice. Now she begins to notice other things that tend to heap up doubt and double-mindedness in her heart. Resentment tells her of something which the mist amplifies; a sense of loss of direction and uncertainty.

Presumably, the reason Much-Afraid does not call for the ear plugs is that she's not yet learned to recognize the voice of Resentment. Hence, this lesson, like the others, will include more training in discernment of spirits. This applies to our training, too.

Commencing with the planting of the thorny seed of Love in her heart, Much-Afraid's training has included Acceptance-with-Joy, Bearing-the-Cost, Peace in the storm and now patience; a pattern emerging of the fruits of the Spirit identified in Galatians 5:22–23. Like seed for the farmer trained in patience, the fruits are certain. She is being renewed in the spirit of her mind (Eph.4:23).

QUESTIONS AND PRAYER: How good is your discernment to the spirit of resentment working in you? How do you deal with it?_____

_____

How good are your "ear-plugs"? Does it require "Bearing-the-Cost" in some situations?_____

_____

At that the voice of Bitterness broke in quite clearly, "You might at least be willing to go back a little way and look, instead of insisting on going on and on along what may prove to be a wrong path leading you round in circles."

Sorrow and Suffering took absolutely no notice, but unfortunately Much-Afraid did, and said with still greater petulance, "I think you ought to consider the suggestion. Perhaps it would be better to go back a little way and see if we have missed the right path. Really, it is no use going on and on in circles, getting nowhere."

To this they replied, "Well, if we are going round in circles, we shall eventually arrive back where we went wrong, and if we keep our eyes open we shall be able to see the path we missed—always provided that it does exist and is not just a bit of imagination on the part of Bitterness."

"You poor little thing," came the whisper of Self-Pity through the mist. "It is too bad that you have been put in the charge of such obstinate mule-like creatures. Just think of the time you are wasting, getting nowhere at all. Trudge, trudge, day after day, nothing to show for it, and you ought to be getting up onto the High Places."

So they went on, whispering and talking at her through the clinging mist, which shrouded everything and made it all seem so ghostly and dreary. Of course, she ought not to have listened to them, but the mist was so bewildering and the path so unspeakably tame that she found something in her heart responding to them almost against her will.

Suffering doggedly led the way, and Sorrow just as doggedly was her rearguard, so that there was no possibility of turning back, but Much-Afraid found herself limping and slipping and stumbling far more often and badly than at any other stage of the journey. It made her very disagreeable and difficult to deal with. It is true that after every stumble her conscience smote her and she apologized sorrowfully and abjectly to her companions, but that did not prevent her slipping

Circles of the Mind

READ: Hind's Feet... facing page & **Mark 1:1–3**

"..Let your eyes look directly ahead, and let your gaze
be fixed straight in front of you." —Proverbs 4:25

"O LORD, lead me in Thy righteousness because of my foes;
make Thy way straight before me." —Psalm 5:8

The Bible makes clear that the pathways of the Lord are to be made straight. The scripture of Isaiah 40:3 recited above by Mark is one of the few passages which all four gospel writers cite in their recounting of the coming of Jesus Christ. Yes! Our paths are to be made straight, but natural man wants to make them crooked—or circular!

How easily misled we can be by doubting or uncertainty, boredom or impatience to stray from the straight path. It is not the path she is walking upon that is going in circles; it is the pathway of Much-Afraid's mind! Sorrow and Suffering give her some "straight" talk about the ease of discovery of the truth if they will just remain faithful to the path; but Much-Afraid can't see things at all. Her mind is fogged in. Yet, if the fog were to lift, wouldn't we expect to discover that the path has been straight all along?

Self Pity works in partnership with Resentment, tormenting Much-Afraid with her lack of attainment, working to convince her she is "wasting" time. Much-Afraid can actually feel something in her heart responding to the tempting voices of the spirits "almost against her will". This is the power of sin over the flesh of which Paul speaks in Romans, chapter 7, identifying the bondage of flesh in sin, and the dilemma of finding power to do right when our flesh always wants to do wrong. (Note Romans, chapter 8, which answers this dilemma!)

In close company with Sorrow and Suffering, Much-Afraid slips and stumbles her way, badly impeded by the tormenting spirits. Apologizing for her stumbles does not defeat the enemy or improve her walk. She is miserable, but persevering.

QUESTIONS AND PRAYER: How do you view the dilemma described by Romans, chapter 7, based on your own experience?_____

_____

_____

What actions would you recommend to build up Much-Afraid's spirit?_____

_____

_____

_____

again almost directly afterwards. Altogether it was a miserable time, and the mist, instead of clearing, seemed to get thicker and colder and drearier than ever.

At last, one afternoon, when the only word which at all described her progress is to say that she was slithering along the path, all muddy and wet and bedraggled from constant slips, she decided to sing.

It has not been mentioned before, but Much-Afraid did not possess the gift of a sweet voice any more than a pretty face. It is true that she was fond of singing and that if the Shepherd sang with her she could keep in tune and manage quite nicely, but if she tried alone the results were by no means so good. However, the mist was so thick and clammy that she was nearly stifled, and she felt she must do something to try to cheer herself and to drown the ghostly voices which kept whispering to her through the trees.

It was not pleasant to think of her relatives now having the opportunity to entertain themselves at the expense of her very unmelodious voice, but she de-cided to risk their ribald comments. "If I sing quite loudly," she told herself, "I shall not be able to hear what they say." The only song which she could think of at the moment was the one which Sorrow had taught her in the hut, and though it seemed singularly inappropriate she lifted up her voice and sang quaveringly:

> *How lovely and how nimble are thy feet,*
> *O prince's daughter!*
> *They flash and sparkle and can run more fleet*
> *Than running water.*
> *On all the mountains there is no gazelle,*
> *No roe or hind,*
> *Can overtake thee nor can leap as well—-*
> *But lag behind.*
> *(Cant 7:1)*

There was perfect silence as she sang. The loud, sneering voices of her enemies had died away altogether. "It is a good idea," said Much-Afraid to herself jubilantly.

Out of the Mud

READ: Hind's Feet... facing page & **Psalm 56**

"Sing to the LORD a new song." —Psalm 149:1

"He brought me up out of the pit of destruction, out of the miry clay; and He set my feet upon a rock making my footsteps firm. And He put a new song in my mouth, a song of praise to our God." —Psalm 40:2–3

From deep within her inner being, having no external instruction, an idea comes to Much-Afraid. Sing a song to stifle the thick and clammy mist! She works the idea back and forth through her head. We recognize this as an alternative to ear plugs, but Much-Afraid is first perturbed by other things; her poor voice, the risk of embarrassment. She is afraid of entertaining her enemies at the expense of her voice, but arrives at an interesting conclusion; if she sings loud enough, she won't be able to hear what they say"! Not bad!

Have we ever sung purely for the purpose of freeing our spirits from torment? We should follow King David's example more. He wrote many of his psalms while he was being oppressed.

Psalm 56 was written for the choir director by David at a time he had been seized (trampled upon, vs. 1 & 3), by the Philistines in Gath. How did he learn to do such things? Can we learn from his instruction? What is the connection between godly music and the uplifting of spirit? What is the connection between uplifting of spirit and God "delivering our feet from stumbling, so that we may walk before God in the light of the living"? Something mighty for the soul! Bless the LORD, O my soul!

Much-Afraid lifts her voice and, quavering, sings her new song, taught to her by Sorrow regarding her quest for new hinds' feet. Unbeknownst to her, the song also portrays her as the lovely bride of the Prince, the Bridegroom, the Shepherd. The song is His view of her now and in the future; also His view of you and me.

QUESTIONS AND PRAYER: What desires do you now have regarding the deformities you listed at the beginning of this study?_____

_____

_____

Would you sing the same song as Much-Afraid, or memorize such a song so that you could sing it at any time?_____

_____

_____

"I wish I had thought of it before. It is a much better way to avoid hearing what they are saying than putting cotton in my ears, and I believe, yes, I really do believe, there is a little rift in the mist ahead. How lovely, I shall sing the verse again." And she did so.

"Why Much-Afraid," said a cheery voice close beside her, "I have not heard that song before. Where did you learn it?"

There, striding toward her was a particularly pleased smile on His face, was the Shepherd Himself. It is just impossible to describe in words the joy of Much-Afraid when she saw Him really coming toward them on that dreary mountain path, where everything had been swallowed up for so long in the horrible mist and everything one touched had been so cold and clammy. Now with His coming the mist was rapidly clearing away and a real gleam of sunshine—the first they had seen for days—broke through at last.

"O Shepherd," she gasped, and caught hold of His hand and could say no more. It really had seemed as though she would never see Him again.

"Tell me," He repeated cheerily as He smiled at them all, "where did you learn that song, Much-Afraid?"

"Sorrow taught it to me," she replied. "I didn't think that she knew any songs, Shepherd, but she said the words and the music came to her as we were climbing up through the forest. I asked her to teach it to me because—I know I am a goose, but it makes me think of the time when You will have made my feet like hinds' feet and I won't ever have to slither along again," and she looked shamefacedly at her bedraggled and muddy condition.

"I am glad you sing it," said the Shepherd more pleasantly than ever. "I think it is a particularly nice song. Indeed," he added smiling, "I think I will add another verse to it Myself," and at once He began to sing these words to the same tune:

Blessed Sonshine!

READ: Hind's Feet... facing page & **Psalm 33**

"Let me sing now for my well-beloved a song of my
beloved concerning His vineyard." —Isaiah 5:1

"...but be filled with the Spirit, speaking to one another in psalms and hymns and
spiritual songs, singing and making melody with your heart to the LORD."
—Ephesians 5:18–19

Mountaineers receive an incredible experience when the sun breaks through and drives away mountain mist. Especially if you've been walking through mud and vegetation that over days have muddied your feet and drenched your clothes, it is nothing short of awesome. The warmth of the sun, appearance of blue sky, emergence of the high peaks, flowers, colors, etc. is an experience of earthly glory. Clothes soon dry, views delight, well-being pervades the soul. The sun brings life!

I have also sung songs and whistled loudly through the drenched heather and blueberries of high mountain mists. It has helped, but seldom has the sun appeared as a result. I was slower to learn than Much-Afraid to sing more unto the LORD, using His poetry!

Author Hurnard captures the key element; "With His coming the mist was rapidly clearing away and a real gleam of sunshine broke through at last". God has designed both the creation and our souls to easily relate to the "radiance of His glory and the exact representation of His nature", Jesus Christ (Heb.1:3)!

Much-Afraid catches hold of the Shepherd's hand and is struck between real reality and what "really had seemed" to be reality; i.e., that "she would never see Him again." Do we ever believe that lie? Maybe not. Yet we sometimes take actions that appear we do not know what is "really real" while we are fogged in by the mists.

Sorrow "taught" her the song, she says. At once the Shepherd begins to sing another poetic verse to the same tune. It will turn out to be based on the same verse of scripture as that which she has just sung (Song 7:1)

QUESTIONS AND PRAYER: Please look at Song of Solomon 7:1 and rephrase the thoughts as you would express them to your wife about her nature or beauty. (Bachelors, imagine you have a wife! Wives, imagine the words of Solomon directed at you!)_____

_____

_____

Thy joints and thighs are like a supple band
On which are met
Fair jewels which a cunning master hand
Hath fitly set.
In all the palace, search where'er you please,
In every place
There's none that walks with such a queenly ease,
Nor with such grace.

(Cant. 7:1)

"O shepherd," exclaimed Much-Afraid, "where did You find that verse to fit in so nicely to the tune which Sorrow taught me?"

Again He smiled at her in the nicest possible way and answered, "The words came to Me just now as I followed you along the path."

Poor Much-Afraid, who knew that she had been slipping and stumbling in the most dreadful way, indeed worse than at any other time, flushed painfully all over her face. She said nothing, only looked at Him almost reproachfully.

"Much-Afraid," said He very gently in answer to that look, "don't you know by now that I never think of you as you are now but as you will be when I have brought you to the Kingdom of Love and washed you from all the stains and defilements of the journey? If I come along behind you and notice that you are finding the way especially difficult, and are suffering from slips and falls, it only makes Me think of what you will be like when you are with Me, leaping and skipping on the High Places. Wouldn't you like to learn and sing My verse just as much as the one which Sorrow taught you?"

"Yes, said Much-Afraid thankfully, and taking His hand again, "certainly I will learn it and sing about the cunning master hand which takes such pains with me."

By this time the mist had actually melted away and the sun, shining brilliantly, was making the dripping trees and grass sparkle with joy and brightness.

Eyes of the Bridegroom

READ: Hind's Feet... facing page & **Song of Solomon 7:1–9**

"It goes down smoothly for my beloved, flowing gently through the lips of
those who fall asleep. I am my beloved's and his desire is for me."
—Song of Solomon 7:9–10

When the LORD makes love with words, it puts men to shame. Yet, we are to take instruction from Him in speaking words of love. We are not to lie nor hold back to our brides. He does not lie when He uses such profound and evocative words on His bride as we read in today's reading from Song of Solomon. This is His view! It becomes obvious why the Jews supposedly did not let young men read these scriptures until they were age 18!

Everyone knows how women respond to words of true love. As we pointed out before, they are creatures of the ears and depend upon the words of their bridegroom to know their unique value and receive affirmation. Why are men so weak at it? Is it because we are unwilling to conform to Christ (Phil. 3:10), who inspired these words of how we appear to him as a bride? The need for exercise is what was behind the previous lesson's closing request. How many men responded to write their own verse of poetry to their wives?

Consider what happens in a woman's heart when she knows she is loved; the key to setting any woman or the church of Christ free. See how she is overflowed by and yielded to the words of her Bridegroom; "It goes down smoothly for my beloved, flowing gently through the lips of those who fall asleep. I am my beloved's and his desire is for me." She is yielded. It is the yielding of one who is loved and trusts in her bridegroom.

This is what God says to His bride and it is what all believing husbands need to speak to their wives. Of course, we have to be trustworthy, too! Failure of trust causes our words to turn into lies. "Take heed then, to your spirit, and let no one deal treacherously against the wife of your youth" (Malachi 2:14). Let's seek after the faithfulness of Christ by dwelling in Him, and seek the fulfillment of men with contented brides, now.

QUESTIONS AND PRAYER: How may this text be applied to building your character and the affirmation of your wife as one who is cherished? What prayer does it produce in you?_____

_____

How about the protection of your daughters?_____

_____

All three thankfully accepted the suggestion of the Shepherd that they should sit down for a short time and rest and rejoice in the sunshine. Sorrow and Suffering withdrew a little, as they always did when the Shepherd was present, leaving Him to talk with Much-Afraid alone. She told Him all the dismal tale of their long wanderings in the mist, the way Resentment, Bitterness, and Self-Pity had been bothering her and her fear that perhaps, after all, they had wandered from the path and lost their way.

"Did you really think that I would let you stray from the right path to the High Places without doing anything to warn you or to prevent it?" asked the Shepherd quietly.

She looked at him sorrowfully and said with a sigh, "When Resentment and the others are shouting at me I am almost ready to believe anything, no matter how preposterous."

"You had better become a singer," said He, smiling. "Then you won't hear what they say to you. Ask Sorrow and Suffering if they have any more songs which they can teach you. Do you find them good guides, Much-Afraid?"

She looked at Him earnestly and nodded her head. "Yes, very good. I never could have believed it possible, Shepherd, but in a way I have come to love them. When I first saw them they looked so terrifyingly strong and stern, and I was sure that they would be rough with me and just drag me along without caring how I felt. How I dreaded it, but they have dealt with me very, very kindly indeed. I think they must have learned to be so gentle and patient with me by seeing Your gentleness.

"I never could have managed without them," she went on gratefully, "and the queer thing is I have a feeling that they really like helping an ugly little cripple like me in this way. They do truly want to get me up to the High Places, not just because it is the commandment which You have given them, but also because

Ministering Angels

READ: Hind's Feet... facing page & Luke 22:42–46

"But to which of the angels has He ever said, 'Sit at My right hand, until I make Thine enemies a footstool for Thy feet'? Are they not all ministering spirits, sent out to render service for the sake of those who will inherit salvation?" —Hebrews 1:13–14

Author Hurnard portrays Much-Afraid's companions Sorrow and Suffering. She sees personality and character traits that seem to reflect the fruits of the Spirit. Whether or not she intends these to reflect the changing lens of Much-Afraid's eyes, herself, or portray them as types of angels is not evident. Still, we can see certain things that she wants to bring out:

(1) They "always withdraw" from the immediate presence of the Shepherd. Privacy between disciple and Shepherd is insured; interaction of Sorrow and Suffering is diminished at this time.

(2) They obey "commandment" by the Shepherd, but are constrained to His personality. This supports I Corinthians 10:13, which promises that all temptation that comes to us is within God's provisions, who also provides a way of escape.

(3) They exhibit at least two fruits of the Spirit in the form of patience and gentleness. It seems that Much-Afraid senses that they love her, too, and want to help her. She is beginning to love them. They also exhibit faithfulness and peace; perhaps other fruits will show up soon!

(4) They at one time "looked" terrifyingly strong and stern, but it seems their terrifying aspects are fading away.

The Bible states that those who are in the Spirit are becoming conformed to the image of Christ (Rom.8:29). This involves sorrow and suffering (Isa. 53:3–5, 7–10). However, we see Sorrow and Suffering themselves also being transformed as they carry out their tasks of delivering Much-Afraid to the High Places. Are they not both ministering spirits sent out to render her service (Heb. 1:14)?

QUESTIONS AND PRAYER: Can you see other things in this portrait that haven't been mentioned?_____

_____

How about similar experiences which you've had and can describe based on the word of God?_____

_____

they want a horrid coward like myself to get there and be changed. You know, Shepherd, it makes a great difference in my feelings toward them not to look upon them any longer with dread, but as friends who want to help me. I know it seems ridiculous, but sometimes I get the feeling that they really love me and want to go with me of their own free will."

As she finished speaking she looked up in His face and was surprised to see that He actually looked as though He was trying not to laugh. He said nothing for a moment or two, but turned slightly so that He could look round at the two guides. Much-Afraid looked too.

They were sitting apart in the background and were unaware that they were being watched. They sat close to one another and were looking away up to the mountains toward the High Places. Their veils had been thrown back, although she still could not see their faces because their backs were toward the Shepherd and herself. She was struck by the fact that they seemed even taller and stronger than when she had first seen them waiting for her at the foot of the mountains.

There was something almost indescribably majestic about them at that moment, a sort of radiant eagerness expressed in their attitude. They were talking quickly to one another, but their voices were so low that she could not catch what they were saying. Was it possible—yes it was! They were actually laughing! That they were talking about something which thrilled them with eagerness and expectation, she felt quite sure.

The Shepherd watched them for a few moments without speaking, then He turned back to Much-Afraid. His eyes were laughing at her, but He said quite gravely, "Yes, I really believe you are right, Much-Afraid. They do look to Me as though they really enjoy their task, and perhaps even feel a little affection for the one they serve." Then He really did laugh out loud.

The Lens of the Eye

READ: Hind's Feet... facing page & I Corinthians 15:45–58

"Or how can you say to your brother, 'Let me take the speck out of your eye,' and behold, the log is in your own eye?" —Matthew 7:4

"And the blind and the lame came to him in the temple, and He healed them." —Matthew 21:14

A man coming into town asked a resident what kind of people lived there. When asked what kind of people lived in his last town, he answered, "Oh, bitter and resentful, always making trouble." The resident said, "You'll find people here much the same." An hour later another traveler came by and asked the same question. When asked what kind of people lived in his last town, he said, "Very nice! Always kind, generous and helpful." He was told, "You'll find people here much the same."

Much-Afraid discusses how she has come "to look upon them"; referring to Sorrow and Suffering. She is describing her own attitudes through which her perceptions are shaped; the condition of her spiritual eyes. A similar ability of spirit of expectant glory of the future is seen in I Corinthians 15 as Paul speaks of our putting on immortality. This is "radiant eagerness".

We perceive the two companions as they expectantly anticipate the future through Much-Afraid's eyes. They are looking forward to something with "a sort of radiant eagerness expressed in their attitude." The Bible says that the "anxious longing of the creation waits eagerly for the revealing of the sons of God" (Rom.8:19). Is this what we are witnessing? The two appear to have the knowledge of God; the certitude of His love, personality and character and His focus on their behalf (or is it Much-Afraid's behalf?). Much-Afraid's eye is able to see this. Perhaps it is her eye that shapes it.

In British-style understatement the Shepherd speaks "gravely" that it really appears as though the two feel "a little" affection for Much-Afraid. Then he laughs!

QUESTIONS AND PRAYER: What do you believe about the "lens of the eye" in shaping perceptions of other people and of situations?_____

_____

_____

What is required to change our eyes?_____

_____

_____

Sorrow and Suffering dropped the veils back over their faces and looked round to see what was happening, but the Shepherd had something more to say before He sped them farther on the journey.

The laughter died out of His face, and very seriously He asked, "Do you love Me enough to be able to trust Me completely, Much-Afraid?"

She looked at Him in the usual startled fashion so natural to her whenever she sensed that He was preparing her for a new test, then faltered, "You know that I do love You, Shepherd, as much as my cold little heart is capable. You know that I love You and that I long to trust You as much as I love You, that I long both to love and trust You still more."

"Would you be willing to trust Me," He asked, "even if everything in the wide world seemed to say that I was deceiving you—indeed, that I had deceived you all along?"

She looked at him in perplexed amazement. "Why, yes," she said, "I'm sure I would, because one thing I know to be true, it is impossible that You should tell a lie. It is impossible that You should deceive me. I know that I am often very frightened at the things which You ask me to do," she added shamefacedly and apologetically, "but I could never doubt You in that way. It's myself I am afraid of, never of You, and though everyone in the world should tell me that You had deceived me, I should know it was impossible."

"O Shepherd," she implored, "don't tell me that You think I really doubt You, even when I am most afraid and cowardly and despicably weak. You know—You know I trust You. In the end I know I shall be able to say Thy gentleness hath made me great."

He said nothing for a little, only looked down very tenderly, almost pitifully at the figure now crouching at His feet. Then, after a time, He said very quietly, "Much-Afraid, supposing I really did deceive you? What then?"

Levels of Trust

READ: Hind's Feet... facing page & **John 21:6–19**

"Jesus said therefore to the twelve, 'You do not want to go away also,
do you?' Simon Peter answered Him, "Lord, to whom shall we go?
You have words of eternal life." —John 6:67–68

"And Saul got up from the ground, and though his eyes
were open, he could see nothing." —Acts 9:8

Much-Afraid still has yet to see the faces of Sorrow and Suffering. They drop the veils back over their faces and turn to her and the Shepherd. The Shepherd asks her a question she has answered before. She senses a new test. She is not the first to address this question numerous times, nor the first to have it carry on to new tests. Peter, Paul and, we presume, all the apostles went through it repeatedly, as do all of Jesus' disciples.

One aspect of response relates to knowing there is no life alternative. Is there anyone else who offers eternal life; whose words themselves offer life?! Peter knew this early on, but it did not finally resolve the issue. Jesus took him to greater and greater depths of faith. Paul, at his first meeting with the Lord, had his eyes opened, but beyond knowing the Savior, and receiving initial instruction, saw nothing more. He was later challenged at incredible levels of faith and suffering.

God is faithful to walk with us at all levels. We are first called to trust and walk; then, He turns out to be/have been walking ahead of us. Only the omniscient God of all time and space, the Alpha and Omega, can do such things. But the challenge of our faith remains always the same. "Do you trust Me?"

Much-Afraid seems to give good responses. She has only her weakness and longings to claim, plus her knowledge of the Shepherd's character. She comes to a foundational claim, "It is impossible that You should deceive me." Then He takes her to another level. "Supposing I really did deceive you? What then?"

QUESTIONS AND PRAYER: Are there incidents in your life where you feel later that you had your eyes opened to things you did not expect?

_____

_____

Is this true of marriage? Did God lead you into these things?

_____

_____

It was then her turn to be quite silent, trying to grasp this impossible thing He was suggesting and to think what her answer would be. What then? Would it be that she could never trust, never love Him again? Would she have to be alive in the world where there was no Shepherd, only a mirage and a broken lovely dream? To know that she had been deceived by one she was certain could not deceive? To lose Him?

Suddenly she burst into a passion of weeping, then after a little while looked straight up into His face and said, "My Lord—if You can deceive me, You may. It can make no difference. I must love You as long as I continue to exist. I cannot love without loving You."

He laid His hands on her head, then with a touch more tender and gentle than anything she had ever felt before, repeated as though to Himself, "If I can, I may deceive her." Then without another word He turned and went away.

Much-Afraid picked up a little icy-cold pebble which was lying on the ground where He had stood, put it in her bag, then trembling rejoined Sorrow and Suffering, and they continued their journey.

Limit(s) on Deception?

READ: Hind's Feet... facing page & John 14:1–6

"For false Christs and false prophets will arise and will show great signs and wonders, so as to mislead, if possible, even the elect." —Matthew 24:24

"If you abide in My word, then you are truly disciples of Mine; and you shall know the truth and the truth shall make you free." —John 8:31–32

What a question the Shepherd asks! "Supposing I really did deceive you? What then?" Think about it. What are the differences between ignorance, good intentions, foolishness, mistakes, lies, bad intentions, etc. Are not our whole lives involved with being surprised with things we've not expected? Is this what is meant by the question? Does it address intentions or results; character or obedience?

Certainly God does not lie or mislead, but many forces are at work in the world to capture and lead us if we have no knowledge of God's will or provisions. We can get into some awful difficulties, even death, because of lack of knowledge (Hos.4:6). How many times have we been brought to say, "If I'd known it would turn out like this, I'd never have done it!" Is there foreknowledge by God involved? Is there fault? Is there a moral issue between God and us when we are led (by whom?) into a situation where we are deceived, causing us extreme pain and distress? Who is responsible?

Much-Afraid is stunned, "trying to grasp this impossible thing". What would she do if she was *actually* deceived by the one she was convinced couldn't deceive? Lose Him? In tears she responds. The Shepherd is given permission to do as He wishes. Much-Afraid resolves there is no life without loving Him.

In extremely tender and gentle care the Shepherd quietly repeats her assent in the words that are significant from His view: "If I *can*, (in terms of His character or other constraints or desires), I *may* (in terms of having her permission) deceive her."

QUESTIONS AND PRAYER: Is there a deceiver? What are his purposes?

_____

How do they compare with those of Christ (See John, chapter 15)._____

_____

Also see Genesis 3:1–5 and Revelation 12:9 and organize a few of your own thoughts on this subject in the war between good and evil. _____

_____

_____

CHAPTER 13

In the Valley of Loss

The mist had cleared from the mountains and the sun was shining, and as a consequence the way seemed much more pleasant and easy than it had for a very long time. The path still led them along the side of the mountain rather than upward, but one day, on turning a corner, they found themselves looking down into a deep valley. To their surprise, their path actually plunged straight down the mountainside toward it, exactly as at the beginning of the journey when Much-Afraid had been led down into Egypt.

All three halted and looked first at one another, then down into the valley and across to the other side. There the ascent was as steep and even higher than the Precipice of Injury and they saw that to go down and then ascend again would not only require an immense amount of strength and effort, but also take a very long time.

Much-Afraid stood and stared, and at that moment experienced the sharpest and keenest test which she had yet encountered on the journey. Was she to be turned aside once again, but in an even more terrible way than ever before? By now they had ascended far higher than ever before. Indeed, if only the path they were following would begin to ascend, they could not doubt that they would soon be at the snowline and approaching the real High Places, where no enemies could follow and where the healing streams flowed.

Now instead of that the path was leading them down into a valley as low as the Valley of Humiliation itself. All the height which they had gained after their

Seeing Ahead

READ: Hind's Feet... facing page & **Acts 9:1–16**

"Do not turn to mediums or spiritists; do not seek them out to be defiled by them. I am the LORD your God." —Leviticus 19:31

"Who has performed and accomplished it, calling forth the generations from the beginning? I, the LORD, am the first, and with the last. I am He" —Isaiah 41:4

The little boy turns to its father and says, "Daddy, are we there, yet?" Isn't it good he doesn't know the time and effort it will require to get there? A young mind struggles for the goal, but finds his answers in his father. Nothing is visible beyond that. It is good that we cannot see further ahead. It would dismay us, no doubt. We are also to trust in our Father.

God holds the future for us and shows us portions. However, He desires that we trust in Him, not knowledge of the future. In fact, we are forbidden to seek knowledge of the future apart from God. The Bible doesn't make much reference to our pathways ahead, other than involving trials and tribulation. Our future is simply in Him. He holds our future. Does this sound too simple? Our future is in a Person, not a pathway.

A potential difficulty of seeing our future pathway is shown in this scene with Much-Afraid. She is dismayed at seeing the tremendous depth to which she must descend and the precipice she must again climb. What is it that dismays her? It is the "strength and effort" required as well as the "very long time" it will take. Not only that, she is also able to relate it to past effort which proved to be such a trial. This appears worse!

Paul, who brought much suffering to the church prior to his salvation, was also shown little of his future, except "how much he must suffer" for the sake of Christ. His first missionary trip brought much persecution and tribulation, including abandonment and stoning. He must have often been confronted with Much-Afraid's decision whether or not to go ahead and been thankful God did not show Him more of his future.

QUESTIONS AND PRAYER: What personal desires do you have to know more of your future?_____

_____

_____

Have you any dissatisfaction with what God provides you?_____

_____

_____

long and toilsome journey must now be lost and they would have to begin all over again, just as though they had never made a start so long ago and endured so many difficulties and tests.

As she looked down into the depths of the valley the heart of Much-Afraid went numb. For the first time on the journey she actually asked herself if her relatives had not been right after all and if she ought not to have attempted to follow the Shepherd. How could one follow a person Who asked so much, Who demanded such impossible things, Who took away everything? If she went down there, as far as getting to the High Places was concerned she must lose everything she had gained on the journey so far. She would be no nearer receiving the promise than when she started out from the Valley of Humiliation.

For one black, awful moment Much-Afraid really considered the possibility of following the Shepherd no longer, of turning back. She need not go on. There was absolutely no compulsion about it. She had been following this strange path with her two companions as guides simply because it was the Shepherd's choice for her. It was not the way which she naturally wanted to go. Now she could make her own choice. Her sorrow and suffering could be ended at once, and she could plan her life in the way she liked best, without the Shepherd.

During that awful moment or two it seemed to Much-Afraid that she was actually looking into an abyss of horror, into an existence in which there was no Shepherd to follow or to trust or to love—no Shepherd at all, nothing but her own horrible self. Ever after, it seemed that she had looked straight down into Hell. At the end of that moment Much-Afraid shrieked—there is no other word for it.

"Shepherd," she shrieked, "Shepherd! Shepherd! Help me! Where are You? Don't leave me!" The next instant she was clinging to Him trembling from head to foot, and sobbing over and over again, "You may do anything, Shepherd. You may ask anything—only don't let me turn back. O my Lord, don't let

Real Horror

READ: Hind's Feet... facing page & **Acts 13:44–14:20**

"Now Paul and his companions put out to sea from Paphos and came to Perga in Pamphylia; and John left them and returned to Jerusalem." —Acts 13:13"

"But Jesus said to him, "No one, after putting his hand to the plow and looking back, is fit for the kingdom of God." —Luke 9:62

The apostle Paul became deeply involved with those to whom he ministered, taking jealous personal interest in them (II Cor. 11:2) on God's behalf and desiring greatly that they experience the benefits of true discipleship to Christ. He took it hard when young John Mark turned back. Mark was a nephew of Barnabus and may not have related well to discipleship under Paul on Paul's first missionary journey. We can speculate that he wearied in turning back early on that first trip. In view of the severe trials that followed, it may have been providential. Though it produced difficulties (Acts 15:38), Paul and Mark were later reconciled to work effectively together (Col. 4:10, II Tim. 4:11). Each had different paths!

In this scene we consider a horror worse than failure of a journey. Or is it? Much-Afraid first sees the issue as one of keeping to the pathway or not. Then it transforms into another; by turning away from the path, she could plan her "life in the way she liked best, without the Shepherd." This opens her to see the pit of Hell; eternal separation from the Shepherd. This close relationship of journey and eternal relationship with the Shepherd is a goal of author Hurnard depicted here with Much-Afraid. Do we agree with this view?

Much-Afraid never seems to get angry, only fearful. I wonder if others would instead get angry with the Shepherd, or if other authors could depict an "Often-Angry" boy or girl on the walk with the Shepherd.

In fright over this horror, Much-Afraid cries out for the Shepherd and immediately pleads her first priority, "Don't let me leave You".

QUESTIONS AND PRAYER: As a man in Much-Afraid's situation, would you be angry or fearful?_____

_____

Would the prospect of quitting the journey produce horror and fear in you or some other reaction?_____

_____

_____

me leave You. Entreat me not to leave Thee nor to return from following after Thee." Then as she continued to cling to Him she sobbed out, "If You can deceive me, my Lord, about the promise and the hinds' feet and the new name or anything else, You may, indeed You may; only don't let me leave You. Don't let anything turn me back. This path looked so wrong I could hardly believe it was the right one," and she sobbed bitterly.

He lifted her up, supported her by His arm, and with His own hand wiped the tears from her cheeks, then said in His strong, cheery voice, "There is no question of your turning back, Much-Afraid. No one, not even your own shrinking heart, can pluck you out of My hand. Don't you remember what I told you before? This delay is not unto death but for the glory of God. You haven't forgotten already the lesson you have been learning, have you?"

"It is no less true now that 'what I do thou knowest not now, but thou shalt know hereafter.' My sheep hear my voice, and they follow me. It is perfectly safe for you to go on in this way even though it looks so wrong, and now I give you another promise: Thine ears shall hear a word behind thee saying, 'This is the way, walk ye in it,' when ye turn to the right hand or to the left."

He paused a moment, and she still leaned against him, speechless with thankfulness and relief at his presence. Then he went on. "Will you bear this too, Much-Afraid? Will you suffer yourself to lose or to be deprived of all that you have gained on this journey to the High Places? Will you go down this path of forgiveness into the Valley of Loss, just because it is the way that I have chosen for you? Will you still trust and still love Me?"

She was still clinging to Him, and now repeated with all her heart the words of another woman tested long ago, "Entreat me not to leave Thee, or to return from following after Thee: for whither Thou goest I will go; Thy people shall be my people and Thy God my God." She paused and faltered

218

Exchanging Loss for Gain

READ: Hind's Feet... facing page & **Ruth 1:1–17**

"I count all things to be loss in view of the surpassing value of knowing Christ Jesus my LORD, for whom I have suffered the loss of all things, and count them but rubbish in order that I may gain Christ." —Philippians 3:8

"When he puts forth all his own, he goes before them, and the sheep follow him because they know his voice." —John 10:4

While clinging and weeping, Much-Afraid pours out her tears and begins a new relationship with the Shepherd; a relationship in which He is more important than His promises. "Things" now take a backseat to the One who provides "things". Being *in* personal relationship with Him is now resolved as paramount for her, even if the "things" are lost forever.

The Shepherd lifts her up and in a strong, cheery voice uses honest words with no condemnation to describe her "shrinking heart" and the fact that no one can pluck her out of His hand (John 10:28). He repeats earlier words, then gives her a new promise from Isaiah 30:21. She will have His guidance on when to turn "to the right hand or to the left". While still in this embrace, He spells this loss out in words to which we would be attentive. Is she willing "to lose or to be deprived" of all that she has gained in her walk with the Shepherd? What things have we gained or lost in our walk with Christ? Stewardship? Position? Material possessions? Reputation? Children?

Ruth, the Moabitess, leaving her own county to follow Naomi back to Israel, is the model of this. She left everything to pursue relationship with the God of Israel and her mother-in-law, both of whom she had come to love. God blessed her with a godly husband, Boaz, the model of the kinsman-redeemer and true manhood, and a place in the lineage of Jesus Christ.

QUESTIONS AND PRAYER: A study of Jesus' words and the lives of the apostles indicates that God may not ask disciples to renounce spouses for His work. Still, the consequences of "walking" with a spouse into work for the Lord frequently results in loss of spouse. What are your views on this?_____

_____

_____

_____

_____

_____

_____

a moment, then went on in a whisper, "And where Thou diest, will I die, and there will I be buried. The Lord do so to me, and more also, if aught but death part Thee and me" (Ruth 1:16,17).

So another altar was built at the top of the descent into the Valley of Loss and another stone added to those in the bag she still carried in her bosom. After that they began the downward journey, and as they went she heard her two guides singing softly:

> *O whither is thy Beloved gone,*
> *Thou fairest among women?*
> *Where dost thou think he has turned aside?*
> *That we may seek him with thee.*

The Shepherd Himself sang the next verse:

> *He is gone down into his garden,*
> *To the beds of spices sweet,*
> *For he feedeth among the lilies,*
> *'Tis there we are wont to meet.*

Then Much-Afraid herself sang the last two verses, and her heart was so full of joy that even her unmelodious voice seemed changed and sounded as sweet as the others.

> *So I went down into the garden,*
> *The valley of buds and fruits,*
> *To see if the pomegranates budded,*
> *To look at the vinestock shoots.*

> *And my soul in a burst of rapture,*
> *Or ever I was aware,*
> *Sped swifter than chariot horses,*
> *For lo! he was waiting there.*

(Cant. 6:1–3)

Considering how steep it was, the descent down into the valley seemed surprisingly easy, but perhaps that was because Much-Afraid desired with her whole

220

Getting High Going Low

READ: Hind's Feet... facing page & Matthew 25:1–13

"...the friend of the Bridegroom, who stands and hears him, rejoices
greatly because of the bridegroom's voice." —John 3:29

"Rejoice with those who rejoice, and weep with
those who weep." —Romans 12:15

Much-Afraid builds another altar and adds another stone to her bag. Do we yet have an idea of the scriptural significance of these stones? As she starts downward a new phenomena takes place. The two companions, (should we now say friends?) Sorrow and Suffering, begin to sing about *her!*

Paraphrasing in an alternative poetic form the words of the poet, Solomon, they sing of Much-Afraid in the third person. They play the role of the chorus, or "Daughters of Jerusalem" in singing of the bride. The Shepherd identifies Himself as the Bridegroom by referring to Himself in the first person as "meeting" the bride. Then, Much-Afraid sings of herself as the bride, in the first person, rejoicing in rapture of her meeting with the Bridegroom where He waits for her!

Does it sound like only a woman could write such stuff? Remember, guys, a guy wrote Song of Solomon!

The 'voice of joy' over the bride is portrayed in the modern day by the tradition of bridesmaids, girls not yet married who rejoice in the bride's happiness, as John the Baptist rejoiced over the joy of the Bridegroom. A lesson in this regard may be found in the parable of the foolish virgins. All wanted to go to the wedding, but only the wise resolved to take oil in their flasks to keep their lamps lighted.

What does it mean to "renew" a lighted lamp? What does "oil" signify for this purpose? Most believe that oil signifies the Holy Spirit, His power in us to hear the truth, be convicted of sin and of righteousness and speak of Jesus Christ in a dark and unbelieving world. What do you think?

QUESTIONS AND PRAYER: Are you in relationship with Christ through the Holy Spirit? How often does He convict you of sin for confession and cleansing? Is your "light" being thereby renewed in the darkness? Can you identify others who are "lighting" off you?_____

_____

_____

will to make it in a way that would satisfy and please the Shepherd. The awful glimpse down into the abyss of an existence without Him had so staggered and appalled her heart that she felt she could never be quite the same again. However, it had opened her eyes to the fact that right down in the depths of her own heart she really had but one passionate desire, not for the things which the Shepherd had promised, but for Himself. All she wanted was to be allowed to follow Him forever.

Other desires might clamor strongly and fiercely nearer the surface of her nature, but she knew now that down in the core of her own being she was so shaped that nothing could fit, fill, or satisfy her heart but He Himself. "Nothing else really matters," she said to herself, "only to love Him and to do what He tells me. I don't know quite why it should be so, but it is. All the time it is suffering to love and sorrow to love, but it is lovely to love Him in spite of this, and if I should cease to do so, I should cease to exist." So, as has been said, they reached the valley very quickly.

The next surprising thing was that though the valley did seem at first a little like a prison after the strong bracing air of the mountains, it turned out to be a wonderfully beautiful and peaceful place, very green with flowers covering the fields and the banks of the river which flowed quietly through it.

Strangely enough, down there in the Valley of Loss, Much-Afraid felt more rested, more peaceful, and more content than anywhere else on the journey. It seemed, too, that her two companions also underwent a strange transformation. They still held her hands, but there was neither suffering nor sorrow in the touch. It was as though they walked close beside her and went hand in hand simply for friendship's sake and for the joy of being together.

Also, they sang continually, sometimes in a language quite different from the one which she had learned from them, but when she asked the meaning of the words they only smiled and shook their heads. This is one of the many songs which all three sang

The Promiser, Not the Promises

READ: Hind's Feet... facing page & Philippians 3:1–14

"One thing I have asked from the LORD, that I shall seek; that I may dwell in the house of the LORD all the days of my life, to behold the beauty of the LORD, and to meditate in His temple." —Psalm 27:4

"I in them, and Thou in Me, that they may be perfected in unity, that the world may know that Thou didst send Me, and didst love them, even as Thou didst love Me." —John 17:23

Much-Afraid reviews her resolution. Her eyes have been opened to the fact that she really has "but one passionate desire, not for the things which the Shepherd had promised, but for Himself." Yes, indeed! Lord, may it be so for all of us! Amen.

In today's scriptures the psalmist, the apostle Paul and Christ with His Father (and us), all come to the same resolution of priority at all costs, even death on the cross. That is, relationship with God! Lord, fill the "God-shaped vacuum" in us! Enable us to look loss in the face without tears that turn us away. We count the Valley of Loss for gain for the sake of having You.

Running down the hill "like water", Much-Afraid does not come to another desert. Instead it is a lovely green valley with fields and a river flowing through it. She finds "more rest", more "peace" and more "contentment" than ever before. The touch of Sorrow and Suffering now no longer convey these qualities to Much-Afraid. Can some of us relate to this? Is it possible to walk together in fellowship with Sorrow and Suffering in real fellowship and the joy of being together?

Jesus the Promise Maker made it clear in His prayer in John 17, that His work was to glorify the Father and share His place with us and that we would find joy in conforming to Him in the same way. By this means we will enable others to know also that the Father sent Him.

QUESTIONS AND PRAYER: Can you relate to the proposition of Sorrow and Suffering losing their grip on us while still walking in this world? What peace is there with Christ in "giving up" even our desire for His promises in exchange for Him?_____

_____

What possible misgivings have you over this idea?_____

_____

down in the Valley of Loss, and it was another from the collection in the old songbook which Much-Afraid so loved.

I am my Love's and he is mine,
And this is his desire,
That with his beauty I may shine
In radiant attire.
And this will be—when all of me
Is pruned and purged with fire.

Come, my Beloved, let us go
Forth to the waiting field;
And where thy choicest fruit trees grow,
Thy pruning knife now wield
That at thy will and through thy skill
Their richest store may yield.

And spices give a sweet perfume,
And vines show tender shoots,
And all my trees burst forth in bloom,
Fair buds from bitter roots.
There will not I my love deny,
But yield thee pleasant fruits.

(Cant. 7:10–13)

It is true that when Much-Afraid looked at the mountains on the other side of the valley she wondered how they would ever manage to ascend them, but she found herself content to wait restfully and to wander in the valley as long as the Shepherd chose. One thing in particular comforted her; after the hardness and slipperiness of the way on the mountains, where she had stumbled and limped so painfully, she found that in those quiet green fields she could actually walk without stumbling, and could not feel her wounds and scars and stiffness at all.

All this seemed a little strange because, of course, she really was in the Valley of Loss. Also, apparently, she was farther from the High Places than ever before.

Gain of Contentment

READ: Hind's Feet... facing page & **Philippians 4:10–19**

"But godliness actually is a means of great gain, when
accompanied by contentment." —I Timothy 6:6

"Let your way of life be free from the love of money, being content with what you
have; for He himself has said, 'I will never desert you, nor will I ever forsake you.'" —
Hebrews 13:5

Much-Afraid sings another song from her beloved songbook, in which the pictures of
pain portrayed also evidence contentment at the process being accomplished by God upon
the singer. In the first verse she sings contentedly of being pruned and purged by fire and in
the second she sings of being submitted to the pruning knife. Although worded somewhat
differently from the scriptures referred, the poem makes a beautiful statement of one submitted to the Savior's purification process, by which one may bear much fruit (John 15:2).

The third verse summarizes in the first person the desire of the fruit bearer to put forth
sweet perfume (Eph.5:2), tender shoots (Isa.53:2) and blossoms (Song 2:12), to yield the
divine fruit which God is raising from His bride (Gal. 5:22–23). It is powerful, personally
motivating poetry for submitting to the work God is doing, both method and result.

After singing a song of contentment, we hear explicitly that Much-Afraid finds herself
"content" to wait restfully and wander in the valley as long as the Shepherd chooses. She
finds that her deformities seem no longer to give her trouble in her walking. In fact, a
picture quite the opposite of "loss" is painted in the Valley of Loss. For whatever Much-
Afraid has lost, she has gained great contentment in its place. Counting all things as loss as
Paul did (Phil. 3:8) has instead brought much blessing to her. Deciding to be empty-handed,
she has been made full. Perhaps this is related to being made "full" in the manner Jesus
spoke of in John 15:11 when He explained the process of pruning.

QUESTIONS AND PRAYER: How may we identify things we are refusing to
part with that are interfering with greater contentment?_____
_____
_____

What clues can our discontents provide?_____
_____
_____

She asked the Shepherd about it one day, for the loveliest part of all was that He often walked with them down there, saying with a beautiful smile that it was one of His favorite haunts.

In answer to her question, He said, "I am glad that you are learning to appreciate the valley too, but I think it was the altar which you built at the top, Much-Afraid, which has made it so easy for you."

This also rather puzzled her, for she said, "But I have noticed that after the other altars which You told me to build, the way has generally seemed harder and more testing than before."

Again He smiled, but only remarked quietly that the important thing about altars was that they made possibilities of apparent impossibilities, and that it was nice that on this occasion it had brought her peace and not a great struggle. She noticed that He looked at her keenly and rather strangely as He spoke, and though there was a beautiful gentleness in the look, there was also something else which she had seen before, but still did not understand. She thought it held a mixture of two things, not exactly pity—no, that was the wrong word, but a look of wonderful compassion together with unflinching determination.

When she realized that, she thought of some words which one of the Shepherd's servants had spoken down in the Valley of Humiliation before ever the Shepherd had called her to the High Places. He had said, "Love is beautiful, but it is also terrible—terrible in its determination to allow nothing blemished or unworthy to remain in the beloved."

When she remembered this, Much-Afraid thought with a little shiver in her heart, "He will never be content until He makes me what He is determined that I ought to be," and because she was still Much-Afraid and not yet ready to change her name, she added with a pang of fear, "I wonder what He plans to do next, and if it will hurt very much indeed?"

Gain of Fellowship

READ: Hind's Feet... facing page & **Genesis 45**

"Just as a father has compassion on his children, so the LORD has compassion on those who fear Him. For He Himself knows our frame; he is mindful that we are but dust." —Psalm 103:13–14

"Repent therefore and return, that your sins may be wiped away, in order that times of refreshing may come from the presence of the LORD." —Acts 3:19

It's easy to slip into "talk" and forget just how difficult some of these things we "walk" really are. We must "walk" to enable God to correct our deformities. After all, the deformities are the result of sin and the sin must be corrected to get rid of the deformities. Jacob, in finally deciding to let Benjamin go with Judah and the rest of the boys back to Egypt (where Simeon was still in prison) had been forced into a situation where he could no longer play favorites with his sons. He had to risk losing Benjamin. It was an occasion of "loss" for Jacob. He gave up the person of greatest value in his heart. After the loss of his wife and Joseph, Benjamin was his last comfort. God knew the value of Benjamin as well as his value to Jacob, but it was essential that all idols be removed.

We find that the Valley of Loss is one of increased fellowship. Much-Afraid identifies increased fellowship with the Shepherd. For Jacob it was restoration of relationship with *all* of his sons, including long "dead" Joseph. It is fellowship based on resurrection power over death. That which "dies" comes back alive with more than we could ask or think! The crucifixion of Christ was the greatest such "Valley of Loss", but it applies to all of us. God's beautiful plan of salvation through Israel and Christ was demonstrated beforehand in a powerful example through Jacob, Joseph and Judah, to show us the principles of redemption and resurrection from the dead!

Much-Afraid senses and identifies two things in the Shepherd; first His deep compassion for her in what she is going through and second, determination to get the job of her purification accomplished.

God loves us too much to leave us as we are. He will bring us to the end of ourselves. The false idols, means of comfort and worldly support must go.

QUESTIONS AND PRAYER: What events in your life might relate to this?

_____

Can you identify an idol God might desire to discuss with you?_____

_____

What is your greatest source of comfort?_____

CHAPTER 14

The Place of Anointing

As it happened, the next thing which the Shepherd had planned was very beautiful indeed. Not long after this conversation the path finished its winding way through the valley and led them to the foot of the mountains on the other side to a place where they rose up like a wall, far higher and steeper than the Precipice of Injury.

However, when Much-Afraid and her two companions reached this place they found the Shepherd waiting for them beside a little hut, and lo! just where the cliffs were steepest and highest was an overhead cable suspended between that spot and the summit far above. On this cable hung chairs, in which two could sit side by side and be swung right up to the top without any effort on their part at all. It is true that at first the very sight of these frail-looking aerial chairs swinging along so high above the ground made Much-Afraid feel giddy and panicky. She felt she could never voluntarily place herself in one of them and be swung up that frightful-looking precipice, with only a little footrest and nothing to prevent her casting herself out of the chair if the urge should come upon her.

However, that passed almost at once, for the Shepherd smiled and said, "Come, Much-Afraid, we will seat ourselves in the first two chairs and Sorrow and Suffering will follow in the next. All you have to do is to trust yourself to the chair and be carried in perfect safety up to the place to which I wish to take you and without any struggling and striving on your part."

Much-Afraid stepped into one of the seats, and the Shepherd sat beside her while the two companions occupied the next pair. In a minute they were

Trust the Lift!

READ: Hind's Feet... facing page & **I Samuel 30:1–25**

"For He will give His angels charge concerning you, to guard you in all
your ways. They will bear you up in their hands, lest you strike your
foot against a stone." —Psalm 91:11–12

"Those that wait for the Lord will gain new strength; they will mount up
with wings like eagles, they will run and not get tired, they will walk
and not become weary." —Isaiah 41:31

Well, now, what have we here? A chair lift? Much-Afraid is going to go up in a chair
lift? That seems like cheating, doesn't it?! Shouldn't she have to labor up this hill all over
again? No! We see another gain coming to Much-Afraid. After her voluntarily giving up all
that she had previously gained in order to enter the Valley of Loss, she is going to get it all
back and more. It is another allegorical illustration of resurrection power abundantly restoring all that we give up to the Savior. It is far-and-away a net gain!

In this case, we also have a vivid personal lesson that was given by God to Hannah
Hurnard, who was afraid of heights and the prospect of riding in a chair lift. God worked it
out abundantly for her once she resolved the matter in her mind. On vacation in Switzer-
land, she experienced the very lesson she is teaching.

Nearly all who have skied have experienced some form of Much-Afraid's concerns. It is
one thing to seat oneself in a dining room chair and quite another to ride scores or hundreds
of feet above rocks and cliffs in an open swinging chair. Yes! What if the urge should come
to jump? How many possible arguments might there be not to trust the chair?

But once the matter is resolved, it is resolved. This is one of those words with finality.
RESOLVED! Once resolved, there is only a matter of sitting and letting the lift do the
work; less work for the rider even than that involved in eagles' wings.

**QUESTIONS AND PRAYER: Can you attempt to think of another allegory on
how trusting in something enables one to "fly" over obstacles?**_____

_____

_____

How does it matter how reliable the object is in which the trust is placed?_____

_____

_____

_____

moving smoothly and steadily toward the High Places which had looked so impossibly out of reach, supported entirely from above, and with nothing to do but rest and enjoy the marvelous view. Though the chairs swung a little in places, they felt no giddiness at all, but went upward and still upward until the valley below looked like a little green carpet and the gleaming white peaks of the Kingdom of Love towered around and above them. Soon they were far above the place to which they had climbed on the mountains opposite, and still they swung along.

When at last they stepped out of the aerial chairs they were in a place more beautiful than anything Much-Afraid had seen before, for though these were not the real High Places of the Kingdom of Love, they had reached the borderland. All around were alps with grassy meadows almost smothered in flowers. Little streams gurgled and splashed between banks of kingcups, while buttercups and cowslips, violets and pink primulae carpeted the ground. Clumps of delicate purple soldanella grew in vivid clusters, and all over the fields, glowing bright as gems, were gentians, more blue than the sky at midday, looking like jewels on a royal robe.

Above were peaks of pure white snow which towered up into a cloudless sky like a roof of sapphire and turquoise. The sun shone so brilliantly it almost seemed that one could see the flowers pushing their way up through the earth and unfolding themselves to receive the glory of its rays. Cowbells and goatbells sounded in every direction, and a multitude of bird notes filled the air, but above the rest was one voice louder and more dominant than them all, and which seemed to fill the whole region.

It was the voice of a mighty waterfall, leaping down another great cliff which towered above them, and whose rushing waters sprang from the snows in the High Places themselves. It was so unspeakably lovely that neither Much-Afraid nor her companions could utter a word, but stood, drawing deep breaths and filling their lungs with the spicy, pine-scented mountain air.

Gain Toward the High Places

READ: Hind's Feet... facing page & **II Samuel 22:30–34**

"Thus says the LORD, 'Heaven is My throne, and the earth is My footstool. Where then is a house you could build for Me? And where is a place that I may rest?" —Isaiah 66:1

"For behold, the winter is past, the rain is over and gone. The flowers have already appeared in the land;...." —Song of Solomon 2:11–12

Up, up goes Much-Afraid, far above the place "to which they had climbed" opposite the Valley of Loss. Still they go up higher. It is hard now to discern what it was that Much-Afraid lost! At last they reach a place more beautiful than anything she has seen before. How can it get better than this?

There in the high meadows are reds, violets, purples, yellows, blues and pinks in the flowers glowing brightly as gems! What contrast of color in the blue sky, the flowered green meadows, pure white snow and gleaming peaks. The sounds, too, are beautiful, filled with bird notes, bells and little streams gurgling and splashing. It is like paradise. But one voice sounds "louder and more dominant" than them all. Listen to the incredible illustration God reveals in the waterfall!

A somewhat similar scene of "leaping" and "running" is given by David in which the mountains represent the strong fortress of God, and upon which David said, "He makes my feet like hinds' feet, and sets me on my high places". It is a scene of power and grace. But in this scene with Much-Afraid it is the waterfall that will become an even more powerful illustration of the High Places in Christ.

The mighty waterfall "leaping down another great cliff" captures her attention. The key words may very well be "leaping down". Do you remember the lesson of the water Much-Afraid learned in her early walk? The earlier water flowed down. This water "leaps". Does this speak to you?

QUESTIONS AND PRAYER: When David says that He "leaps" over a wall, what does this portray to you?_____
When mountain deer leap the rocks, what does this portray?

_____

What do these pictures evoke as motivation in us beyond the mere leaping of waterfalls?_____

_____

As they wandered forward, they stooped down at every other step, gently touching the jewel-like flowers or dabbling their fingers in the splashing brooks. Sometimes they just stood still amid the profusion of shining beauty around them and laughed aloud with pure joy. The Shepherd led them across meadows where the warm, scented grass grew nearly waist high, toward the mighty waterfall.

At the foot of the cliffs they found themselves standing in cool shadows with a light spray sometimes splashing their faces, and there the Shepherd bade them stand and look up. There stood Much-Afraid, a tiny figure at the foot of the mighty cliffs, looking up at the great, never-ending rush of waters as they cast themselves down from the High Places. She thought that never before had she seen anything so majestic or so terrifyingly lovely. The height of the rocky lip, over which the waters cast themselves to be dashed in pieces on the rocks below, almost terrified her. At the foot of the fall, the thunderous voice of the waters seemed almost deafening, but it seemed also to be filled with meaning, grand and awesome, beautiful beyond expression.

As she listened, Much-Afraid realized that she was hearing the full majestic harmonies, the whole orchestra as it were, playing the original of the theme song which all the little streamlets had sung far below in the Valley of Humiliation. Now it was uttered by thousands upon thousands of voices, but with grander harmonies than anything heard down in the valleys, yet still the same song.

> *From the heights we leap and go*
> *To the valleys down below,*
> *Always answering to the call,*
> *To the lowest place of all.*

"Much-Afraid," said the Shepherd's voice in her ear, "what do you think of this fall of great waters in their abandonment of self-giving?"

So Terrifyingly Lovely

READ: Hind's Feet... facing page & **I John 4:7–21**

"And I will most gladly spend and be expended for
your souls." —II Corinthians 12:15

"Everyone who drinks of this water shall thirst again; but whoever
drinks of the water that I shall give him shall never thirst; but the
water that I shall give him shall become in him a well of water
springing up to eternal life." —John 4:14–15

We are caught up in a dazzling scene touching most of the human senses; lovely things which are perceived through sight, sound, touch and smell. It is all good for Much-Afraid and for us to grasp a bit of the reality of the glory which awaits the children of God (Rom.8:21). Then the Shepherd leads Much-Afraid to the waterfall.

What a splendid portrait is pictured as the waters "cast themselves down from the High Places." Not a single random word here! Picture each aspect as the water flings itself over the precipice, dashing downward with wild abandon into such seeming destruction!! Much-Afraid senses in its roaring thunder a grand and awesome meaning to it, "beautiful beyond expression". Then she recalls the simple theme she heard in the waters of the valley below; that water loves to go downward, ever downward in service. She hears this now in majestic orchestral tones with "thousands upon thousands of voices" in the abandonment of self-giving, on the grandest scale.

Then one who surely knows how the voice of Love is designed to come to a woman, uses choice words to describe her romance with the Shepherd. She hears, *"the Shepherd's voice in her ear,"* as he asks her what she thinks of this great fall of waters.

We almost anticipate her answer, even as can the Shepherd. Does this draw our hearts? How does the Shepherd's voice draw us to self-giving? Can prophetic beauty in God's design of nature and His inspired word activate us in Christ as a fountain of life to others?

QUESTIONS AND PRAYER: To what extent do you feel God's design of nature teaches us the complete truth also described in the Bible? In your opinion is this completely or only partly true?_____

_____

_____

How does Romans 1:20 apply?_____

_____

She trembled a little as she answered. "I think they are beautiful and terrible beyond anything which I ever saw before."

"Why terrible?" He asked.

"It is the leap which they have to make, the awful height from which they must cast themselves down to the depths beneath, there to be broken on the rocks. I can hardly bear to watch it."

"Look closer," He said again. "Let your eye follow just one part of the water from the moment when it leaps over the edge until it reaches the bottom."

Much-Afraid did so, and then almost gasped with wonder. Once over the edge, the waters were like winged things, alive with joy, so utterly abandoned to the ecstasy of giving themselves that she could almost have supposed that she was looking at a host of angels floating down on rainbow wings, singing with rapture as they went.

She gazed and gazed, then said, "It looks as though they think it is the loveliest movement in all the world, as though to cast oneself down is to abandon oneself to ecstasy and joy indescribable."

"Yes," answered the Shepherd in a voice vibrant with joy and thanksgiving, "I am glad that you have noticed that, Much-Afraid. These are the Falls of Love, flowing from the High Places in the Kingdom above. You will meet with them again. Tell Me, does the joy of the waters seem to end when they break on the rock below?"

Again Much-Afraid looked where he pointed, and noticed that the lower the water fell, the lighter it seemed to grow, as though it really were lighting down on wings. On reaching the rocks below, all the waters flowed together in a glorious host, forming an exuberant, rushing torrent which swirled triumphantly around and over the rocks.

234

Casting Downward with Joy

READ: Hind's Feet... facing page & **Hebrews 11:24–12:2**

> "..and though you have not seen Him, you love Him, and though you do not see Him now, but believe in Him, you greatly rejoice with joy inexpressible and full of glory." —I Peter 1:8

> "For whatever is born of God overcomes the world; and this is the victory that has overcome the world—our faith." —I John 5:4

The contrast with which we read of the joy of the waterfall and contemplate our own "casting ourselves down" in service is perhaps the central challenge of this book, and all discipleship in Jesus Christ. Certainly, as long as the flesh lives and has a voice to contest with the Spirit of God working within us, we find it difficult to die, must less do so with joy.

Of course, the water 'knows' a secret by nature. Perhaps it is built into all forms of nature upheld by the word of God's power (Heb.1:3). Nothing is self-destructing which is upheld by the word of God, because it is by its nature indestructible! It all lives to serve again. The issue is not suicide, but service.

Droplets of water form from the stream. They break up into smaller droplets as they accelerate and are broken up in the windy downdraft. They seem to "float" down on the air, like a "host of angels floating down on rainbow wings", singing with rapture.

Then below, as the water meets the rocks, the water's joy does not end. Rocks are only obstacles to be overcome. The water flows around and over the rocks. It is the rocks that are defeated. "Oh, death, where is thy sting?" (I Cor.15:55) The rocks slowly wear away. It is the waters, not the rocks, which are indestructible. Water says there is resurrection.

QUESTIONS AND PRAYER: What more complex examples of "nature" giving itself up for service might you identify? _____

_____

Name some that actually involve loss of life on behalf of mankind? (i.e., Wood for heat? Food for sustenance? Soldiers or police for protection? Fathers for families?)_____

_____

What portion of each can be held back in self interest without effecting success?_____

_____

Laughing and shouting at the top of their voices, they hurried still lower and lower, down through the meadows to the next precipice and the next glorious crisis of their self-giving. From there they would again cast themselves down to the valleys far below. Far from suffering from the rocks, it seemed as though every obstacle in the bed of the torrent was looked upon as another object to be over-come and another lovely opportunity to find a way over or above it. Everywhere was the sound of water, laughing, exulting, shouting in jubilation.

"At first sight perhaps the leap does look terrible," said the Shepherd, "but as you can see, the water itself finds no terror in it, no moment of hesitation or shrinking, only joy unspeakable, and full of glory, because it is the movement natural to it. Self-giving is its life. It has only one desire, to go down and down and give itself with no reserve or holding back of any kind. You can see that as it obeys that glorious urge the obstacles which look so terrifying are perfectly harm-less, and indeed only add to the joy and glory of the movement." When He had said this, He led them back to the sunny fields, and gently told them that for the next few days they were to rest themselves there in preparation for the last part of their journey.

On hearing these words, "the last part of the journey," Much-Afraid felt al-most as though she would sink to the ground with happiness. Moreover, the Shep-herd Himself remained there with them the whole time. Not for a single hour was He apart from them, but walked and talked with them. He taught them many things about the Kingdom to which they were going, and it was as though grace flowed from His lips and sweet ointments and spices were diffused wherever He went. How thankfully Much-Afraid would have stayed there for the rest of her life; she would have cared no more about reaching the High Places, had it not been that she still walked on crooked feet, still had a twisted mouth, still had a fearing heart.

Natural Movement

READ: Hind's Feet... facing page & **John 13**

"For whoever wishes to save his life shall lose it, but whoever loses his life for My sake, he is the one who will save it." —Luke 9:24

"For He whom God has sent speaks the words of God; for He gives the Spirit without measure." —John 3:34

Author Hurnard completes her picture of the nature of water with sketches of exuberant child-like shouting and laughter as it hurries "still lower and lower" down the precipices and each "next glorious crisis", of self-giving. She observes that each opportunity brings no hesitation, but that water by its own desire pursues "the movement natural to it".

Does this help us identify with the Savior? Let us grasp in our spirit the movement natural to Him, Jesus Christ, the Son of God, who came from His throne to give Himself as a ransom in the flesh for our salvation. Recall His washing the feet of the disciples shortly before He was to die. Washing feet! Is this our basic desire? Yes! The desire is there isn't it? What is it that prevents us from responding to this call of the heart? "The spirit is willing, but the flesh is weak" (Matt. 26:41). God can bring these spirits of our flesh (that avail nothing) into submission under the Holy Spirit, which gives life (Jn.6:63). What is it that we truly want? Will we pray for what we really want?

Much-Afraid is quickened by the Shepherd's gently informing her to prepare for "the last part of the journey". Now she has a different sort of momentary temptation; she is so happy and thankful in her surroundings and in the Shepherd's continuously flowing grace that she would thankfully stay here the rest of her life. However, she still walks on crooked feet, still has a twisted mouth and still has a fearing heart. And, she still wants to be perfected.

QUESTIONS AND PRAYER: Do you know any scriptures where God tells us that we are to be perfect?_____

_____

How does this build your faith that this is indeed His purpose and, therefore, also our ultimate position in Christ?_____

_____

Please try to identify several such scriptures and describe your attitudes toward them._____

_____

_____

It was not, however, that the sun always shone, even there on that borderland of the High Places. There were days of mist when all the gleaming peaks were completely blotted out by a curtain of cloud, so that if one had never seen them it would have been impossible to be sure that they really existed and were round about, quite close at hand, towering high above the mist and clouds into the clear blue sky above.

Every now and again, however, there would be a rent in the veil of mist, and then, as though framed in an open window, would appear a dazzling whiteness. For a moment one of the vanished peaks would gleam through the opening as if to say, "Be of good courage, we are all here, even though you cannot see us." Then the mist would swirl together again and the window in heaven would close.

On one such occasion the Shepherd said to Much-Afraid, "When you continue your journey there may be much mist and cloud. Perhaps it may even seem as though everything you have seen here of the High Places was just a dream, or the work of your own imagination. But you have seen reality and the mist which seems to swallow it up is the illusion.

"Believe steadfastly in what you have seen. Even if the way up to the High Places appears to be obscured and you are led to doubt whether you are following the right path, remember the promise, "Thine ears shall hear a word behind thee saying, 'This is the way, walk ye in it, when ye turn to the right hand and when ye turn to the left.' Always go forward along the path of obedience as far as you know it until I intervene, even if it seems to be leading you where you fear I could never mean you to go.

"Remember, Much-Afraid, what you have seen before the mist blotted it out. Never doubt that the High Places are there, towering up above you, and be quite sure that whatever happens I mean to bring you up there exactly as I have promised." As He finished speaking another rent appeared in

238

Mist is the Illusion

READ: Hind's Feet... facing page & **Colossians** 1:1–23

"For now we see in a mirror dimly, but then face to face;
now I know in part, but then I shall know fully just as
I also have been fully known." —I Corinthians 13:12

"He Himself has said, "I will never desert you, nor
will I ever forsake you." —Hebrews 13:5

Many illustrations and exhortations in the Bible teach that we are to proceed in our walk of faith according to the way things ARE, not according to the way they appear to be. It is the "substance of things unseen, the assurance of things hoped for" (Heb.11:1) that is to quicken and activate us. There are, though, many "veils" that hide the reality of God from the world and those without faith. One of these is our own flesh. Just as there was a veil which shielded man (except for the High Priest, once a year) from seeing the Holy of Holies in the temple, our flesh is also a veil and in the flesh, no man can see God (Exod.33:20, I Tim.6:16).

But, on occasion, the veil is briefly torn open, as happened historically upon the sacrifice of Christ (Matt.27:51) and we see the abundant glory of God. This is reality; not the other way round. As the mountains and their snow-capped glory are always there, mist or not, so God and His glory are there always, even when we are unable to see clearly.

One thing is among the certainties; our LORD is, and is responsible for us. He is our Shepherd; we are the sheep of His pasture. He has declared no one can take us out of His hand. He has promised He will never leave us nor forsake us; He will be with us until the end of the age (Matt. 28:20). What could be plainer and more thorough? Having been "begun by the Spirit are we to be perfected in the flesh" (Gal. 3:3)? No!

The Shepherd reiterates, "Always go forward along the path of obedience as far as you know it until I intervene".

QUESTIONS AND PRAYER: In Paul's confidence that God "who began a good work in you will perfect it" (Phil 1:6), what is being perfected?_____

_____

Who is responsible for the work? What doubts about this do you have?_____

_____

_____

_____

_____

the curtain of mist, and one of the peaks of the High Places framed in blue sky shone down on them.

Before the curtain closed again Much-Afraid stooped down and picked a few of the gentians growing near her feet as a reminder of what she had seen, for, said she to herself, "These actually grew on the lower slopes of the High Places and are a reminder that though the peaks may again become invisible they are there all the time."

On the last day they stayed there the Shepherd did a very wonderful thing. He took Much-Afraid apart by herself and carried her right up to the summit of one of the High Places—in the Kingdom of Love itself. He took her to a high peak, dazzling white, uplifted like a great throne with numberless other peaks grouped round about.

Up there on the mountaintop He was transfigured before her, and she knew Him then to be what she had dimly sensed all along—the King of Love Himself, King of the whole Realm of Love. He was clothed in a white garment glistening in its purity, but over it He wore a robe of purple and blue and scarlet studded with gold and precious gems. On His head He wore the crown royal, but as Much-Afraid bowed herself and knelt at His feet to worship, the face that looked down upon her was that of the Shepherd whom she had loved and followed from the very low places up to the heights. His eyes were still full of gentleness and tenderness but also of strength and power and authority.

Putting out His hand, without a word He lifted her up and led her to a place where on the topmost pinnacle of all they could look right out on the whole realm around them. Standing there beside Him and so happy as to be scarcely conscious of herself at all, Much-Afraid looked out over the Kingdom of Love. Far, far below were the valleys and the plains and the great sea and the desert. She even thought she could recognize the Valley of Humiliation itself, where she had lived so long and had first learned to know the Shepherd, but that seemed so long ago it was like remembering another existence altogether.

Beyond the Veil

READ: Hind's Feet... facing page & **Hebrews 9:1–5**

"—having also believed, you were sealed in Him with the Holy Spirit
of promise, who is given as a pledge of our inheritance,
with a view to the redemption of God's own possession,
to the praise of His glory." —Ephesians 1:13–14

"And He was transformed before them; and His face shone like the
sun, and His garments became as white as light." —Matthew 17:2

Realization by Much-Afraid of the deceptive nature of the mountain mists to hide reality causes her to pick some flowers. She picks them while the peaks of the High Places are in view, as an "earnest"; i.e., "something given or done as an indication or assurance of what is to come"[1]. It will serve as a reminder and "seal" upon what she has seen.

Much-Afraid is then brought to her third mountaintop experience; this one being a true depiction of the transfiguration of Christ in Matthew 17. She is taken beyond the veil to see things as they truly are. As with the disciples Peter, James and John, she is given a view of the Promise, the Future and the Hope of eternity, all in the Shepherd, from a mountaintop viewpoint. She sees clearly what every human heart perceives at least dimly; that the Shepherd is the King of Love, Himself, the Christ, the Holy One of God, to whom all things belong through His redemption by His blood. Hence, the unmistakable identity of His strength and power and authority over all things in the creation.

Standing beside Him on the topmost pinnacle, she is "scarcely conscious of herself at all". Is this part of transfiguration? Is this happening to all? Are there experiences the Shepherd has given us in which we can attest that this is indeed true?

Perhaps we recall what followed Much-Afraid's previous mountaintop experiences, and Christ's. Author Hurnard may also be sensitive to "patterns of threes" which follow throughout the Bible.

QUESTIONS AND PRAYER: Could you perhaps write out some short notes on an incident in which God has taken you behind the veil? _____

_____

_____

_____

[1] Webster's New World Dictionary, Second College Edition —1970

All around her, in every direction, were the snowy peaks of the High Places. She could see that the bases of all these mountains were extremely precipitous and that higher up they were all clothed with forests, then the green slopes of the higher alps and then the snow. Wherever she looked, the slopes at that season of the year were covered with pure white flowers through those half-transparent petals the sun shone, turning them to burning whiteness.

In the heart of each flower was a crown of pure gold. These white-robed hosts scented the slopes of the High Places with a perfume sweeter than any she had ever breathed before. All had their faces and golden crowns turned down the mountains as if looking at the valleys, multitudes upon multitudes of them, which no man could number, like "a great crowd of witnesses," all stooping forward to watch what was going on in the world below. Wherever the King and His companion walked, these white-robed flowers bowed beneath their feet and rose again, buoyant and unsullied, but exuding a perfume richer and sweeter than before.

On the utmost pinnacle to which He led her was an altar of pure gold, flashing in the sun with such splendor that she could not look at it but had to turn her eyes away at once, though she did perceive that a fire burned on it and a cloud of smoke perfumed with incense rose from it.

Then the King told her to kneel and with a pair of golden tongs brought a piece of burning coal from off the altar. Touching her with it He said, "Lo! this hath touched thy lips; and thine iniquity is taken away, and thy sin purged" (Isa. 6:7).

It seemed to her that a burning flame of fire too beautiful and too terrible to bear went through her whole being, and Much-Afraid lost consciousness and remembered no more.

When she recovered she found that the Shepherd was carrying her in His arms and they were back on the lower slopes of the borderland. The royal robes

242

Transfiguration Views

READ: Hind's Feet... facing page & **Revelation 7:9–17**

"Therefore, since we have so great a cloud of witnesses surrounding us, let us also lay aside every encumbrance, and the sin which so easily entangles us, and let us run with endurance the race that is set before us." —Hebrews 12:1

The human eye has remarkable capabilities, usually taken for granted unless one becomes a photographer. A photographer must continuously change camera lenses to capture the content and meaning of a photo, changing from wide-angle to telephoto depending upon circumstances. The human eye does not have to do this, but can perceive both incredible breadth and minute detail at the same time.

The human eye, in turn, only depicts in a temporal sense the capacity of the human spirit to discern, to "see", things in minute detail or incredible scope as they pertain to the Kingdom of God.

Much-Afraid views her entire journey, as well as the expansive kingdom in which she stands. Her past seems so long ago it is like another existence. In every direction the mountains reveal their precipitous lower slopes guarding access to the high places, their forests, green alps and rock and snow leading to the pinnacles. Then she begins to study the flowers.

She captures the nature of the narcissus, a flower which, robed as the saints of God in pure white, spread in myriads over the slopes. She notes the crown of pure gold in the heart of each flower. Then she notices a remarkable thing, reflecting the insights of Hannah Hurnard in her visit to the Swiss Alps in 1949. All the narcissus, "without exception", face downward! The insight is clothed in meaning relevant to us. The hosts in the High Places are all looking downward to observe our progress in overcoming the entanglements of sin.

In a ritual of fire common to purging, Much-Afraid then experiences the seeming frightful touch of Isaiah's coal to her lips.

QUESTIONS AND PRAYER: Briefly sketch the purification by fire that worked in some of the following: Abraham, Moses, Joseph, Judah, David, Daniel, Esther, Boaz, Jeremiah or others you may recall._____

_____

_____

_____

_____

_____

and the crown were gone, but something of the expression on His face remained, the look of utmost authority and power. Above them towered the peaks, while everything below was shrouded in cloud and mist.

When He found that she was sufficiently recovered, the Shepherd took her by the hand, and they walked together down into the white mist and through a little wood where the trees were scarcely visible and there was no sound but drops of water splashing onto the ground. When in the middle of the wood a bird burst into song. They could not see it for the mist, but high and clear and indescribably sweet the bird sang and called the same series of little notes over and over again. They seemed to form a phrase constantly repeated, always with a higher chirrup at the end which sounded just like a little chuckling laugh. It seemed to Much-Afraid that this was the song the bird was singing:

> *He's gotten the victory, Hurrah!*
> *He's gotten the victory, Hurrah!*

The wood rang with the jubilant notes, and they both stood still among the dripping trees to listen.

"Much-Afraid," the Shepherd said, "you have had a glimpse of the Kingdom into which I am going to bring you. Tomorrow you and your companions start on the last part of your journey which will bring you thither."

Then with wonderful tenderness He spoke words which seemed too glorious to be true. "Thou hast a little strength and hast kept My word, and hast not denied My name ... Behold I will make thine enemies to come and worship before thy feet, and to know that I have loved thee. Behold, I come quickly: Hold fast that which thou hast, that no man take thy crown, and she that overcometh will I make a pillar in the temple of My God, and she shall go no more out: and I will write upon her the name of My God ... I will write upon her My new name" (Rev. 3:8–12).

Into the Mists Again

READ: Hind's Feet... facing page & **Matthew 17:8–27**

"This is My beloved Son, with whom I am well-pleased; hear Him!" —Matthew 17:5

"He who has an ear, let him hear what the Spirit says to the
churches." —Revelation 2:7, 11, 17, 29, 3:6, 13, 22

Upon His descent from the mountain of transfiguration, Jesus set His face toward the cross and drew His disciples into His most difficult teachings. The immediate lessons Matthew records following the transfiguration include discerning prophetic identities, difficult healing, pronouncement of His impending death and the principle that His own avoiding of offense prevailed over His own personal "rights". Things became difficult indeed for both Christ and His disciples as He journeyed toward His death and subsequent return to His High Places.

Back into the mist and listening to the sounds, Much-Afraid hears the pronouncement of nature regarding Christ's victory over death. How much more attentive our ears could be to the messages of nature extolling its Creator and Redeemer—ours, too (Rom.8:19–21)!

Men should be most attentive to the bride's spirit as she (Hannah Hurnard through Much-Afraid) personalizes the promise of Christ to the church of Philadelphia. It is spoken in "wonderful tenderness". Female pronouns are used in the promises to those who overcome. The church of Philadelphia is the only of seven to which Christ did not ascribe sin.

Men should be attentive to the fact that we are sin-bearers for our wives and are building a "free woman" in the same manner in which Christ builds His church. Correction needs to be without reproach. Freedom is power to do what is right, and grants freedom to others to make mistakes, even when they demonstrate misuse of freedom for wrong.

Girls and women are always looking for Christ in a man, a "knight in shining armor", who will value them and confirm their safety.

QUESTIONS AND PRAYER: How may this lesson be applied to keeping faith, building character, fulfilling responsibilities and building value for yourself and your family in Christ?_____

_____

_____

It was then that Much-Afraid took courage to ask Him something which she had never dared to ask before. With her hand held in His she said, "My Lord, may I ask one thing? Is the time at last soon coming when You will fulfill the promise that You gave me?"

He said very gently, yet with great joy, "Yes—the time is not long now. Dare to begin to be happy. If you will go forward in the way before you, you will soon receive the promise, and I will give you your heart's desire. It is not long now, Much-Afraid."

So they stood in the mist-filled wood, she trembling with hope and unable to say a word, worshiping and wondering if she had seen a vision, or if this thing had really happened. Upon His face was a look which she would not have understood even if she had seen it, but she was too dazed with happiness even to look at Him. High over the dripping trees the little bird still sang his jubilant song, "He's gotten the victory," and then in a burst of trills and chuckles, "Hurrah! Hurrah! Hurrah!"

A little later they were down in the meadows where Sorrow and her sister were waiting for their return. It was time to go forward on the journey, but after the Shepherd had blessed them and was turning to go His way again, Sorrow and Suffering suddenly knelt before Him and asked softly, "Lord, what place is this where we have been resting and refreshing ourselves during these past days?"

He answered very quietly, "This is the place to which I bring my beloved, that they may be anointed in readiness for their burial."

Much-Afraid did not hear these words, for she was walking a little ahead, repeating over and over again, "He said, 'Dare to begin to be happy, for the time is not long now, and I will give you your heart's desire.'"

Did This Really Happen?

READ: Hind's Feet... facing page & Judges 6:11–40

"I know a man in Christ who fourteen years ago—whether in the body I do not know, or out of the body I do not know, God knows—such a man was caught up to the third heaven." —II Corinthians 12:2

"Now while Peter was greatly perplexed in mind as to what the vision which he had seen might be, behold, the men who had been sent by Cornelius, having asked directions for Simon's house, appeared at the gate." —Acts 10:17

Many are the perplexities that attend discipleship in Christ. One is being unsure as to whether a vision or "voice" from God really took place or if it has only been "our own thoughts" which have deceived us. The Bible reveals this problem among many who have walked before us and shows what we will also experience: God will confirm Himself. He Himself will validate direction to us where true uncertainty and obedience are at stake.

Back in the mist filled world, Much-Afraid wonders this question in a related form. Perhaps it was a vision and not an "in body" experience. Things in the Shepherd's face beyond her comprehension are kept from her now. Nature continues to sing of His victory over death. She doesn't realize the victory pertains to her own death.

We are told now what we might be otherwise too slow to comprehend. Using the method of informing her companions, we're told what Much-Afraid does not know; she has been anointed for burial. She is beloved and yet has been anointed for burial. Like a young woman joyfully pregnant, she walks along in wonder, reciting things of her future, prior to onset of birth pangs.

The transfiguration beholds what is on the other side of the cross. There is no way to the other side except through the cross. "For if we have become united with Him in the likeness of His death, certainly we shall be also in the likeness of His resurrection" (Rom.6:5).

QUESTIONS AND PRAYER: Do you have some ideas on what might be the nature of Much-Afraid's coming death? _____

_____

Can you relate this to things in your early walk with Christ?_____

_____

CHAPTER 15

The Floods

The path they followed did not go straight up to the heights but sloped gently up the mountainside. The mist still shrouded everything, and indeed grew a little thicker. All three walked in silence, occupied with different thoughts. Much-Afraid was thinking of the promise the Shepherd had so recently given her, "Behold, I come quickly ... and will give thee thy heart's desire." Sorrow and Suffering perhaps were thinking of the answer they had received to the question asked of Him at parting. Whether or not this was so there was no indication, for they walked in complete silence, though the help they gave their lame companion was, had she noticed it, even more gentle and untiring than before.

Toward evening they came to another log cabin standing at the side of the path with the Shepherd's secret mark inscribed upon the door, so they knew that they were to rest there for the night.

Once inside they noticed that someone must have been there quite recently, for a fire was burning brightly on the hearth and a kettle of water was singing on the hob. The table, too, was laid for three, and a supply of bread and fruit upon it. Evidently their arrival had been expected and these kindly preparations made, but of the one who had thus gone in the way before them there was no sign. They washed themselves and then sat down at the table, gave thanks, and ate of the prepared meal. Then, being weary, they lay down to rest and immediately fell asleep.

How long she had slept Much-Afraid could not tell, but she woke suddenly while it was still quite dark. Her companions slumbered peacefully beside her,

Approaching the Storm

READ: Hind's Feet... facing page & **I Samuel 1**

"Therefore every one who hears these words of Mine, and acts upon them, may
be compared to a wise man, who built his house upon the rock. And the rain
descended, and the floods came, and the winds blew, and burst against that house;
and yet it did not fall, for it had been founded upon the rock."
—Matthew 7:24–25

"Delight yourself in the LORD; and He will give you the
desires of your heart." —Psalm 37:4"

Quietly, inexorably, the path leads through the mist up to the heights. Much-Afraid
follows it according to the word of the Shepherd. He has promised to come quickly.... to
give her her heart's desire. Has she resolved what her greatest desire is? Do you recall what
she resolved? In I Samuel 1, what was Hannah's greatest desire? How did Hannah resolve
it?

Hannah resolved her need by giving it away to the LORD. In her case, she gave her
son *away* before she had him. But it was resolved. The matter had been cast before God
ever evidenced His answer. Even the foul reputation of Eli the priest and his sons did not
later turn her aside from the commitment of her son to serve God through them as God's
servants in the temple. As a result of her faith, "the boy Samuel grew before the LORD" (I
Sam. 2:21).

Near evening Much-Afraid and her companions find their needs met by a cabin and
food already prepared. God has always evidenced Himself as One who "goes ahead" and
prepares a way for His servants. Illustrated in both the Old and New Testament, as a pillar
of smoke and fire (Gen. 15:17, Exod.13:21, 14:19), and as a Shepherd (Jn.10:3–4), God
also prepared the way for His Son, "The Righteous One, My Servant" (Isaiah 53:11) by
John the Baptist, scores of prophets, and generations of believers. Though His signs are
hidden from many who do not believe, all who serve the living God see evidence of a way
prepared for them beforehand (Eph.2:10).

**QUESTIONS AND PRAYER: Jesus calls Himself "The Way" in John 14:6. Is it
possible to find this outside of Jesus, Himself? How do we tend to get this confused?**_____

_____

_____

_____

but she knew that someone had called her. She waited in silence, then a Voice said: "Much-Afraid."

"Behold me, here I am, my Lord," she answered.

"Much-Afraid," said the Voice, "take now the promise you received when I called you to follow Me to the High Places, and take the natural longing for human love which you found already growing in your heart when I planted My own love there and go up into the mountains to the place that I shall show you. Offer them there as a Burnt Offering unto Me."

There was a long silence before Much-Afraid's trembling voice spoke through the darkness.

"My Lord—am I understanding you right?"

"Yes," answered the Voice. "Come now to the entrance of the hut and I will show you where you are to go."

Without waking the two beside her, she rose silently, opened the door of the hut, and stepped outside. Everything was still shrouded in mist, and the mountains were completely invisible, swallowed up in darkness and cloud. As she looked, the mist parted in one place and a little window appeared through which the moon and one star shone brightly. Just below them was a white peak, glimmering palely. At its foot was the rocky ledge over which the great waterfall leaped and rushed down to the slopes below. Only the lip of rock over which it poured itself was visible, all below being shrouded in the mist.

Then came the Voice, "That is the appointed place."

Much-Afraid looked, and replied, "Yes, Lord. Behold me—I am thy handmaiden, I will do according to Thy word."

She did not lie down again, but stood at the door of the hut waiting for daybreak. It seemed to her that the voice of the fall now filled the whole night and

The Narrow Gate

READ: Hind's Feet... facing page & **Genesis 22:1–19**

"But God said, 'No, but Sarah your wife shall bear you a son, and you shall call his name Isaac; and I will establish My covenant with him for an everlasting covenant for his descendants after him.'" —Genesis 17:19

"It is easier for a camel to go through the eye of a needle than for a rich man to enter the kingdom of God." —Mark 10:25

Probably the greatest events in history prior to the fulfillment of the New Covenant in Jesus Christ are those which foreshadowed it. The greatest of these, enabling us to see both the heart of the Father and of the obedient Son, is the call to Abraham to give up all that God had promised him through his son by Sarah, Isaac. The anguish of a father offering up such a desire seems mostly incomprehensible to me; much greater than that of his son being put to death (John 3:16). Soldiers and others voluntarily offer their lives in service and sacrifice them as a result; but none by the hands of their fathers.

Imagine the wrath of a father for those who would despise such an offering as his son!

In conformation with God's example, Much-Afraid is asked to offer up her "Isaac", the promise she received when she was called to follow the Shepherd, along with "the natural longing for human love" she already had found in her heart when His love was planted there. There follows a long silence. . . . . "My Lord—am I understanding you right?"

Her only issue is *understanding*. She obeys and gets up for more directions. By moonlight she sees the rock where the great waterfall "pours itself down".

Abraham is recorded rising "early in the morning", a sign of earnestness throughout scripture, to sacrifice his son. Much-Afraid declares the words of Mary (Luke 1:38, after being told of her pregnancy by the Holy Spirit), then stands at the door of the hut until daybreak.

QUESTIONS AND PRAYER: Can you describe your own spirit as you share with Much-Afraid her coming sacrifice?_____

_____

Do you see other historic events since Christ which portray the New Covenant sacrifice? _____

was thundering through her trembling heart, reverberating and shouting through every part and repeating again and again, "Take now the promise that I gave you, and the natural human love in your heart, and offer them for a burnt offering."

With the first glimmer of dawn she bent over her sleeping companions and said, "We must start at once. I have received commandment to go up to the place where the great fall pours itself over the precipice."

They rose immediately, and after hurriedly eating a meal to strengthen themselves, they started on their way. The path led straight up the mountainside toward the thunderous voice of the fall, though everything was still shrouded in mist and cloud and the fall itself remained invisible.

As the hours passed they continued to climb, though the path was now steeper than ever before. In the distance thunder began to roll and flashes of lightning rent the veil of mist. Suddenly, higher up on the path, they heard the sound of running feet, slipping and scraping on the rocks and stones. They stopped and pressed themselves closely to one side of the narrow path to allow the runners to pass, then out of the ghostly mist appeared first Fear, then Bitterness, followed by Resentment, Pride, and Self-Pity.

They were running as though for their lives, and as they reached the three women they shouted, "Back! Turn back at once! The avalanches are falling ahead, and the whole mountainside is shaking as though it will fall too. Run for your lives!"

Without waiting for an answer, they clattered roughly past and fled down the mountainside.

"What are we to do?" asked Sorrow and Suffering, apparently at a loss for the very first time. "Shall we turn back to the hut and wait until the avalanches and the storm are over?"

Separation

READ: Hind's Feet... facing page & **Revelation 6:9–17**

"Take now your son, your only son, whom you love, Isaac, and go to the
land of Moriah; and offer him there as a burnt offering on one of the
mountains of which I will tell you." —Genesis 22:2

"......do not eat or drink for three days, night or day. I and my maidens
will fast in the same way. And thus I will go in to the king, which is
not according to the law; and if I perish, I perish." —Esther 4:16

At the first glimmer of dawn Much-Afraid, quite contrary to her old nature, wakes
her companions and leads the way up the steep slope toward the roaring waterfall. She
seems resolute to obey.

Signs of heavenly wrath and judgment gather as they go higher. As portrayed at Cal-
vary (Matt. 27:45, 51) and in Revelation (Rev. 6:12–14), the heavens and earth begin to
quake, penetrating the veil of mist. Suddenly the relatives of Much-Afraid's, the companions and tormentors of her life, flee down the pathway! Who would have known they had
reached this height of ascent with her?! As the kings of the earth are judged, they are now
being judged in her life. In her conformance with Christ, there is no longer room for the
enemy to stand.

Now, Sorrow and Suffering, apparently at a loss for the very first time, look to
Much-Afraid for leadership. It is a submittal, a test of servant-hood and a test of leadership.
Shall we turn back to the hut? Have the issues been resolved in Much-Afraid?

Hear the low, steady voice. "No," she says. The matter is resolved. She has received
direction. She speaks with authority. As with Esther, "If I perish, I perish".

**QUESTIONS AND PRAYER: Do you believe women are superior at resolving
to perish, if necessary, in carrying out their obedience to Christ? Should that be
the normal function of wives for their husbands, or only for their children?**_____
Has God ordained men to take first position in dying for their families?

_____

**Why do you think most men are inferior in their ability to do this? Can you cite
scripture in discussing your views?**_____

_____

_____

"No," said Much-Afraid in a low, steady voice, speaking for the first time since she had called them to rise and follow her. "No, we must not turn back. I have received a commandment to go up to the place where the great fall pours over the rock."

Then the Voice spoke close at hand. "There is a place prepared for you here beside the path. Wait there until the storm is over."

In the rocky wall beside them was a little cave so low that it could be entered only if they stooped right down, and with just enough room for them to crouch inside. Side by side, they sat huddled together, then all of a sudden the storm burst over them in frightful fury. The mountains reverberated with thunder and with the sound of falling rocks and great avalanches. The lightning flashed incessantly and ran along the ground in sizzling flames.

Then the rains descended and the floods came, and the winds blew and beat upon the mountains until everything around them seemed to be shivering and quaking and falling. Flood waters rushed down the steep cliffs and a torrent poured over the rocks which projected over the cave so that the whole entrance was closed with a waterfall, but not a single drop fell inside the cave where the three sat together on the ground.

After they had been there for some time and the storm, far from abating, seemed to be increasing in strength, Much-Afraid silently put her hand in her bosom and drew out the leather bag which she always carried. Emptying the little heap of stones and pebbles into her lap, she looked at them. They were the memorial stones from all the altars which she had built along the way, from the time that she stood beside the Shepherd at the pool and allowed Him to plant the thorn in her heart and all along the journey until that moment of crouching in a narrow cave upon which the whole mountain seemed to be ready to topple. Nothing was left to her but a command to offer up the promise on which she had staked her all, on the strength of which she had started on the journey.

Alone, with Companions

READ: Hind's Feet... facing page & **Esther 4**

"Let the words of my mouth and the meditation of my heart be acceptable
in Thy sight, O LORD, my rock and my redeemer." —Psalm 19:14

"And it will come about, while My glory is passing by, that I will
put you in the cleft of the rock and cover you with My hand until
I have passed by." —Exodus 33:22

Sorrow and Suffering are subordinated to the will of Much-Afraid as she has subordinated to the will of the Shepherd. Love has done a miracle in leading her into such surroundings under such fearsome conditions. Upon her taking mastery of the situation, a Voice immediately speaks to her "close at hand". She is shown a protective cleft. "Stooping down" they are able to enter and find safety.

The nature of small caves is much as the "eye of the needle" placed in the protective walls of ancient cities. The only way a person or baggage animal could get through the hole was to divest of all baggage. Usually, it required the animal or person to go through on their knees, a humble and helpless position. Similarly, a cleft in the rock requires one to become conformed with the rock!

While the world outside rages in fury and the cleft is closed off with a waterfall, the companions find complete protection and Much-Afraid contemplates things. Our sentences give us away! God asks us to think about Him, and we want to think about "things". She takes out her bag of stones and considers them. She considers "the promise on which she had staked her all". Even the promise, as high sounding and wonderful as it seemed, was over a "thing" which Much-Afraid earnestly desired for herself.

Can we imagine that this promise may be discarded for a greater desire for God Himself, the Shepherd, our LORD? What about a desire for a relationship with Him in which trust and security produce complete compliance with His desire?

QUESTIONS AND PRAYER: Describe some situations where you refuse to put away "things" in favor of people._____

_____

Does this relate in some way to sorrow and suffering?_____
Do you have testimony you could share about this or, perhaps, where the reverse is true? _____

_____

She looked at the little pile in her lap and asked herself dully, "Shall I throw them away? Were they not all worthless promises which He gave me on the way here?" Then with icy fingers she picked up the first stone and repeated the first words that He had spoken to her beside the pool. "I will make thy feet like hinds' feet and set thee upon thine High Places" (Hab. 3:19). She held the stone in her hand for a long time, then said slowly, "I have not received hinds' feet, but I am on higher places than ever I imagined possible, and if I die up here, what does it matter? I will not throw it away."

She put the stone back in the bag, picked up the next and repeated, "What I do thou knowest not now; but thou shalt know hereafter" (John 13:7); and she gave a little sob and said, "Half at least of that is true, and who knows whether the other half is true or not—but I will not throw it away."

Picking up the third stone, she quoted, "This is not unto death, but for the glory of God" (John 11:4). "Not unto death," she repeated, "even though He says, 'Offer the promise as a Burnt Offering'?" But she dropped the stone back into the bag and took the fourth. "Bread corn is bruised ... but no one crushes it forever" (Isa. 28:28). "I cannot part with that," she said, replaced it in the bag, and took the fifth. "Cannot I do with you, as the Potter? saith the Lord" (Jer. 18:6). "Yes," said she, and put it back into the bag.

Taking the sixth, she repeated, "O thou afflicted, tossed with tempest, and not comforted, behold, I will lay thy stones with fair colors..." (Isa. 54:11), then could go no farther but wept bitterly. "How could I part with that?" she asked herself, and she put it in the bag with the others, and took the seventh. "My sheep hear My voice, and they follow Me" (John 10:27). "Shall I not throw this one away?" she asked herself. "Have I really heard His voice, or have I been deceiving myself all the time?"

Then as she thought of His face when He gave her that promise she replaced it in the bag, saying, "I will keep it. How can I let it go?" and took the eighth.

Soul Searching in Storms

READ: Hind's Feet... facing page & Ecclesiastes 3:1–11

"Thy word is a lamp to my feet, and a light to my path." —Psalm 119–105

"I remember the days of old; I meditate upon all Thy doings; I muse on the work of Thy hands. I stretch out my hands to Thee." —Psalm 143:5

Two storms are in progress. One outside and one in Much-Afraid. She uses the inactivity imposed by the outside weather to review her only possessions, in the silent presence of her companions. With icy fingers, denoting death, she picks up her stones one by one. In words similar to those of Esther (Esth.4:16), she concludes that perishing does not matter all that much. Despite not having received hinds' feet, she has reached higher places that she had ever imagined possible.

She recognizes some promises not yet received (Heb.11:39–40). She is still in hope and will not throw that away (Rom.8:24). She works through the word of God given her for each major event in her journey, meditating on their meaning and resolving one thing or another on each. She confronts the meaning of "Not unto death", in "offering the promise as a Burnt Offering", just as Abraham offered his promise, his son, Isaac as forerunner of The Promise, Jesus Christ. We all have promises unfulfilled, earnestly sought for. But God in Christ is The Promise Whom we must seek above all. Apart from sacrifice of all other things, we have idols that prevent Him possessing us fully.

Again, she is brought back to some of the Shepherd's words to her. Did she just imagine them? How can she know? She considers the memory of His face when he spoke the promise of John 10:27 to her and decides to keep the stone representing it. This is a promise not based upon her ears, mind or character, but upon the One who gave her the promise.

QUESTIONS AND PRAYER: When Much-Afraid recalls the memory of the Shepherd's face when He gave her the promise of being able to hear His voice, how did this help her resolve the question of keeping the stone?_____

_____

_____

Have you an opinion as to whether our faces reflect spirit or character?

_____

"Now shalt thou see what I will do" (Ex. 6:1). Remembering the precipice which had seemed so terribly impossible and how He had brought her to the top, she put the stone with the others and took the ninth. "God is not a man, that He should lie ... hath He said, and shall He not do it? or hath He spoken, and shall He not make it good?" (Num. 23:19).

For a very long time she sat trembling with that stone in her hand, but in the end she said, "I have already given the only answer possible when I told Him, 'If Thou canst, Thou mayest deceive me."

Then she dropped the icy-cold little pebble into the bag and took the tenth. "Thine ears shall hear a word behind thee, saying, 'This is the way, walk ye in it, when ye turn to the right hand, and when ye turn to the left.'" (Isa. 30:21). At that she shuddered, but after a while added, "Thou hast a little strength, and hast not denied My name ... Hold that fast which thou hast, that no man take thy crown" (Rev. 3:8:11).

Returning the tenth stone to the bag, after a long pause she picked up an ugly little stone lying on the floor of the cave and dropped it in beside the other ten saying, "Though He slay me, yet will I trust in Him" (Job 13:15). Tying up the bag again, she said, "Though everything in the world should tell me that they are worthless—yet I cannot part with them," and put the bag once again in her bosom.

Sorrow and her sister had been sitting silently beside her watching intently as she went over the little heap of stones in her lap. Both gave a strange laugh, as though of relief and thankfulness, and said together, "The rain descended, and the floods came, and the winds blew, and beat upon the house; and it fell not: for it was founded upon a rock" (Matt. 7:25).

By this time, the rain had ceased, the cataract was no longer pouring over the rocks, and only a light mist remained. The rolling of the thunder and the roar of

Reaffirmation in Death

READ: Hind's Feet... facing page & **Matthew 26:31–46**

"And as for me, I know that my Redeemer lives, and at the last He
will take His stand on the earth. Even after my skin is flayed, yet
without my flesh I shall see God." —Job 19:25–26

"Let your heart hold fast my words; keep my
commandments and live." —Proverbs 4:4

Reviewing the last of the stones, Much-Afraid approaches her covenant with death. In manner similar to millions of saints, only few of whom have been briefly resurrected to this life to the glory of God, she reaffirms her faith in Him; it is okay for God to deceive her through His words, "if He can".

Then she picks up an "ugly little stone" on the floor of the cave, adds it to the previous ten and declares the words of Job saying, "Though He slay me, yet will I trust in Him" (Job 13:15). Does it not seem amazing that even in this perhaps oldest book of the Bible, the work of God remains the same and has been so clearly given to those called as His sheep. In spite of all our eyes tell us, we can grasp Him, His love and character, and trust Him though He slay us. Do we really believe this? "When the Son of Man comes, will He find faith on the earth" (Lu.18:8)? He has asked this for each man to answer. What is our answer? It is a personal, historical question.

So, she agrees to be conformed to His death. That is the covenant. She has established herself upon the rock. Far from being shaken, she is more settled than ever. Her companions breath relief and speak the word of God. The storms have raged as upon the mountain, but her house has fallen not, "for it was founded upon a rock".

By contrast with the mountain outside, from which avalanches have been pouring, Much-Afraid has come through the storm much the better. She has been protected in the shelter of the Most High, abiding in the shadow of the Almighty (Ps. 91:1) and resolved that trusting Him is her course, though the world testify that the stones are worthless.

QUESTIONS AND PRAYER: What does Much-Afraid's covenant have to do with you?_____

_____

Do you feel drawn to do the same as she? What concerns can you see that make you reluctant?_____

_____

the avalanches were fading away into the distance, and as they looked out of the cave, up from the depths beneath came through the wreaths of mist the clear jubilant notes of a bird. It might have been brother to that which sang in the dripping woods at the foot of the High Places:

> *He's gotten the victory, Hurray!*
> *He's gotten the victory, Hurray!*

As the pure clear notes came floating up to them the icy coldness in the heart of Much-Afraid broke, then melted away. She pressed her hands convulsively against the little bag of stones as though it contained priceless treasure which she had thought lost, and said to her companions, "The storm is over. Now we can go on our way."

From that place on, it was very steep going, for the path now went straight up the mountainside, so straight and steep that often Much-Afraid could hardly do more than crawl forward on hands and knees. All along she had hoped that the higher she went and the nearer she got to the High Places, the stronger she would become and the less she would stumble, but it was quite otherwise.

The higher they went, the more conscious she was that her strength was leaving her, and the weaker she grew, the more she stumbled. She could not help dimly realizing that this was not the case with her companions. The higher they went, the more vigorous and strong they seemed to become, and this was good, because often they had almost to carry Much-Afraid, for she seemed utterly spent and exhausted. Because of this they made very slow progress indeed.

On the second day they came to a place where a little hollow in the mountainside formed a tiny plateau. Here a spring bubbled out of the cliff and trickled across the hollow and down the side of the mountain in a little waterfall. As they paused to rest, the Voice said to Much-Afraid, "Drink of the brook at the side of the way and be strengthened."

Higher Levels of Exhaustion

READ: Hind's Feet... facing page & **Daniel 10:1–19**

"The LORD is my strength and my shield; my heart trusts in Him,
and I am helped; therefore my heart exults, and with my song
I shall thank Him." —Psalm 28:7

"...whoever serves, let him do so as by the strength
which God supplies;....." —I Peter 4:11

Is it not likely that all those who have celebrated God as their strength have prior to this been brought to exhaustion in their own strength? Without doubt, human endeavor will continue until the point where it is exhausted; where it is resolved without question that God must deliver or there is to be no delivery at all.

Much-Afraid has some respite from the icy death in her heart, presses the stones in her bosom, "the seat of inmost thoughts"[1], as "priceless treasures" and continues her way. Though they should prove worthless, they motivate her to higher levels of ascent. They are all she has . . . . the Shepherd, the One who gave her the promises, is who draws her.

Her consciousness now shifts to developing symptoms of exhaustion. Contrary to her hopes and expectations she is getting weaker, not stronger. Would we agree that this is also contrary to what we expect? This reflects misunderstanding by human wisdom regarding God's requirements of weakness for His strength to be perfected (II Cor.12:5–10). One symptom of her exhaustion is "very slow progress". Could this perhaps also be a mark of being near the end of her journey? Sorrow and Suffering seem to become stronger and often almost to be carrying Much-Afraid.

Then, a pleasant oasis appears, offering refreshment. The Voice directs Much-Afraid to "be strengthened" by drinking of the wayside brook. Might we discern what could be offered here? Is this part of a picture of dying?

QUESTIONS AND PRAYER: Does "very slow progress" mark any of your work, fatherhood, counseling or relationships?_____

_____

Is it accompanied by evidence of exhaustion in you or others? Are there other symptoms?_____

[1] Webster's New World Dictionary, Second College Edition, 1970

Stooping down at the spring where it bubbled up from between the rocks, she filled her mouth with the water, but as soon as she swallowed it she found it so burning and bitter that her stomach rejected it altogether and she was unable to retain it. She knelt by the spring, gasping for a moment, and then said very quietly and softly through the silence, "My Lord, it is not that I will not, but that I cannot drink of this cup."

"There is a tree growing beside this spring of Marah," answered the Voice. "Break off a piece of branch, and when you have cast it into the waters they will be sweetened."

Much-Afraid looked on the other side of the spring and saw a little stunted thorn tree with but one branch growing on either side of the splintered trunk, like the arms of a cross. They were covered all over with long, sharp spines.

Suffering stepped forward, broke off a piece of the thorn tree, and brought it to Much-Afraid, who took it from her hand and cast it into the water. On doing this she stooped her head again to drink. This time she found that the stinging, burning bitterness was gone, and though the water was not sweet, she could drink it easily. She drank thirstily and found that it must have contained curative properties, for almost at once she was wonderfully refreshed and strengthened. Then she picked up her twelfth and last stone there beside the water of Marah and put it into her bag.

After they had rested a little while she was able to resume the journey, and for a time was so much stronger that although the way was even steeper than before, she was not nearly so faint and exhausted. This greatly comforted her, for by that time she had only one desire in her heart, to reach the place appointed and fulfill the command which had been given her before her strength ebbed away altogether. On the third day, "they lifted up their eyes and saw the place afar off," the great rock cliff and the waterfall, and continuing up the rocky path, at midday they came through the shrouding mist to the place which had been appointed.

Nearing Sacrifice

READ: Hind's Feet... facing page & **Exodus 15:22–27**

"Therefore strengthen the hands that are weak and the
knees that are feeble." —Hebrews 12:12

"And after you have suffered for a little, the God of all grace,
who called you to His eternal glory in Christ, will Himself perfect,
confirm, strengthen and establish you." —I Peter 5:10

The beauty of Hannah Hurnard's graphic picture on this page is stunning. It is taken from scripture, and additionally placed in a setting immediately prior to sacrificial death. The water tasted is burning and bitter as the spring of Marah, where God led Israel into the desert. By throwing in a branch of tree, waters that could not be drunk became drinkable. What is the meaning of this? What is the bitterness that cannot be drunk without the branch? What is the branch? How does it strengthen?

Who is "The Branch" (Zech.3:8, 6:12)? Who first drank the cup of bitterness (Matt. 26:39)? How does adding the Branch sweeten the waters of bitterness? Prior to death? Who actually tasted the sponge filled with vinegar just prior to giving up the ghost (Mark 15:36–37)? Far be it that the Holy Spirit be unable to explain these things to the Bride of Christ.

The Shepherd is present in the piece of thorn tree thrown into the waters. He not only removes the bitterness, but strengthens the weak and the lame. It is almost a figure of speech now to say that the Shepherd is not visibly present! Refreshed and strengthened, Much-Afraid picks up her "last stone". Why are we told this? Do we need to know? Does Much-Afraid already know?

Pursuing the one desire in her heart, and comforted in her capacity to do so, she lifts her eyes, the eyes of Abraham about to slay his own son, to see the designated "place afar off" (Gen. 22:4). She is going to the very place where the waterfall hurls itself off the great rock cliff.

QUESTIONS AND PRAYER: How do you feel about Hannah Hurnard's power as an inspired story teller?_____

_____

About God's story-telling of salvation in the Bible? _____

_____

Is there any part of this story you cannot believe or enjoy?_____

_____

CHAPTER 16

Grave on the Mountains

The path led forward to the edge of a yawning chasm, then stopped dead. The grave-like gorge yawned before them in each direction as far as they could see, completely cutting off all further progress. It was so filled with cloud and mist that they could not see how deep it was, nor could they see across to the other side, but spread before them like a great gaping grave, waiting to swallow them up. For a moment Much-Afraid wondered whether this could be the place, after all, but as they could plainly hear the sound of mighty, swirling waters, and she realized that they must be standing somewhere near the lip of the great fall and that this was indeed the place appointed.

Looking at her companions, she asked quietly, "What must we do now? Can we jump across to the other side?"

"No," they said, "it would be impossible."

"What, then, are we to do?" she asked.

"We must leap down into the canyon," was the answer.

"Of course," said Much-Afraid at once. "I did not realize at first, but that is the thing to do."

Then for the last time on that journey (though she did not know it at the time) she held out her hand to her two companions that they might help her. By this time she was so weak and exhausted that instead of taking her hands, they came close up to her and put their hands beneath her arms so that she leaned with her full weight against them. Thus with Sorrow and Suffering supporting her, Much-Afraid cast herself down into the yawning grave.

264

Leap in the Mist

READ: Hind's Feet... facing page & **I John 4:1–18**

"And your ears will hear a word behind you, 'This is the way, walk in it,' whenever you turn to the right or to the left. And you will defile your graven images overlaid with silver, and your molten images plated with gold. You will scatter them as an impure thing; and say to them, 'Be gone!'" —Isaiah 30:21–22

"But knowledge is easy to him who has understanding." —Proverbs 14:6

Much-Afraid has reached a point where everything becomes easy. Her flesh is dead. The only thing important is to serve the LORD; to find His will and obey Him. This she understands. Nothing else counts for anything. She has peace to have and hold, to dwell in this knowledge. Although she is not yet passed through the final fire, everything else has dropped away. Idols can't be carried by the dead. A dead person can't fear or be tempted.

How simple is the process. She comes to the grave; a yawning chasm. She cannot see the "other side". There is a moment of perplexity, which God has told us we will have (but not despair —II Cor.4:8). A brief exchange with her companions and the answer becomes obvious; they must leap down into the canyon. She must exercise "casting herself down" in conformance with the great waterfall and its water, free to cast itself downward. She submits and casts herself into the yawning grave.

Perhaps it should be obvious we are not speaking of suicide. We are speaking of submission and service in love. It is the love of God which has grown in Much-Afraid's heart to bring her to this. No outside onlooker can see the whole truth. Only the Shepherd. He knows and she knows. She loves Him. She knows she is not misunderstanding His will for her. You and I cannot exactly understand until we have experienced it ourselves with the Savior and follow Him. We can only be onlookers until we follow.

QUESTIONS AND PRAYER: What motivations of the flesh normally cause a man to serve his family (or refuse to serve his family)?_____

_____

By what motivations of the Spirit is God calling us to serve instead? What scriptures have you to confirm this?_____

_____

265

The place into which they had thrown themselves was deep, and had she been alone she would have been badly hurt by the fall. However, her companions were so strong that the jump did not seem to harm them at all, and they bore her so easily between them and broke the fall so gently that she was no more than bruised and shaken. Then, because the canyon was so filled with mist and cloud that nothing was visible, they began to feel their way slowly forward and saw, looming up before them, a flat, oblong rock. On reaching it, they found it to be some kind of stone altar with the indistinct figure of someone standing behind it.

"This is the place," said Much-Afraid quietly. "This is where I am to make my offering." She went up to the altar and knelt down. "My Lord," she said softly through the mist. "Will You come to me now and help me to make my burnt offering as You have commanded me?"

But for the first time on all that journey there seemed to be no answer—no answer at all—and the Shepherd did not come.

She knelt there quite alone in the cold, clammy mist, beside the desolate altar in this valley of shadow, and into her mind came the words which Bitterness had flung at her long before when she walked the shores of loneliness: "Sooner or later, when He gets you up on the wild places of the mountains He will put you on some sort of a cross and abandon you to it."

It seemed that in a way Bitterness had been right, thought Much-Afraid to herself, only he had been too ignorant to know and she too foolish at that time to understand that in all the world only one thing really mattered, to do the will of the One she followed and loved, no matter what it involved or cost. Strangely enough, as she knelt there by the altar, seemingly abandoned at that last tremendous crisis, there was no sign or sound of the presence of her enemies.

In the Grave

READ: Hind's Feet... facing page & **Psalm 22**

"For I will go through the land of Egypt on that night, and will strike down all the first-born in the land of Egypt, both man and beast; and against all the gods of Egypt I will execute judgments—I am the LORD" —Exodus 12:12

"And Jesus, crying out with a loud voice, said, 'Father into Thy hands I commit My spirit.' And having said this, He breathed His last." —Luke 23:46

Into a place the enemy cannot follow, Much-Afraid and her companions cast themselves. Born up as if by angels she is no more than bruised and shaken. Finding the altar, she calls upon the Shepherd to help her with her sacrifice—no answer.

We follow the One called Branch, who drank the bitter waters and who was forsaken by the Father for us. For us the cross and grave are not places of our judgment. They are places where enemy spirits cannot follow; but are left behind. In the silence of her Shepherd, Much-Afraid is not dismayed, but continues to think clearly, and find answers.

The lying words of Bitterness come with understanding of his ignorance; "too ignorant to know" and she "too foolish at that time to understood" the truth. No wonder the evil one can distort the truth to such a degree; he does not understand love. Now she has understanding and knowledge. Her foolishness has passed. She knows the only thing that matters.

It is evident that Hannah Hurnard, missionary to Palestine in 1932 who wrote this allegory in 1955, speaks from the voice of personal knowledge. She knew the love of the Savior and experienced the agony of individuals, Arabs and Jews, during the war-torn years that eventually gave re-birth to the nation of Israel in 1948. Like Much-Afraid, she also had a personal speech handicap and dealt for years with unreasoning fear that God would abandon her. She learned eventually to ignore the enemy's voice and deal with obedience above all else.

QUESTIONS AND PRAYER: What do you think Hannah Hurnard means when she refers to Much-Afraid, "seemingly abandoned at that last tremendous crisis"?_____

_____

_____

_____

The grave up on the mountains is at the very edge of the High Places and beyond the reach of Pride and Bitterness and Resentment and Self-Pity, yes, and of Fear too, as though she were in another world altogether, for they can never cast themselves down into that grave. She knelt there feeling neither despair nor hope. She knew now without a shadow of a doubt that there would be no Angel to call from heaven to say that the sacrifice need not be made, and this knowledge caused her neither dread nor shrinking.

She felt nothing but a great stillness in which only one desire remained, to do that which He had told her, simply because He had asked it of her. The cold, dull desolation which had filled her heart in the cave was gone completely; one flame burned there steadily, the flame of concentrated desire to do His will. Everything else had died down and fallen into ashes.

After she had waited for a little and still He had not come, she put out her hand and with one final effort of failing strength grasped the natural human love and desire growing in her heart and struggled to tear them out. At the first touch it was as though anguish pierced through her every nerve and fiber, and she knew with a pang almost of despair that the roots had wound and twined and thrust themselves into every part of her being. Though she put forth all her remaining strength in the most desperate effort to wrench them out, not a single rootlet stirred.

For the first time she felt something akin to fear and panic. She was not able to do this thing which He had asked of her. Having reached the altar at last, she was powerless to obey. Turning to those who had been her guides and helpers all the way up the mountains, she asked for their help, and for them to do what she could not for herself, to tear the plant out of her heart. For the first time Sorrow and Suffering shook their heads.

Yielded Clay

READ: Hind's Feet... facing page & **II Corinthians 4:1–14**

"But the LORD was pleased to crush Him, putting Him to grief; if He would render Himself as a guilt offering." —Isaiah 53:10

"And the blood will be a sign for you on the houses where you live; and when I see the blood I will pass over you, and no plague will befall you to destroy you when I strike the land of Egypt." —Exodus 12:13

More knowledge is revealed to Much-Afraid that causes "her neither dread nor shrinking". There is to be no substitute as there was in Abraham's case; no ram in the thicket to take her place (Gen. 22). She carries this knowledge full in her mind. But it has no influence on her responses. She has become the word of the LORD GOD in her, Lord over human flesh, in which complete softness and purity of clay in the hands of the potter is manifested. There is no resistance. She is fully conformed. She is fully given over to death.

She learns a final lesson. Even the final sacrifice cannot be accomplished by her own hand. This is not suicide. As ordained by God with Adam and Eve in the garden of Eden, no amount of self-help will accomplish anything with God. Our own "fig leaves" are unacceptable (Gen. 3:7); He must provide for us the skins of animals (Gen. 3:21). He is our merciful and faithful High Priest (Heb.7:17–28) and must do the work of our sacrifice, also. Despite her best effort to wrench out the natural human love and desire growing in her heart, she is unable to stir "a single rootlet".

This is yet another picture, also, of distinction between suicide and obedient response to serve the LORD in trust. We never take our own lives. We are serving the LORD. All our motivation and purpose, no matter how high minded and worthwhile our effort may sound, is in service to the LORD (Eph.6:5–7). Even service to wives and children is to be "as to the LORD, and not to men." Nothing else has eternal value.

QUESTIONS AND PRAYER: In I Cor. 3:11–14, what is it that is referred to in "the foundation that is already laid"?_____
Explain the difference between suicide and letting God put us to death.

_____
What prompts our willingness to let Him put us to death?_____
_____
_____

"We have done all that we can for you," they answered, "but this we cannot do."

At that the indistinct figure behind the altar stepped forward and said quietly, "I am the priest of this altar—I will take it out of your heart if you wish."

Much-Afraid turned toward him instantly, "Oh, thank you," she said. "I beg you to do so."

He came and stood beside her, his form indistinct and blurred by the mist, and then she continued entreatingly, "I am a very great coward. I am afraid that the pain may cause me to try to resist you. Will you bind me to the altar in some way so that I cannot move? I would not like to be found struggling while the will of my Lord is done."

There was complete silence in the cloud-filled canyon for a moment or two, then the priest answered, "It is well said. I will bind you to the altar." Then he bound her hand and foot.

When he had finished, Much-Afraid lifted her face toward the High Places which were quite invisible and spoke quietly through the mist. "My Lord, behold me—here I am, in the place Thou didst send me to—doing the thing Thou didst tell me to do, for where Thou diest, will I die, and there will I be buried; the Lord do so to me, and more also, if aught but death part Thee and me" (Ruth 1:17).

Still there was silence, a silence as of the grave, for indeed she was in the grave of her own hopes and still without the promised hinds' feet, still outside the High Places with even the promise to be laid down on the altar. This was the place to which the long, heartbreaking journey had led her. Yet just once more before she laid it down on the altar, Much-Afraid repeated the glorious promise which had been the cause of her starting for the High Places. "The Lord God is my strength, and He will make my feet like hinds' feet and He will make me to walk upon mine High Places." (Hab 3:19)

Conformance with the Grave

READ: Hind's Feet... facing page & Isaiah 53

"..that I may know Him, and the power of His resurrection and the fellowship of His sufferings, being conformed to His death; in order that I may attain to the resurrection from the dead." —Philippians 3:10–11

"knowing this, that our old self was crucified with Him, that our body of sin might be done away with, that we should no longer be slaves to sin." —Romans 6:6

With aid of the priest, Much-Afraid's desires are accomplished. Her moment of death comes, fully conformed, bound as Isaac, and as Jesus has indicated his disciples shall also be (Jn.21:18). Moments such as this mark the journey from one altar to the next for all who are disciples of Christ, yielding idols and strongholds of the flesh which separate us from God. In this allegory of Much-Afraid, author Hurnard has depicted human love as the fleshly lie to be rooted out and put to death; necessary if the Spirit-led love of God is to rule. Otherwise human love and godly love will forever war with each other (Gal. 5:16–18).

There is also a time destined for all of us where we lay down our earthly tent for our heavenly dwelling place, a place not made with human hands, eternal in the heavens (II Cor.5:1–2). No fleshly desires at all can follow this event. It seems likely that Hurnard's allegory covers both types of death events.

Which is worse, yielding fleshly idols or yielding life in the flesh? Are they different? From each there is resurrection in Christ. Perhaps the two types of this event on earth are allegories of each other or perhaps there is no difference. What do you think?

This grave has a name, "the grave of her own hopes". Much-Afraid still is without the promised hinds' feet and has now yielded even her precious promises back to the Shepherd. Nevertheless, at the moment of death she speaks the promise that drew her.

QUESTIONS AND PRAYER: Do you feel like an outside observer to Much-Afraid's death or can you identify with her? _____

Have you ever closely accompanied someone "crucified" in their deepest attachments in human love; someone who has "died" in a divorce or lost a child? How does it appear to illustrate this lesson or not?_____

_____

_____

_____

The priest put forth a hand of steel, right into her heart. There was a sound of rending and tearing, and the human love, with all its myriad rootlets and fibers, came forth.

He held it for a moment and then said, "Yes, it was ripe for removal, the time had come. There is not a rootlet torn or missing."

When he had said this he cast it down on the altar and spread his hands above it. There came a flash of fire which seemed to rend the altar; after that, nothing but ashes remained, either of the love itself, which had been so deeply planted in her heart, or of the suffering and sorrow which had been her companions on that long, strange journey. A sense of utter, overwhelming rest and peace engulfed Much-Afraid. At last, the offering had been made and there was nothing left to be done. When the priest had unbound her she leaned forward over the ashes on the altar and said with complete thanksgiving, "It is finished."

Then, utterly exhausted, she fell asleep.

Climax

READ: Hind's Feet... facing page & **John 19:23–30**

"for he who has died is freed from sin." —Romans 6:7

"'Then you call on the name of your god, and I will call upon the name
of the LORD, and the God who answers by fire, He is God.' And all the people
answered and said, 'That is a good idea.'" —I Kings 18:24

We should probably not be puzzled as to who the priest is, who does such a masterful job of removing the human love from Much-Afraid's heart. "There is not a rootlet torn or missing." Nevertheless, at the moment of death, there is a horrendous sound of "rending and tearing". Indeed the sound of death must resound throughout the body, soul and spirit of all who have submitted to it.

We tend to picture fire as from the enemy, but nearly all Bible uses of it are for purification, refinement, the adding of quality and resilience. Think about it for a moment. Is our abhorrence of "fire" another trick of the enemy to protect his residence in our minds and flesh?

Twentieth century physicists discovered matter can be transformed into energy; pure heat. From the relationships of the theory of relativity came understanding of nuclear fission and fusion. II Peter 3:10 depicts such a scene in the day of the LORD, "in which the heavens will pass away with a roar and the elements will be destroyed with intense heat, and the earth and its works will be burned up." From this and other biblical portraits of fire "burning up" earthly things, we grasp that the entire universe depicts an unseen world where removal of things which would hurt us is accomplished by fire and transformed. No earthly thing, no fleshly spirit may come into the Kingdom of God. What comes in is fit for royalty; for company with the Kings of Kings, patterned after the Seed of Woman, who placed Life in us according to His likeness, as royal offspring of God. By His hand, "It is finished."

QUESTIONS AND PRAYER: By expending His life on the cross for us, Jesus enabled planting of His Seed in us (Jn.12:24). By receiving Him, we are born again. What is the likeness between this and raising vegetable crops (Hebrews 6:7–8)? Sexual intercourse (Luke 1:35)?_____

_____

_____

_____

Part Two

"Joy cometh in the morning" (Psalm 30:5)

CHAPTER 17

Healing Streams

When at last Much-Afraid awoke, the sun was high in the sky, and she looked down through the mouth of the cave in which she found herself lying. Everything was shimmering in a blaze of radiant sunshine which burnished every object with glory. She lay still a little longer, collecting her thoughts and trying to understand where she was.

The rocky cave into which the sunbeams were pouring was warm and quiet and drenched with the sweet perfume of spikenard, frankincense, and myrrh. This perfume she gradually realized was emanating from the wrappings which covered her. She gently pushed back the folds, sat up, and looked about her. Then the memory of all that had happened returned to her.

She and her two companions had come to a cloud-filled canyon high up on the mountains and to an altar of sacrifice, and the priest had wrenched out of her heart her flower of human love and burned it on the altar. On remembering that, she glanced down at her breast and saw it was covered with a cloth soaked in the spices whose perfume stole out and filled the cave with sweetness. She pushed the cloth aside a little curiously and was astonished to find no trace of a wound—not even a scar, nor was there any hint of pain or aching or stiffness anywhere in her body.

Arising in the Tomb

READ: Hind's Feet... facing page & **Psalm 19:1–6**

"But on the first day of the week, at early dawn, they came to the
tomb, bringing the spices which they had prepared. And they
found the stone rolled away from the tomb." —Luke 24:1–2

"and walk in love, just as Christ also loved you, and
gave Himself up for us, an offering and a sacrifice to God
as a fragrant aroma" —Ephesians 5:2

God has done a great work in Hannah Hurnard's allegory. Always her portraits seem to accentuate the beauty and glory of the gospel. Even in the case of Much-Afraid's awakening, her first sight is to see the sun having gone ahead of her, being "high in the sky", pouring out its blazing, radiant sunshine in glory. The glory of God has gone ahead in the Son, who went ahead of us in death and resurrection in glory.

In a similar manner of speaking, other "lights" begin to go on in Much-Afraid. The aromas of death and sacrifice fill the tomb; sweet aromas. They are those which were brought to the Christ as a child by the wise men, thus portraying His coming death and burial (Matt. 2:11). They portray those of every pleasing sacrifice made unto the LORD.

Then she remembers all that happened to her and discovers that despite the horrible pain of her sacrifice, there is no scar at all. By His stripes we are healed (Isa.53:6, I Pet. 2:24). By some miracle we can't understand we are healed of all pain or wounding of things given to the LORD in sacrifice.

The scene is one of rest and peace. It introduces Part Two of the allegory; yet only 26 pages remain. Less than 17% of the story is given to this remainder. Perhaps this is because we know much less about the "other side" and can effectively report and teach only of that in which we have experienced the living power of the word of God. This portion, then, is a glimpse into life in the resurrection power of God, that which we can see, not all of which is reserved for the future.

QUESTIONS AND PRAYER: Have you ever been in a resurrection scene such as described here? Can you testify of the truth or falsehood of this scene pertaining to a disciple of Christ? _____

_____

_____

_____

Rising quietly, she went outside, then stood still and looked about her. The canyon, which had been so shrouded in mist that nothing had been distinguishable, now shimmered in the golden sunlight. Soft, verdant grass grew everywhere, starred with gentians and other little jewel-like flowers of every variety. There were banks of sweet-smelling thyme, moss, and myrtle along the sides of the rocky walls, and everything sparkled with dew.

In the center of the canyon, at a little distance from the cave, was the long stone altar to which she had been bound, but in the sunlight she saw that the flowers and mosses grew all about it and clothed its sides with verdure. Little birds hopped about here and there, scattering the dewdrops off the grasses and chirping merrily as they preened their plumage.

One was perched on the altar itself, its little throat throbbing as it trilled forth a song of joy, but the most beautiful and wonderful thing of all was that out from under the rock altar there gushed a great "river of water, clear as crystal." It then flowed in a series of cascades and through rock pools right through the canyon till it came to a broad lip of rock, over which it poured with a noise of shouting and tumultuous gladness. She was at the very source of the great fall and knew now that it flowed from under the altar to which the priest had bound her.

For some time she stood looking about her, her heart leaping and thrilling with a growing joy which was beyond her understanding and a peace indescribably sweet which seemed to enfold her. She was quite alone in the canyon. There were no signs of her companions Sorrow and Suffering nor of the priest of the altar. The only things which breathed and moved in the canyon beside herself were the cheerful little chirping birds and the insects and butterflies flitting among the flowers. High overhead was a cloudless sky, against which the peaks of the High Places shone dazzlingly white.

The first thing she did, after she had taken in her surroundings, was to step toward the river which gushed out from under the altar. It drew her irresistibly.

276

New Life

READ: Hind's Feet... facing page & **Isaiah 65:17–25**

"And when He had said these things, He cried out with a loud voice, "Lazarus, come forth. He who had died came forth....." —John 11:43–44

"And He showed me a river of the water of life, clear as crystal, coming from the throne of God and of the Lamb." —Revelation 22:1

What do people notice when they are given new life, or a resurrection rebirth? It is usually filled with intensity, breadth and meaning even in minute detail.

We see through Much-Afraid's eyes that she is still in the same canyon in which she died. She is in the High Places, but under different conditions. Now everthing is shimmering and radiant. Every distinct plant is evident in its own unique beauty. Little birds are seen moving and even "scattering of dewdrops" observed. She is still and quiet in her observations.

Now she observes that the great waterfall issues forth with its life-giving character from under the rock altar upon which she made her sacrifice. We have previously noted "water of life" identified in scripture and see these words explicitly referenced in the Revelation of John (Rev. 21:6, 22:1). How does it work? Perhaps it works much like the water Much-Afraid sees, joyfully casting itself down to bring life to dead places. Jesus knows and we will see someday.

In peaceful amazement and tranquility, the beauty of the high mountains is observed. From "cheerful birds" and "insects and butterflies" to the majestic grandeur of the dazzling high peaks, it is all a marvelous scene in which to contemplate the Savior's creation. No one else is there. This is her moment. This is all there just for her enjoyment.

QUESTIONS AND PRAYER: How do you specifically set time aside to contemplate the work and word of God?_____

_____

Does your life tend to become hectic and filled with distractions, pushing time with God to the side?_____

How do you view "re-creation"?_____

Do you think God overrules our plans when He determines it necessary to stop and enable us to be "re-created" in the fashion of Much-Afraid?_____

_____

She stooped down when she got to the bank and dabbled her fingers in the crystal water. It was icy cold, but it sent a shock of ecstasy tingling through her body, and without further delay she put off the white linen robe she was wearing and stepped into one of the rocky pools. Never had she experienced anything so delicious and exhilarating. It was like immersing herself in a stream of bubbling life. When at last she again stepped out of the pool she was immediately dry and tingling from head to foot with a sense of perfect well-being.

As she stood on the mossy bank by the pool she happened to glance down and noticed for the first time that her feet were no longer the crooked, ugly things which they always had been, but were "straight feet," perfectly formed, shining white against the soft green grass.

Then she remembered the healing streams of which the Shepherd had spoken which gushed out of the ground on the High Places. Stepping straight back into the pool with a shock of sweetest pleasure and putting her head beneath the clear waters, she splashed them about her face. Then she found a little pool among the rocks, still and clear as a mirror. Kneeling down, she looked into its unruffled surface and saw her face quite clearly. It was true, the ugly, twisted mouth had vanished and the face she saw reflected back by the water was as relaxed and perfect as the face of a little child.

After that she began to wander about the canyon and noticed wild strawberries and blueberries and other small berries growing on the banks. She found a handful of these as refreshing and sustaining a meal as ever she had eaten.

Then she came to the lip of the rock cliff over which the river cast itself, and stood a long time watching the water as it leaped over the edge with the noise of its tumultuous joy drowning every other sound. She saw how the sun glorified the crystal waters as they went whirling downward and far below she saw the green alps where the Shepherd had led her

Healing

READ: Hind's Feet... facing page & **Ezekiel 47:1–12**

"...behold, a great multitude, which no one could count, from every nation and all tribes and peoples and tongues, standing before the throne and before the Lamb, clothed in white robes, and palm branches were in their hands." —Revelation 7:9

"...And on either side of the river was the tree of life, bearing twelve kinds of fruit, yielding its fruit every month; and the leaves of the tree were for the healing of the nations." —Revelation 22:2

This page is filled with beautiful symbols of the Kingdom of God and God's work in the lives of the saints. Much-Afraid wears a white linen robe, portraying the bride who "has made herself ready" for the marriage of the Lamb. The fine linen is declared to be "the righteous acts of the saints" (Rev. 19:7–8). It is not difficult to grasp what the righteousness of Much-Afraid is, what her acts were and what they were founded upon.

Drawn to bathe in the "water of life", she discovers healing in her feet, and recalling the words of the Shepherd, applies the water also to her face. Both her lame feet and ugly, twisted mouth depart forever.

She eats the fruit of the high meadows, also nurtured by the "water of life" (Rev. 22:1); as "refreshing and sustaining a meal" as she's ever eaten.

Then at the lip of the rock cliff over which the river cast itself she hears the "noise of its tumultuous joy drowning every other sound." It is the "voice of many waters" described by John of the LORD in Revelation 1:15. We read in Revelation 19:6, that the voice of the "great multitude" of saints is "as the sound of many waters and as the sound of mighty peals of thunder". It is yet another aspect of transfiguration of the children of God to the likeness of Christ. Each droplet of the falls is glorified by the sun. The LORD shares His glory (John 17:22).

QUESTIONS AND PRAYER: How might we receive rest and restoration in reading of the restoration of others?_____

_____

_____

Do you feel these things which the Bible pictures are to be fulfilled literally or are the scriptures also only allegorical?_____

_____

_____

and where they had stood at the foot of this same fall. She felt completely encompassed by peace, and a great inner quietness and contentment drowned every feeling of curiosity, loneliness and anticipation.

She did not think about the future at all. It was enough to be there in that quiet canyon, hidden away high up in the mountains with the river of life flowing beside her, and to rest and recover herself after the long journey. After a little she lay down on a mossy bank and slept, and when she woke again, bathed herself in the river. So the long, quiet day passed like a sweet dream while she rested and bathed and refreshed herself at intervals with the berries and then slept again.

When at last the shadows lengthened and the sun sank in the west and the snow peaks glowed glorious in rose and flame color she went back into the cave, laid herself down among the spice-perfumed coverings and slept as deeply and dreamlessly as she had the first night when the priest laid her there to rest.

Peace Like a River

READ: Hind's Feet... facing page & Isaiah 66:7–15

"But My servant Caleb, because he has had a different spirit and has followed Me fully, I will bring into the land which he entered, and his descendants shall take possession of it." —Numbers 14:24

"There remains therefore a Sabbath rest for the people of God. For the one who has entered His rest has himself also rested from his works, as God did from His." —Hebrews 4:9–10

When God sentenced the children of Israel to forty years of wandering in the desert (Nu.14), it was because of their lack of faith and obedience. As Psalm 95 summarizes it in the last verse, "Therefore I swore in my anger, truly they shall not enter into My rest." This is some of the history that the author of Hebrews has reviewed before concluding that there is indeed a rest into which obedient servants of God may enter, as did Caleb.

Much-Afraid has apparently entered into such a rest. She has entered the promises of God for her through faith and obedience, but the primary fruit she enjoys first is rest. She feels "completely encompassed by peace"; with "great inner quietness and contentment." She is not lonely, curious or even looking forward to the future. She is at rest. Godliness with contentment is "great gain" (I Tim. 6:6).

"Peace like a river" is promised for a rebirth of Israel, the Old Testament picture for the New Testament bride of Christ. It is all to be done in a single day (Isa.66:8, Zech.12:9–14) to a nation yet not believing in the character or promises of God. All through the Isaiah 66 passage read today, God portrays Himself as the full-breasted nurturer of life for Jerusalem. He is the source of milk and honey in the Promised Land. But giants guard the land; we must overcome the giants if we are to enter.

QUESTIONS AND PRAYER: What were the "giants" which discouraged Israel from entering the Promised Land? _____

_____

How are these giants any different today?_____

_____

What was different about Caleb's spirit? Much-Afraid's?_____

_____

How does one overcome giants? _____

CHAPTER 18

Hinds' Feet

On the third day, while it was still almost dark, she woke suddenly, and sprang to her feet with a shock of joy tingling through her. She had not heard her name called, had not even been conscious of a voice, yet she knew that she had been called. Some mysterious, poignantly sweet summons had reached her, a summons which she knew instinctively she had been awaiting ever since she woke up for the first time in the cave. She stepped outside into the fragrant summer night. The morning star hung low in the sky, and in the east the first glimmer of dawn appeared. From somewhere close at hand a solitary bird uttered one clear, sweet note and a light breeze stirred over the grasses. Otherwise there was no sound save the voice of the great waterfall.

Then it came again—tingling through her—a call ringing down from some high place above. Standing there in the pale dawn, she looked eagerly around. Every nerve in her body surged with desire to respond to the call, and she felt her feet and legs tingling with an almost irresistible urge to go bounding up the mountains, but where was the way out of the canyon? The walls seemed to rise smooth and almost perpendicular on all sides, except at the end which was blocked by the waterfall.

Then, as she stood straining every nerve to find a possible means of exit, up from a nearby mossy bank sprang a mountain hart with the hind close behind him, just as she had seen them at the foot of the great Precipice of Injury. As she watched, the hart sprang onto the altar of rock, and from there with a great leap he reached a projecting ledge on the wall on the farther side of the ravine. Then,

Early Morning Call

READ: Hind's Feet... facing page & **I Samuel 3:1–10**

"Now on the first day of the week Mary Magdalene came early
to the tomb, while it was still dark, and saw the stone already
taken away from the tomb." —John 20:1

"Behold, as for the proud one, his soul is not right within him;
but the righteous will live by his faith." —Habakkuk 2:4

Neat things happen in the wee hours. A person who gets up early in the morning in response to God's call is in good Bible company. It is the mark of earnestness that, almost without exception from Abraham onward, God calls upon responses of His people during the wee hours of the night, before dawn. The list includes Lot's escape from Sodom, Abimelech's response to God's warning, several responses by Abraham, Jacob and Laban (each in response to covenants), Moses (many times), Joshua, Gideon, Samuel, David and others.

Christ's resurrection also took place before dawn and scriptural promise would seem to be that the rapture shall be likewise, sometime prior to the dawning of the sun in the east, by the "bright morning star" (Rev. 2:28, 22:16). Levitical law requires wages "not to be withheld until morning". It appears the LORD's accounts are all resolved prior to sunrise.

Many have tried to imagine the stupendous moment when the Father raised the Son from the dead (Rom. 6:4). In the stillness of the tomb on the morning of the third day, a word was spoken and it all took place, perhaps as depicted with Much-Afraid. Since we who follow Jesus are to be raised even as He was, we shall fully know that moment. Hallelujah! It is almost too stupendous to grasp, but the promise is ours regardless of what happens in this life, if we remain faithful until the end (Rev. 2:7, 10, 17, 26–28, 3:5, 12, 21).

QUESTIONS AND PRAYER: Are you confident of resurrection life; that you will be raised from the dead on the last day (John 6:44)?_____

_____

Have you experienced enough of resurrection power in things you've sacrificed to Christ, to know that this power is demonstrated to God's servants in this life?

_____

Do you desire more of it?_____

closely followed by the hind, he began springing up the great wall of the canyon.

Much-Afraid did not hesitate one instant. In a moment she was on the rock altar herself, the next, with a flying leap, she, too, reached the ledge on the wall. Then, using the same footholds as the hart and the hind, leaping and springing in a perfect ecstasy of delight, she followed them up the cliff, the hooves of the deer ringing on the rocks before her like little silver hammers.

In a moment or two all three were at the top of the canyon, and she was leaping up the mountainside toward the peak above, from which the summons had come. The rosy light in the east brightened, the snow on the summits of the mountains caught the glow and flushed like fire, and as she skipped and jumped from rock to rock excitedly the first sunbeams streamed over the mountaintop. He was there—standing on the peak—just as she had known He would be, strong and grand and glorious in the beauty of the sunrise, holding out both hands and calling to her with a great laugh, "You—with the hinds' feet—jump over here."

She gave one last flying spring, caught His hands and landed beside Him on the topmost peak of the mountain. Around them in every direction towered other and greater ranges of snow mountains, whose summits soared into the sky higher than her sight could follow them. He was crowned, and dressed in royal robes, just as she had seen Him once before when He had carried her up to the High Places, and had touched her with the live coal from off the golden Altar of Love. Then His face had been stern in its majesty and gravity, now it was alight with glory of joy which excelled anything which she had ever imagined.

"At last," He said, as she knelt speechless at His feet, "at last you are here and the 'night of weeping is over and joy comes to you in the morning.' " Then, lifting her up, He continued, "This is the time when you are to receive the fulfillment of

Fulfillment of Promises

READ: Hind's Feet... facing page & **Psalm 30**

"For the vision is yet for the appointed time; it hastens
toward the goal, and it will not fail. Though it tarries, wait for it;
For it will certainly come, it will not delay." —Habakkuk 2:3

"Behold, as for the proud one, His soul is not right within him;
But the righteous will live by his faith." —Habakkuk 2:4

In an instant, up from the grave Much-Afraid leaps! Up to the mountain top, this time with resurrection power. The rosy light in the east brightens and fires the peaks. She reaches the summit as "the first sunbeams stream over the mountaintop"! What brilliant, graphic words!

Perhaps we grasp before Much-Afraid does what the descriptions of the prior page depicted, especially with respect to her "feet and legs tingling" and her urge to go to the mountaintops. She has been equipped to do things which normal mortal bodies cannot do. As Jesus could appear anywhere and pass through walls (Luke 24:36, Jn. 20:26), Much-Afraid is now also equipped to do in the allegory of her resurrection.

Everything is now transformed. Her "knowledge" that the Shepherd would be on the peak is confirmed, much as a word of knowledge is provided in ministry to the body of Christ (I Cor. 12:8) and confirmed. These are gifts of God which are given to those put to death for His sake, whether on this side (partially) or on the other side of this world, when the Perfect comes (I Cor. 13:10). What she was allowed to "see" from the other side now turns out to be reality, not illusion. The Shepherd is crowned and dressed in his "royal robes, just as she had seen Him once before". Now everything is "alight with glory". The portraits of glory continue.

She worships at the Shepherd's feet as He speaks a portion of Psalm 30 over her then "lifts her up" with the announcement of what we already see; "fulfillment of the promises."

QUESTIONS AND PRAYER: How may the text be applied to keeping faith, building character, fulfilling responsibilities and building value in yourself and your family in Christ?_____

_____

_____

_____

the promises. Never am I to call you Much-Afraid again." At that He laughed again and said, "I will write upon her a new name, the name of her God. The Lord God is a sun and shield: the Lord will give grace and glory: no good thing will He withhold from them that walk uprightly" (Psa. 84:11). "This is your new name," He declared. "From henceforth you are Grace and Glory."

Still she could not speak, but stood silent with joy and thanksgiving and awe and wonder.

Then He went on, "Now for the flower of Love and for the promise that when it blooms you will be loved in return."

Grace and Glory spoke for the first time. "My Lord and King," she said softly, "there is no flower of Love to bloom in my heart. It was turned to ashes on the altar at Thy command."

"No flower of Love?" He repeated, and laughed again so gently and joyfully that she could hardly bear it. "That is strange, Grace and Glory. How, then, did you get here? You are right on the High Places, in the Kingdom of Love itself. Open your heart and let us see what is there."

At His word she laid bare her heart, and out came the sweetest perfume she had ever breathed and filled all the air around them with its fragrance. There in her heart was a plant whose shape and form could not be seen because it was covered all over with pure white, almost transparent blooms, from which the fragrance poured.

Grace and Glory gave a little gasp of wonder and thankfulness. "How did it get there, my Lord and King?" she exclaimed.

"Why, I planted it there myself," was his laughing answer. "Surely you remember, down there by the sheep pool in the Valley of Humiliation, on the day that you promised to go with Me to the High Places. It is the flower from the thorn-shaped seed.

286

Grace and Glory

READ: Hind's Feet... facing page & **Ephesians 2:1–10**

"And the glory which Thou hast given Me I have given to them; that they may be one, just as We are one; I in them, and Thou in Me, that they may be perfected in unity, that the world may know that Thou didst send Me, and didst love them, even as Thou didst love Me." —John 17:22–23

Much-Afraid is given a new name. Names portray great significance regarding who the person IS carrying the name. They reflect a state of "BE-ing"; who they BE. It does not reflect only momentary experience. Thus, Abraham was re-named "Father of Multitudes (Gen. 17:5), Sarah was re-named "Princess" (Gen.17:15), Jacob meant "one who usurps or supplants" but was later named Israel, meaning "one who strives with God" (Gen. 32:28). God, Himself, identified to Moses as "I AM" (Ex. 3:14).

Hence, we should expect that Much-Afraid will continue to walk in grace and glory, reflecting who she is in her new name.

She now has explained to her something we have already perhaps perceived; that is, her misunderstanding between God's love which was originally planted in her heart, and the human love which the priest tore out of her heart at the moment of her sacrifice. It is now a big surprise to her that God's love in her has flowered in profusion, despite her thought it had been removed! What she thought she had given up has not been lost at all. It has been restored many-fold, replacing what she gave up of such high personal value. What she actually gave up was worthless; an idol that interfered with her relationship with God and ability to love. What she has received, grown to full fragrant flower, is priceless!

The difference between *Agape*, and what she had been carrying as the weed of human love will become more evident to her and to us as we continue with her.

QUESTIONS AND PRAYER: Provide a short summary of the power of the flesh to deceive us regarding value of fleshly things. (Please provide some examples.)

_____

_____

How does sacrificing things that "seem" valuable enable God to clarify for us what is truly from Him and for our benefit?_____

_____

_____

"Then, my Lord, what was the plant which the priest tore out of my heart when I was bound to the altar?"

"Do you remember, Grace and Glory, when you looked into your heart beside the pool, and found that My kind of love was not there at all—only the plant of Longing-to-be-loved?

She nodded wonderingly.

"That was the natural human love which I tore out from your heart when the time was ripe and it was loose enough to be uprooted altogether so that the real Love could grow there alone and fill your whole heart."

"You tore it out!" she repeated slowly and wonderingly, and then, "O my Lord and King, were You the priest? Were You there all the time, when I thought You had forsaken me?"

He bowed His head and she took His hands in hers, the scarred hands which had sown the thorn-shaped seed in her heart, and the hands with the grasp of steel which had torn out that love which had been the cause of all her pain, and kissed them while tears of joy fell on them.

"And now for the promise," said He, "that when Love flowers in your heart you shall be loved again." Taking her hand in His, He said, "Behold I have set My love upon thee and thou art Mine ... yea, I have loved thee with an everlasting love: therefore with loving-kindness have I drawn thee" (Jer. 31:3) After that He said, "Give Me the bag of stones of remembrance that you have gathered on your journey, Grace and Glory."

She took it out and passed it to Him and then He bade her hold out her hands. On doing so, He opened the little purse and emptied the contents into her hands. Then she gasped again with bewilderment and delight, for instead of the common, ugly stones she had gathered from the altars along the way, there fell into her hands a heap of glorious, sparkling jewels, very precious and very beautiful. As she stood there, half-dazzled by the glory of the flashing gems, she saw in His hand a circlet of pure gold.

Wheat and Tares

READ: Hind's Feet... facing page & Matthew 13:24–30

"But the very hairs of your head are all numbered. Therefore do not fear;
you are of more value than many sparrows." —Matthew 10:31

"Of how much more value then is a man than a sheep! So then,
it is lawful to do good on the Sabbath." —Matthew 12:12

The Shepherd reviews events, explaining to Much-Afraid that what was removed from her was "natural human love". She also discovers He was the one who performed the operation! He remained faithful, though she could not see and understand. All the time He was there leading through trials to enable her to purify her responses. He was the "refiner's fire" and "fuller's soap" that did the job (Mal. 3:2).

In a manner similar to the wheat and tares, God has removed everything that interfered with His love. It is marriage supper time. Much-Afraid has been purified as a bride (Rev. 19:7–8)!

Hannah Hurnard has chosen the transformation of the stones as the first fruit of Much-Afraid's experiencing the promise that she "shall be loved again". *This touches upon something difficult to imbue to the spirit of men,* (although not to women.) It may be taught intellectually but is difficult to convey spiritually the extent to which *value* and uniqueness is inherent in knowing love and receiving the knowledge of God's love. Nevertheless, it is fundamental to the knowledge of God and empowerment of our lives.

Women and the bride of Christ must *know* value in order to know they are loved. Claims of love without manifestation of value are worthless. Hence, significance to the wording of John 3:16; it connects the profession of love with value. Even that profession would be powerless, however, without God's expensive action to redeem us. Actions convey true value.

Likewise, Jesus declared deeds of mercy lawful on the Sabbath because <u>they reflect the value</u> of those who receive mercy.

QUESTIONS AND PRAYER: Would God intervene for us if we had no value? Do you agree that the key to your salvation was the discovery of the fact that you were loved? How did this happen in your case? _____

_____

How can you apply this important lesson to those in your care?_____

_____

"O thou who wast afflicted, tossed with tempest and not comforted," He said, "behold I lay thy stones with fair colors."

First He picked out of her hand one of the biggest and most beautiful of the stones—a sapphire, shining like the pavement of heaven, and set it in the center of the golden circlet. Then, taking a fiery, blood red ruby, He set it on one side of the sapphire and an emerald on the other. After that He took the other stones— twelve in all—and arranged them on the circlet, then set it upon her head.

At that moment Grace and Glory remembered the cave in which she had been sheltered from the floods, and how nearly she had succumbed to the temptation to discard as worthless those stones which now shone with glory and splendor in the crown upon her head. She remembered, too, the words which had sounded in her ears and had restrained her, "Hold fast that thou hast, that no man take thy crown." Supposing she had thrown them away, had discarded her trust in His prom- ises, had gone back on her surrenders to His will? There could have been no jew- els now to His praise and glory, and no crown for her to wear.

She marveled at the grace and love and tenderness and patience which had led and trained and guarded and kept poor faltering Much-Afraid, which had not al- lowed her to turn back, and which now changed all her trials into glory. Then she heard Him speaking again and this time the smile on His face was almost more joyful than before.

"Hearken, O daughter, and consider, and incline thine ears; forget also thine own people, and thy father's house; so shall the King greatly desire thy beauty: for He is thy Lord; and worship thou Him ... The King's daughter is all glorious within. She shall be brought unto the King in clothing of wrought gold, in raiment of needlework. The virgins, her companions that follow her, shall be brought unto thee. With gladness and rejoicing shall they be brought: they shall enter into the King's palace" (Psa. 45:10–15). Then he added, "Now that you are to live with Me here on the High Places, to go where I

Great Value

READ: Hind's Feet... facing page & **Psalm 45**

"An excellent wife, who can find? Her worth is
far above jewels." —Proverbs 31:10

" Charm is deceitful and beauty is vain, but a woman who fears the LORD,
she shall be praised. Give her the product of her hands, and let her
works praise her in the gates." —Proverbs 31:30–31

Much-Afraid's obedient responses to the Shepherd have been gathered up. He bestows upon her His measure of the value of her responses. By so doing He praises her and acknowledges His full understanding of everything that went into each of her resolutions and actions. She is amazed. How close had she come to throwing it all away? God knew all along!

Young husbands perceive little of what their wives invest in them. But grateful hearts cause their appreciation to grow and be expressed in words of admiration. These words express some of the reality of the inexpressible value of a faithful wife. As Psalm 45 and Proverbs 31 so clearly convey, the place of women is unique—different from that of men. The images which convey value as that of a queen (King Lemuel's wife) are authored by God and to be accomplished by men. Women must be praised by their husbands. The reverse is not true.

Men do need affirmation by their wives, but it is not through praise. In fact, nowhere in scripture are wives asked to praise their husbands. They are asked to "respect" and obey them, in the manner in which Much-Afraid has affirmed the Shepherd (Eph.5:22–24, 33, I Pet. 3:1–6). We presume that male disciples of Jesus will not instruct their wives to respect them, but will obey Christ and give themselves up for their wives (without prior response!) This conforms with Christ in a manner that will enable them "to see the results and be satisfied". The results await obedient men on the other side of the cross, as with Christ (Isa.53:11). It is a non-optional command of Christ for men (Eph.5:25–33), with rewards that are certain.

QUESTIONS AND PRAYER: Have you personal experience in which you have been convicted by God of failing to deal rightly with girls or women?

_____

What could you do about it at this time?_____
How may you yield to the Spirit in dealing rightly in the future with wives, sisters, daughters or other women in your circle of stewardship?

_____

go, and to share My work in the valley below, it is fitting, Grace and Glory, that you should have companions and handmaidens, and I will bring them to you now."

At that Grace and Glory regarded Him earnestly, and there were almost tears in her eyes, for she remembered Sorrow and Suffering, the faithful companions whom He had given her before. It had been through their help and gentleness and patience she had been able to ascend the mountains to the High Places. All the time she had been with her Lord and King, receiving her new name, and being crowned with joy and glory, she had been thinking of them and wishing—yes, actually wishing and longing that they were there too, for why should she receive everything? They had endured the same journey, had supported and helped her, had been through the same trials and attacks of the enemy.

Now she was here and they were not. She opened her mouth to make her first request, to beg her Lord to let her keep the companions He had chosen in the beginning and who had brought her to the glory of the High Places. Before she could speak, however, He said with the same especially lovely smile, "Here are the handmaidens, Grace and Glory, whom I have chosen to be with you henceforth and forever."

Two radiant shining figures stepped forward, the morning sunshine glittering on their snowy garments, making them dazzling to look at. They were taller and stronger than Grace and Glory, but it was the beauty of their faces and the love shining in their eyes which caught at her heart and made her almost tremble with joy and admiration. They came toward her, their faces shining with mirth and gladness, but they said not a word.

"Who are you?" asked Grace and Glory softly. "Will you tell me your names?"

Instead of answering they looked at one another and smiled, then held out their hands as though to take hers in their own. At that familiar gesture, Grace

Coronation

READ: Hind's Feet... facing page & **Ruth 4:1–17**

"and to Salmon was born Boaz by Rahab; and to Boaz was born
Obed by Ruth; and to Obed, Jesse; and to Jesse was born
David the king." —Matthew 1:5–7

"She will be led to the King in embroidered work; the virgins, her
companions who follow her, will be brought to Thee." —Psalm 45:14

Of course, what would a coronation be without companions?! There are few Bible accounts of queen coronations, but marriages always provide for witness and companions. When a girl is incorporated into royal lineage, one of her foremost provisions is the sharing of the joy with others.

Even two potentially lonely women coronated into the royal lineage of Christ, Rahab and Ruth, were provided relatives and friends to share in the occasion of their marriages to sons of Israel. Rahab, the harlot of Jericho, was enabled by God to save her relatives when Jericho fell, by hanging a "scarlet thread" outside her window when Israel came in (Josh. 2:18, 6:22–23). She later married Salmon and mothered Boaz, one of the most Godly men of the Bible. A generation later, Ruth, a foreign widow, married Boaz and received the company of her prior mother-in-law Naomi and her friends. A good circle of women friends surrounded them when Obed was born (Ruth 4:14–17). The same idea may also be involved in the parable of the virgins, keeping watch for the arrival of the bridegroom (Matt. 25:1–13).

Now Grace and Glory is given two "companions and handmaidens", fitting for a crowned princess. There is lots of feminine stuff in the account of their stepping forward and capturing Grace and Glory's admiration (worth re-reading and much like the things women share everywhere in celebrating. Also please read again Ruth 4:14–17). It may sound gooey, fellas, but God loves it and provides for it. Grace and Glory is treated as royalty; the bride of Christ.

QUESTIONS AND PRAYER: Do you see yourself as the Bride of Christ being crowned as a princess?_____

_____

Please explain how this applies to those who live as men on earth, but through Christ become members of the Bride. How does the wedding supper of the Lamb fulfill the vision of women for a "knight in shining armor" who will treat them as a princess and "live happily forever after"?_____

_____

and Glory knew them and cried out with a joy which was almost more than she could bear.

"Why! You are Sorrow and Suffering. Oh, welcome, welcome! I was longing to find you again."

They shook their heads. "Oh, no!" they laughed, "we are no more Sorrow and Suffering than you are Much-Afraid. Don't you know that everything that comes to the High Places is transformed? Since you brought us here with you, we are turned into Joy and Peace."

"Brought you here!" gasped Grace and Glory. "What an extraordinary way to express it! Why, from the first to last you dragged me here."

Again they shook their heads and smiled as they answered, "No, we could never have come here alone, Grace and Glory. Sorrow and Suffering may not enter the Kingdom of Love, but each time you accepted us and put your hands in ours we began to change. Had you turned back or rejected us, we never could have come here."

Looking at one another again, they laughed softly and said, "When first we saw you at the foot of the mountains, we felt a little depressed and despairing. You seemed so Much-Afraid of us, and shrank away and would not accept our help, and it looked so unlikely that any of us would ever get to the High Places. We told ourselves that we would have to remain Sorrow and Suffering always, but you see how graciously our Lord the King arranged for all of us, and you did bring us here. Now we are to be your companions and friends forever."

With that they came up to her, put their arms around her, and all three embraced and kissed one another with a love and thankfulness and joy beyond words to express. So with a new name, and united to the King and crowned with glory, Grace and Glory, accompanied by her companions and friends, came to the High Places and was led into the Kingdom of Love.

Transforming Relationships

READ: Hind's Feet... facing page & **Revelation 21:1–22:5**

"Thou hast turned for me my mourning into dancing; Thou hast
loosed my sackcloth and girded me with gladness; that my soul
may sing praise to Thee, and not be silent. O LORD my God, I will
give thanks to Thee forever." —Psalm 30:11–12

"...fixing our eyes on Jesus, the author of our faith, who for the joy
set before Him, endured the cross, despising the shame and has sat
down at the right hand of the throne of God." —Hebrews 12:2

The Bible is clear that God ordains a process for the transformation of sorrow and suffering into joy and peace. The scriptures above and others (Ps.126:5–6, Isa.35:10, 51:11, 60:20, 65:19) promise this. There are principles of relationship, too, which pertain to the ideas seen in this scene with our newly named and crowned heroine, Grace and Glory (recently Much-Afraid).

One principle is that personal relationships exercise and mold both parties in a relationship. "Iron sharpens iron. So one man sharpens another" (Prov.27:17). Author Hurnard postulates this from several standpoints.

First, she says "everything" coming to the High Places is "transformed", and shows that the transformation has been continuous, not sudden and all at once. She shows that Much-Afraid could not have come there alone, nor vice versa. Sorrow and Suffering were themselves transformed into Joy and Peace by the manner in which they were treated by Much-Afraid. They confess effects that were dependent upon the manner in which they were treated. When treated with Much-Afraid's characteristics of fear (shrinking away), they were repelled, depressed and despairing. But when they were accepted, they began to change just as Much-Afraid was also changed.

Joy and Peace, two fruits of the Spirit (Gal. 5:22), are now companions of Grace and Glory for life. In lovely union, they enter the Kingdom of Love.

QUESTIONS AND PRAYER: Can you identify any life relationships where the life invested in the other person does not affect both giver and recipient?_____

How could you apply this to your attitudes toward unpleasant circumstances?
_____
_____
_____

CHAPTER 19

High Places

Grace and Glory with her handmaidens Joy and Peace stayed up on the High Places for several weeks while all three explored the heights and learned many new lessons from the King. He led them himself to many places, and explained to them as much as they were able to understand at that time. He also encouraged them to explore on their own, for there are always new and lovely discoveries to make up there on the High Places.

Even these High Places were not the highest of all. Others towered above them into the sky, where mortal eye could no longer follow them, and where only those who have finished their pilgrim life on earth are able to go. Grace and Glory and her friends were on the lowest, the "beginners' slopes" in the Kingdom of Love, and these were the parts which they were to explore and enjoy at this time. From these slopes, too, they were able to look down on the valleys below, and from that new viewpoint gain an understanding of many things which had been puzzling and mysterious to them before. From beneath they had not been seen clearly, and even then only a small part had been visible.

The first thing, however, which they realized up there on the slopes of the Kingdom of Love was how much more there would be to see and learn and understand when the King took them higher on future occasions. The glorious view which they now enjoyed was but small in comparison with all that lay beyond, and would be visible only from yet higher places above.

It was now perfectly evident to them that there must be ranges upon ranges of which they had never dreamed while they were still down in the narrow

Exploring Perspective

READ: Hind's Feet... facing page & **James 1**

"And also if anyone competes as an athlete, he does not win the prize unless he competes according to the rules." —II Timothy 2:5

"And if your brother sins, go and reprove him in private; if he listens to you, you have won your brother." —Matthew 18:15

There are rules for everything, even walking in the Kingdom of God. Breaking the rules brings penalty. Keeping the rules brings blessing. Some are easy; some, such as Matthew 18:15, are very difficult. The author of James had become an effective "practitioner" of the word of God and wrote up some very "hard" word. He had perspective and extremely practical applications of the word of God to teach to others. He wanted Jesus' disciples to apply actions to love; not just talk about it.

This is like any profession or activity. Certain rules of application lead to success and to learning new skills to advance even further. "Learning how to learn" is a skill needed just to get a college degree; it would be foolish to undertake architecture, heart surgery or Himilayan mountaineering without similar learning and application methods.

The three companions now enjoy a period of new perspective and understanding that will apply to future learning. It's apparent from their perspective that they have far to go and are still in their "pilgrim life" on earth. Yet the plant of Kingdom Love has been manifested now in Grace and Glory's heart. She's got the basics and will prove eager for more.

God is eager that we apply in faith the things we learn. Keeping them "on the shelf" like old books does not produce the practical work of bearing fruit which James and many scriptures such as John 14:21 call us to do. This material is NOT theoretical nor is it experimental! It is practical and proven, but must be applied with faith in God to see any results.

QUESTIONS AND PRAYER: Have you ever noticed how God's grace in your life makes you eager to find more obedience and to experience even more of God's grace? How would you encourage your children or others to apply this?_____

_____

_____

valleys with their extraordinarily limited views. Sometimes, as she looked at the glorious panorama visible from these lowest slopes in the Kingdom of Love, she found herself blushing as she remembered some of the dogmatic statements which she and others had made in the depths of the valleys about the High Places and the ranges of Truth. They had been able to see so little and were unconscious of what lay beyond and above. If that had been the case while down in the valleys, how much more clearly, she now realized, that even up on those wonderful slopes she was only looking out on a tiny corner of the whole.

She never tired of looking from the glorious new viewpoint on the first slopes of the Kingdom of Love and seeing it all from a new perspective. What she could see and could take in almost intoxicated her with joy and thanksgiving, and some-times even with inexpressible relief. Things which she had thought dark and ter-rible and which had made her tremble as she looked up from the Valley because they had seemed so alien to any part of the Realm of Love were now seen to be but parts of a great and wonderful whole. They were so altered and modified that as she saw what they extended into, she wondered at having been so blind and stupid at having had such false ideas about them.

She began to understand quite clearly that truth cannot be understood from books alone or by any written words, but only by personal growth and develop-ment in understanding, and that things written even in the Book of Books can be astonishingly misunderstood while one still lives on the low levels of spiritual experience and on the wrong side of the grave on the mountains.

She perceived that no one who finds herself up on the slopes of the Kingdom of Love can possibly dogmatize about what is seen there, because it is only then that she comprehends how small a part of the glorious whole she sees. All she can do is to gasp with wonder, awe, and thanksgiving, and to long with all her heart to go higher and to see and understand more.

Principles of Perspective

READ: Hind's Feet... facing page & **Ephesians 3**

"...one thing I do know, that, whereas I was blind, now I see." —John 9:25

"The beginning of wisdom is: Acquire wisdom; and with
all your acquiring, get understanding." —Proverbs 4:7

Now that her eyes have been opened, Grace and Glory soaks up views and their lessons. She realizes her narrow perspective down in the Valley, when she thought she had such a grasp of things, was "blind and stupid" and that, really, the proportion of the whole she can see from her new perspective from here is no different. It is only a "tiny corner" of the whole. Realizing this now protects her from making the same presumptuous errors again. Her lesson can be applied to the future.

She also faces the paradox now of knowing things which are "beyond knowing". Consider the extraordinary claims of Ephesians, chapter 3. Is it a contradiction to speak, as Paul does, about "making known" things which are "unfathomable" (v.8–11), "comprehending" and "knowing" the love of Christ which "surpasses knowledge" (v.17–19) and being filled up to the "fullness of God" who is always exceedingly abundant "beyond all that we ask or think" (v.19–20)? Perhaps the point is to confidently know <u>the Person</u> who contains these things and therefore be able to trust Him for all things. Recall the profession of faith that says, "I know not what the future holds, but I know the One who holds the future."

Grace and Glory now "comprehends" how small a part of the glorious whole she sees. All she can do is to "gasp with wonder, awe and thanksgiving." So should we all. We are given much more than the heathen. We know the good news of Jesus Christ. Yet Romans, chapter 1, says, even for the heathen, "...since the creation of the world His invisible attributes, His eternal power and divine nature, have been clearly seen, being understood through what has been made, so that they are without excuse" (Rom.1:20).

QUESTIONS AND PRAYER: Can you think of any valid reasons we should not attain to Grace and Glory, given that we have the same information as Much-Afraid when starting her journey? If not, why not?_____

_____

_____

_____

Paradoxical as it may seem, as she gazed out on dazzling vistas, so glorious that she could not look at them steadily or grasp their magnificent sweep, she often thought that the prayer which best expressed her heart's desire was that of the blind man. "Lord, that I might receive my sight! Help me to open myself to more light. Help me to fuller understanding." Another thing which gave her continual joy was their unbroken communion with the King. Wherever he went she and Peace and Joy went too, springing behind him with a delight which at times was almost hilarious, for he was teaching and training them to use their hinds' feet. Grace and Glory quickly saw, however, that He always chose the way most carefully, and restrained His own amazing strength and power, taking only such springs and bounds as they could manage too.

So graciously did He adapt Himself to what was possible to their newly acquired capacity that they scarcely recognized in the exhilaration of leaping and skipping like hinds on the mountains, that had He really extended His powers, they would have been left behind completely.

For Grace and Glory—who had been lame and limping all her life—the ecstasy of leaping about in this way and of bounding from rock to rock on the High Places as easily as the mountain roes, was so rapturous that she could hardly bear to cease from it even for rests. The King seemed to find great delight in encouraging this, and led her on and on, taking long and longer leaps, until at last she would be quite breathless. Then as they sat side by side on some new crag to which He had led her, while she rested He would point out some of the vistas to be seen from the new viewpoint.

On one of these occasions after they had been up on the High Places for several days, she flung herself down on the lichen and moss-covered crag to which He had led her, and, laughing and breathless, said, "Even hinds' feet seem to need a rest now and then!"

The Desire of Grace

READ: Hind's Feet... facing page & **II Corinthians 5:1–9**

"so that you may walk in a manner worthy of the Lord, to please
Him in all respects, bearing fruit in every good work and increasing
in the knowledge of God:" —Colossians 1:10

"....'The LORD your God gives you rest, and
will give you this land.'" —Joshua 1:13

Grace and Glory meditates upon one of the remarkable aspects of her new name. It is a characteristic of the grace of God, given to those who humble themselves (Jas. 4:6–7, I Pet. 5:5–6), that it produces more eagerness to see and understand more of God. She longs for more obedience and revelation, praying for "sight", "more light", and "fuller understanding"; her heart's desire to live in a way pleasing to the Lord. In the midst of this desire she seems to gain even more insight.

She sees that the King, The Shepherd, always "restrained his own amazing strength and power" to levels which his followers can attain to, in keeping with the word of God not to exceed our capacities (I Cor.10:13). She then restates this proposition in a manner that makes it possible for disciples of Christ to recognize as a necessary characteristic of the mature Christian, as well. Christ, working through parents, teachers and pastors, will not extend his powers to leave the disciple behind completely.

Free from lameness for the first time in her life, Grace and Glory leaps around in her rapturous fellowship with the King, considering many aspects of her new "viewpoint" of truth and reality. Then she comes to some recognition of a need to "rest" even in her ecstasy. The extreme joy and glory of God is itself something that we cannot bear in the flesh for long.

Rest in glory is provided for those in Christ who obey His word, enter the land (though filled with giants that must be slain!), and trust Him for the results.

QUESTIONS AND PRAYER: Does "rest" in the midst of grace and glory sound contradictory to you? What earthly experiences have you had (such as "falling in love") in which you have experienced something similar?

_____

_____

_____

_____

"Grace and Glory," he answered, "do you think you understand now how I was able to make your feet like hinds' feet and to set you on these High Places?"

She drew closer to him and looked earnestly in his face and asked, "How were you able to do this, My Lord and King?"

"Think back over the journey you made," he replied, "and tell me what lessons you learned on the way."

She was silent for a while as she reviewed the whole journey, which had seemed so terribly long and in some places so cruelly difficult and even impossible. She thought of the altars which she had built along the way; of the time when she had stood with him at the trysting-place in the Valley, when he had called her to follow him to the heights. She remembered the walk to the foot of the mountains; the first meeting with Sorrow and Suffering and of learning to accept their help; she recalled the shock of what had seemed such a heartbreaking detour down into the desert, and of the things which she had seen there.

Then their journey along the shores of Loneliness; the empty cove which the sea had filled to the brim; and then the agony of disappointment and frustration experienced in the wilderness when the path once again had turned away from the High Places. She remembered crossing the great sea wall, walking through the woods and valleys until the rapturous moment when the path had turned back toward the mountains. Her thoughts turned to the Precipice of Injury, the Forests of Danger and Tribulation, the great storm during which they had sheltered in the hut. And then the mist—the endless mist, and the awful moment when the path suddenly led down into the Valley of Loss, and the nightmare abyss of horror into which she had looked when she had thought of turning back.

She recalled the descent down into the Valley of Loss and the peace she had found there before reascending to the heights in the aerial chairs, and of the days

Do You Understand?

READ: Hind's Feet... facing page & **John 8**

"Then those who feared the LORD spoke to one another, and the LORD gave attention and heard it, and a book of remembrance was written before Him for those who fear the LORD and who esteem His name." —Malachi 3:16

"But the Helper, the Holy Spirit, whom the Father will send in My name, He will teach you all things, and bring to your remembrance all that I said to you." —John 14:26

We come now to an exercise which may seem to the reader somewhat mundane; it is a review by Grace and Glory of her walk as Much-Afraid which led her to the High Places. But suppose this were your review of your own walk with the Shepherd to the places you are at now? Would that be of more interest? How often do you "rest" and do this?

One of the remarkable things God leaves with us through all of His work of redemption and regeneration is our memories. Why is this? Have you ever thought it might be superior to have removed from your memory some of your ugliest failures and sins? God does indeed have a wonderful reason for leaving us with our ugly memories!

Grace and Glory first silently recollects her journey, recalling events and emotions; lessons and decisions. Using strong words but true, she recalls *"agony of disappointment and frustration"*, and the many surprises along the way. She is actually reviewing the entire allegory we have just read and is being tested regarding her understanding of the parables of her journey. Has she grasped it all? Would you imagine she comprehends and understands each of its lessons?

We recall that the trusting-place in the Valley was where she first met the Shepherd and committed to follow Him. This is not merely a story of a one-time only salvation event, as some sadly treat their salvation. It is the story of one who after meeting Him, then becomes a follower and disciple of Jesus Christ, renewing their journey together over and over again.

QUESTIONS AND PRAYER: When you compare your own journey with Grace and Glory's, does it seem you are progressing toward the High Places? Is what it "seems" important? Or is it not? Is it a journey at all? Write down some of its allegorical lessons for you?_____

_____

_____

_____

spent in that place where she had been prepared for burial. Then that last agonizing ascent, and the cave where they sheltered from the floods and where she had been tempted to cast away the promises. Then the spring called Marah, and finally the mist-shrouded grave up among the peaks where she had been bound to the altar. How little she had imagined, when first she set out on that strange journey, what lay ahead of her and the things which she would be called upon to pass through. So for a long time she sat silent—remembering, wondering and thankful.

At last she put her hand on his and said softly, "My Lord, I will tell you what I learned."

"Tell me," he answered gently.

"First," said she, "I learned that I must accept with joy all that you allowed to happen to me on the way and everything to which the path led me! That I was never to try to evade it but to accept it and lay down my own will on the altar and say, 'Behold me, I am thy little handmaiden Acceptance-with-Joy.'"

He nodded without speaking, and she went on, "Then I learned that I must bear all that others were allowed to do against me and to forgive with no trace of bitterness and to say to thee, 'Behold me—I am thy little handmaiden Bearing-with-Love,' that I may receive power to bring good out of this evil."

Again he nodded, and she smiled still more sweetly and happily.

"The third thing that I learned was that you, my Lord, never regarded me as I actually was, lame and weak and crooked and cowardly. You saw me as I would be when you had done what you promised and had brought me to the High Places, when it could be truly said, 'There is none that walks with such a queenly ease, nor with such grace, as she.' You always treated me with the same love and graciousness as though I were a queen already and not wretched little Much-Afraid."

Propitiation Report

READ: Hind's Feet... facing page & 1 John 1:1–2:2

"Therefore He had to be made like His brethren in all things, that He might become a merciful and faithful high priest in things pertaining to God, to make propitiation for the sins of the people." —Hebrews 2:17

"And the disciples came and said to Him, "Why do You speak to them in parables? And He answered and said to them, "To you it has been granted to know the mysteries of the kingdom of heaven, but to them it has not been granted."
—Matthew 13:10–11

Propitiation is often treated as having no distinction in meaning from *expiation*. But there is a big difference. *Expiation* means to "make amends, satisfaction or atonement" to remove wrongdoing. But *propitiation* means to "make favorable, auspicious or advantageous", not by merely removing something's effects, but by reversing its effects! God's power to work "all things for good", even that "intended for evil", is a mark of greatness going far beyond even His ability to remove sin (Gen.50:20, Rom.8:28).

Grace and Glory continues remembering her journey to the High Places. "How little" she had imagined, of what lay ahead and "the things which she would be called upon to pass through." After a "long time" in silent, thankful thought, she speaks the things she has learned; a testimony of the King's power to propitiate her difficult experiences. Thank God she has not lost her memory!

In the spirit of Mary (Luke 1:38), she describes having learned "acceptance with joy" of all the Shepherd allowed to come upon her. Next she relates the lesson of propitiating power itself; forgiving with no trace of bitterness. *This is key to receiving power to bring good out of evil (Rom.12:21)*. Third, recalling His beautiful words of her and to her, she grasps that she has always been treated as a royal queen by her transforming King. The words of the King have prevailed in the princess (Song of Solomon 6 & 7).

QUESTIONS AND PRAYER: Do you treat others with a sense of their royalty? (See 1 Pet. 3:7) Is this who they actually are? How does this also relate to your own faith and who you are?_____

_____

_____

_____

Then she looked up into his face and for a little time could say no more, but at last she added, "My Lord, I cannot tell you how greatly I want to regard others in the same way."

A very lovely smile broke out on his face at that, but he still said nothing, only nodded for the third time and waited for her to continue.

"The fourth thing," said she with a radiant face, "was really the first I learned up here. Every circumstance in life, no matter how crooked and distorted and ugly it appears to be, if it is reacted to in love and forgiveness and obedience to your will can be transformed.

"Therefore I begin to think, my Lord, you purposely allow us to be brought into contact with the bad and evil things that you want changed. Perhaps that is the very reason why we are here in this world, where sin and sorrow and suffering and evil abound, so that we may let you teach us so to react to them, that out of them we can create lovely qualities to live forever. That is the only really satisfactory way of dealing with evil, not simply binding it so that it cannot work harm, but whenever possible overcoming it with good."

At last he spoke, "You have learned well, Grace and Glory. Now I will add one thing more. It was these lessons which you have learned which enabled me to change you from limping, crippled Much-Afraid into Grace and Glory with the hinds' feet. Now you are able to follow me wherever I go, so that we need never be parted again."

"So remember this; as long as you are willing to be Acceptance-with-Joy and Bearing-in-Love, you can never again become crippled and you will be able to go down into the Valley of the world to work with me there, for that is where the evil and sorrowful and ugly things are which need to be overcome."

"Accept and bear and obey the Law of Love, and nothing will be able to cripple your hinds' feet or to separate you from me. This is the secret of the High Places, Grace and Glory, it is the lovely and perfect law of the whole universe. It is this

Reproduction of Seed

READ: Hind's Feet... facing page & **Galatians** 3:1–19

"And I will put enmity between you and the woman, and
between your seed and her seed; he shall bruise you on the head,
and you shall bruise him on the heel." —Genesis 3:15

"Truly, truly, I say to you, unless a grain of wheat falls
into the earth and dies, it remains by itself alone; but if
it dies, it bears much fruit." —John 12:24

Beginning with creation and God's stated desire to reproduce Himself (Gen. 1:26), we see God's portrait of "seed" as the process by which all reproduction is accomplished. The first name given the Christ is "Seed". Promises given Abraham are all for the "seed". God is reproducing the likeness of Christ in all who receive His "Seed". Our hearts are the wombs of reproduction.

We see now in Grace and Glory evidence that the likeness of Christ is manifesting itself through her. "My Lord," she says, "I cannot tell you how greatly I want to regard others in the same way"; i.e., the same royal way she has been treated by the Shepherd King; as though she had had no defects. This is her spirit speaking; something else has been transformed.

Then to a fourth lesson, another portrait of propitiation: she sees that "every circumstance in life", no matter how ugly, "can be transformed" if it is reacted to in love, forgiveness and obedience to God's will. Perhaps we are here as part of God's propitiating process to "be brought into contact with the bad and evil things" that God wants changed. She grasps that evil is something not merely to be bound, but "whenever possible" to be overcome by good (Rom. 12:21).

The King renews a conditional covenant. Her walk with Him depends upon her will to maintain these lessons in her life. They are summarized as the "Law of Love", perhaps related to the "perfect law" and the "royal law" referred to by James (Jas. 1:25, 2:8). Discipleship requires continued obedience to avoid crippling problems.

QUESTIONS AND PRAYER: What is your opinion whether one can "lose" or "break" discipleship and return to crippling defects previously removed by Christ? How about new "defects" appearing?_____

_____

In your opinion, does this question relate to salvation or to the fruit of salvation? Why?_____

that makes the radiant joy of the Heavenly Places." Then he rose to his feet, drew her up beside him, and said, "Now use your hinds' feet again, for I am going to lead you to another part of the mountain."

Off he went, "leaping on the mountains and skipping on the hills," with Grace and Glory following close behind and the beautiful figures of Peace and Joy springing at her side. As they went she sang this song:

Set me as a seal upon thine heart
Thou Love more strong than death
That I may feel through every part
Thy burning, fiery breath.
And then like wax held in the flame,
May take the imprint of thy Name.

Set me a seal upon thine arm,
Thou Love that burst the grave,
Thy coals of fire can never harm,
But only purge and save.
Thou jealous Love, thou burning Flame,
Oh, burn out all unlike thy Name.

The floods can never drown thy Love,
Nor weaken thy desire,
The rains may deluge from above
But never quench thy fire.
Make soft my heart in thy strong flame,
To take the imprint of thy Name.

(Cant. 8:6)

The Imprint of Thy Name

READ: Hind's Feet... facing page & **Lamentations 1**

"The heart is more deceitful than all else and is desperately
sick; who can understand it? —Jeremiah 17:9

"How lovely on the mountains are the feet of him who brings good
news, who announces peace and brings good news of happiness, who
announces salvation and says to Zion, "Your God reigns!" —Isaiah 52:7

How far we have fallen! What little remains among men to minister the true relationship of bride and bridegroom. True, there is a girl's vision of being imprinted by a faithful bridegroom's name and character. A brave and trustworthy warrior in "shining armor". These precepts once founded a girl's taking of her husband's name, the joyful support and submission of the girl to her bridegroom and in raising up seed to bear his name. But these visions are now shattered for most teen-age girls long before they marry. They are viciously destroyed through sexual exploitation. We are in ruins.

Men die for lack of knowledge (Isa.5:13, Hos.4:6, Prov.29:18). They pour out their seed on the ground, "streams of water in the street" (Prov.5:16); impotent to raise up Godly seed (Mal. 2:15). They deal treacherously with girls and the wives of their youth. Harlotry reigns (Hos.4:14). Our virgins and young men are dead in the streets, before ever seeing their wedding bed. Why would a bride today desire the imprint of a man?

Sexual idolatry, abortion, child molestation and desertion fill our land with abomination. Women learn they will not find fulfillment under men and therefore work to create their own. Unwed mothers and cries of the unborn testify to our loss of manhood. Women's lib rages. The word of Isaiah is fulfilled; "children and women will rule over us" (Isa.3:1–12).

But there is a Bridegroom, the Beautiful One, and a vision for His imprint. Hear a girl's prayer. His Name is that which any woman would desire. Men everywhere should bear His aroma.

QUESTIONS AND PRAYER: How do you feel about being imprinted by the Name of Jesus?_____

_____

Would you pray the poem of the preceding page? If so, would you also please sign and date it? _____

CHAPTER 20

Return to the Valley

The place to which the King of Love now brought them was a most beautiful valley among the peaks of the High Places. The whole of this sheltered spot was laid out in quiet gardens and orchards and vineyards. Here grew flowers of rarest beauty and lilies of every description. Here, too, were trees of spices and of many kinds of fruits, and nut trees, almonds and walnuts, and many other varieties which Grace and Glory had never seen before. Here the King's gardeners were always busy, pruning the trees, tending the plants and the vines, and preparing beds for new seedlings and tender shoots.

These the King Himself transplanted from uncongenial soil and conditions in the valleys below so that they might grow to perfection and bloom in that valley high above, ready to be planted in other parts of the Kingdom of Love, to beautify and adorn it wherever the King saw fit. They spent several delightful days watching the gardeners as they worked under the gracious supervision of the King Himself and accompanying Him as He walked in the vineyards, teaching and advising those who tended the vines.

One day, however, Grace and Glory with her two attendants walked to the end of the valley and found themselves on the very edge of the High Places, from which they could look right down into the Lower Places far below. As they stood there they saw a long, green valley between two chains of mountains through which a river wound like a ribbon of light. Here and there were patches of brown and red which seemed to be villages and dwelling places, surrounded with trees and gardens.

Gardens and Vineyards of the King

READ: Hind's Feet... facing page & **Matthew 21:33–44**

"Like an apple tree among the trees of the forest, so is my beloved among the young men. In his shade I took great delight and sat down, and his fruit was sweet to my taste." —Song of Solomon 2:3

"And they were utterly astonished, saying, "He has done all things well; He makes even the deaf to hear, and the dumb to speak." —Mark 7:37

In an almost anti-climactic sense author Hurnard gives us yet another picture of Christ administering His Kingdom through His servants, raising up many "tender shoots" in the likeness of Him after whom we are being conformed (Isaiah 53:2, Rom.8:29). The imagery is that of Song of Solomon, in which gardens, orchards, lilies, vineyards, flowers, etc. describe profusion of life.

"Pruning" appears graphically in the terms of which Jesus spoke to His disciples; given to those branches which bear fruit in order that they will bear more fruit (Jn.15:1–5). Then a statement is made that all these "plants, vines, new seedlings and tender shoots" have been transplanted by the King Himself from "uncongenial soil and conditions in the valleys below so that they might grow to perfection." What does this portray?

Scripture is lavish in its clarity that growth of people is closely related to their being transplanted, the most outstanding growth being in those for whom the transplanting is most traumatic. Noah and Abraham were "transplants". Jacob, Joseph, Moses, Samuel, David and Daniel were all "transplants". In fact, the most powerful lives in the Bible are usually associated with those removed from their parents and raised by others. Something about adoption brings special promise in enabling one to "grow to perfection and bloom in that valley high above".

Over all is the Chief Gardener, in the gracious splendor of a King who does all things well.

QUESTIONS AND PRAYER: What imagery do you see in the "King who does all things well"?_____

_____

Suppose the portrait were to be applied in your vocational area? Your steward-ship area(s)? What do you imagine "all things" to mean?_____

_____

All of a sudden, Grace and Glory gave a queer little gasp, for she recognized the place. They were looking down into the Valley of Humiliation itself, the place where she had lived in misery for so long and from which the Shepherd had called her to the High Places.

Without a word she sat down on the grassy slope, and as she looked a multitude of thoughts filled her mind. Down there was the little white cottage where she had lived, and the pastures where the shepherds tended the King's flocks. There were the sheepfolds, and the stream where the flocks went to drink and where she had met the Shepherd for the first time. In that valley were all her fellow workers and the friends among whom she had lived and with whom she had enjoyed such happy fellowship.

Others she had known were there, too. Away on the outskirts of the village was the cottage where her Aunt Dismal Forebodings lived and where she had spent her miserable childhood with her cousins Gloomy and Spiteful and Craven Fear. As she thought of them and their wretched existence a pang of compassion and pain shot through her heart.

Poor Aunt Dismal, trying to hide the fact that her heart was broken by the unhappy marriages which her two daughters had made, and embittered by the shameful doings of her darling son. She saw the dwellings of her other relatives; the Manor House, where decrepit old Lord Fearing lived, tortured by his failing powers and his dread of approaching death. There was the house where Pride lived, and near it the homes of Bitterness and Resentment, and under those dark trees lived miserable Self-Pity. She recognized the dwelling places of those who had so harassed her on her journey to the High Places, and round about were the homes of other inhabitants of the Valley, people who hated or despised or rejected the Shepherd.

Compassion for Souls

READ: Hind's Feet... facing page & **Psalm 103**

"For the Lord your God is gracious and compassionate, and will not turn His face away from you if you return to Him." —II Chronicles 30:9

"And when He came out, He saw a great multitude and felt compassion for them and healed their sick." —Matthew 14:14

A transformed creature with "new eyes" looks down upon the valley of her origins. Grace and Glory recognizes the Valley of Humiliation and begins viewing and meditating. Starting with good memories of her home and pastures, she recalls fellow workers and friends and the "happy fellowship they had enjoyed together. Then her thoughts progress.

In terms quite unlike any she had ever thought before about her relatives, she contemplates their unhappy lives and in a sudden pang of compassion she grieves over their "wretched existence". The causes of their "misery" come easily to her understanding. Unhappy marriages, ruined dreams, shame, bitterness, failing powers and fear of approaching death quickly equip her to be supportive and sympathetic. She recognizes those who "hated or despised or rejected the Shepherd."

She is now "seeing" the feelings and problems of those God gave her as "relatives". Instead of observing them as spirits that tormented her, she now views them as living souls being tormented by the same spirits. She feels their pain.

A servant cannot effectively serve his master unless he is given the eyes of his master. He must be able to "see" his vision and his problems in order to support and harmonize with his efforts. That is also why an attitude of service (to aid success of the one being served) is an *absolute prerequisite* in order to "gain the eyes" of those we would assist in relieving misery in their lives. That is why, too, we must be given the eyes of our Shepherd in order to serve Him.

QUESTIONS AND PRAYER: Do you see your employer or supervisor as one to whom you've been sent to help be successful?_____

_____

Do you view your primary role as that of a servant? _____
How do you measure your success at your servant's job?_____

_____

_____

As Grace and Glory sat looking down into the Valley the tears welled into her eyes and her heart throbbed with pain, two sensations which she had completely forgotten up there on the High Places.

Suddenly she discovered that her feelings toward her relatives and those who lived down there in the Valley had undergone a complete change, and she saw them in a new light. She had thought of them only has horrible enemies, but now she realized that they were just miserable beings such as she had been herself. They were indwelt and tormented by their different besetting sins and ugly natures, just as she had been by her fears. They were wretched slaves to the natures which gave them their names, and the more horrible the qualities which characterized them, the more misery they endured, and the more we should show them compassion.

She could scarcely bear the thought, yet for so many years she had not only feared but also condemned them, had actually "disdained their misery," telling herself it was their own fault. Yes, she, detestable, fear-enslaved Much-Afraid had actually dared to disdain them for the things which made them so wretched and ugly when she herself was equally wretched and enslaved. Instead of a fellow feeling of compassion and passionate desire that they might be delivered and transformed from the pride and resentment and bitterness which made them what they were, she had just detested and despised them.

When she thought of that she turned to Joy and Peace, who were sitting beside her, and cried out desperately, "Can nothing be done for them down there in the Valley? Must my Aunt Dismal be left unhelped, and poor Spiteful and Gloomy too, and those cousins who went so far with us on the way to the High Places, trying to turn us back! If the Shepherd could deliver me, Grace and Glory, from all my fears and sins, couldn't He deliver them also from the things which torment them?"

New Light on Slavery

READ: Hind's Feet... facing page & **Isaiah 61**

"And Jesus answered and said to them, 'Go and report to John the things which you hear and see: the Blind receive sight and the lame walk, the lepers are cleansed and the deaf hear, and the dead are raised up and the poor have the gospel preached to them. And blessed is he who keeps from stumbling over me." —Matthew 11:4–6

With the compassion stirred up in Grace and Glory, comes new, sudden revelation. She sees everything regarding her relatives in a new light. They are "wretched slaves". She was no different herself before the Shepherd rescued her. The clarity of what she sees enables her to separate her relatives, themselves, from the sins that enslave them. Her characterizations are clear and scriptural.

The problem is with the "different besetting sins and ugly natures" which "indwell and torment" them. It is clear reference to separate entities and personalities who war against their souls (Jas. 4:1, I Pet. 2:11). She "sees" that they can be separated from her relatives even as her besetting "fears and sins" were separated from her. By the nature of salvation the causes of sin can be separated from us as well as the death penalty for obedience to sin (Rom.6:16).

Of course, now she also sees how she had feared and condemned her relatives, beset by the same Satanic spirits. They caused her to "detest" and despise" her relatives. Now she has been delivered from these detesting and despising demons that warred against her and her relatives and is able to sympathize with their misery. Wow! O Lord, may we also please have such eyes to discern between your precious ones given to our care and the enemies that war against them!

Now, invigorated by compassion and vision, Grace and Glory begins to cast about for some means of helping her relatives. If the Shepherd could deliver her, surely he can do the same for them!

QUESTIONS AND PRAYER: Do compassion and vision stir you to seek the Lord for wisdom in helping others (James 1:5)? What other things motivate your searches for wisdom? _____

_____
_____
_____
_____

"Yes," said Joy (who had been Sorrow). "If He can turn Sorrow into Joy, Suffering into Peace, and Much-Afraid into Grace and Glory, how can we doubt that He could change Pride and Bitterness and Resentment and Self-Pity too, if they would just yield to Him and follow Him? And your Aunt Dismal could be changed into Praise and Thanksgiving, and poor Gloomy and Spiteful also. We cannot doubt that it could be done that they could be completely delivered from all the things which torment them."

"But," cried Grace and Glory, "how can they be persuaded to follow the Shepherd? At present they hate Him and won't go near Him."

Then Peace (who before had been Suffering) said quietly, "I have noticed that when people are brought into sorrow and suffering, or loss, or humiliation, or grief, or into some place of great need, they sometimes become ready to know the Shepherd and to seek His help. We know, for example, that your Aunt Dismal is desperately unhappy over the behavior of poor Craven Fear, and it may be that she would be ready now to turn to the Shepherd. Then poor Gloomy and Spiteful are so wretched that though they felt no need of the Shepherd before, it is very possible that now is the time to try to persuade them to seek His help."

"Yes!" exclaimed Grace and Glory, "I am sure you are right. Oh, if only we could go to them! If only there were some way of helping them to find what we have found."

At that very moment, close at hand, sounded the voice of the King. He came and sat down beside them, looked with them down the Valley so far below, and said gently to Grace and Glory, "Thou that dwellest in the gardens, the companions hearken to thy voice; cause Me to hear it" (Cant. 8:13).

Grace and Glory turned to Him and laid her hand upon His arm. "My Lord," she said, "we are talking about the people who live down there in the Valley of Humiliation. They are my relatives, you know, all of them. They are so wretched

Strategy for Freedom

READ: Hind's Feet... facing page & **Galatians 4:21–31**

"And He called the twelve together and gave them power and authority over all the demons, and to heal diseases. And He sent them out to proclaim the kingdom of God, and to perform healing." —Luke 9:1–2

"If therefore the Son shall make you free,
you shall be free indeed." —John 8:36

How can a slave set another free? It is impossible (Ps. 49:7–9). And how can one plant seed that he does not have? In eastern Europe in 1945 an army appearing much like those of the western allies liberated Nazi occupied nations and helped bring WW II to a close. But they did not have the seed of liberty to plant. Their seed was the spirit of slavery and that was what they reproduced; over 45 years of communist slavery for eastern Europe. Western Europe reaped the opposite, not because the armed forces were different, but because the spirits they served were different.

Now a freed woman, Grace and Glory thinks and speaks freedom. The King has set her free. Freedom is the mark of a secure and fearless woman, able "to do what is right without being frightened by any fear" (I Pet. 3:6). She will sow and reproduce this naturally, by her spirit; the Seed of the Savior in those she has been given to care for in His name.

Conversing with Joy and Peace, Grace and Glory grasps the strategy of sowing freedom. The soil is prepared by sorrow, suffering, loss, humiliation, grief, or some great need. It makes those enslaved ready to turn to the Shepherd, the lowly One who leads lowly sheep to green pastures, still water, peace and rest. No sooner does this result in utterance of desire to "help" the tormented ones, than the Shepherd appears. Note the touch of intimacy of the woman's hand upon His arm. This is a picture of the free woman's spirit for her Bridegroom.

QUESTIONS AND PRAYER: Are you familiar with the story of how Sarah conceived Isaac by Abraham? What do you think was the exact point at which she was convinced that God loved her, was set free and empowered to reproduce the "son of the free woman"?_____

_____
_____
_____

and miserable. What can we do for them, my Lord? They don't know anything about the joy of the High Places and the Kingdom of Love. There is my poor Aunt Dismal Forebodings. I lived with her for a long time, and know that she is utterly wretched."

"I know her," said the King quietly, "she is a most unhappy woman."

"And her daughter Gloomy," went on Grace and Glory, looking at him entreatingly as she spoke. "She married Coward, the son of old Lord Fearing, very rich, but much older than herself and a miserably unhappy and selfish creature. I believe she has not known a moment's peace since. There was talk in the Valley before I came away, that he was likely to desert her."

"He has done so," answered the King quietly, "and she has returned to her mother in the cottage, a miserable and disillusioned woman with a broken heart."

"And her sister Spiteful. Poor, poor soul, with her sharp tongue which makes so many enemies and deprives her of friends. She married Timid-Skulking, and they are desperately poor, and have to live in one little rented room in the house of my cousin Bitterness and his wife. I cannot bear to think of their wretched condition while I live up here in the Kingdom of Love."

"They are wretched indeed," said the King, even more gently and compassionately than before. "They have just lost the little daughter who poor Spiteful had hoped would be such a comfort to them in their dreary circumstances."

"And then," continued Grace and Glory with just a hint of hesitation in her voice, "there is their brother Craven Fear." She did not look at the King as she spoke, but paused a moment, then went on hurriedly. "He is the most unhappy member of the whole family. He has broken his mother's heart; neither of his sisters will speak to him any more, and he goes skulking about the Valley hated by everyone."

Woman's Eye-View

READ: Hind's Feet... facing page & **Genesis 18:1–15**

"And Abraham said to God, 'Oh that Ishmael might live before Thee!" But
God said, 'No, but Sarah your wife shall bear you a son, and you shall
call his name Isaac; and I will establish My covenant with him for an everlasting
covenant for his descendants after him." —Genesis 17:18–19

"But My covenant I will establish with Isaac, whom Sarah will bear
to you at this season next year." —Genesis 17: 21

"The mouth speaks out of that which fills the heart" (Matt. 12:34). Hannah Hurnard makes no pretense of understanding a man's heart or his torments. In her list of concerns, she speaks only of things vital to women, upon which their life fulfillment and happiness depend. Hear what Grace and Glory grieves over:

1. A girl married to a rich, older man, facing desertion (with money but not love).
2. A disillusioned (vision destroyed) woman with a broken heart.
3. A woman who wounds others.
4. A woman with no life-supporting relationships.
5. A woman with a skulking husband who cannot represent her.
6. Desperate economic hardship.
7. A woman who has lost a daughter, her only comfort.
8. A mother broken-hearted over a son (See Prov.29:15).
9. Two sisters who hate their bully and coward brother.

This is an entire list of women!!! No broken and unhappy men, even though "basket case" men are also certain to be involved here. The first man's torment with a fearful, gloomy wife (who married for money and does not love him) is not found; not perceived with compassion even by this "free" woman. But our purpose is not to evoke sympathy for men nor to scold Hannah Hurnard. It is rather to "see" through the eyes of our gifted female author her perspective on life; the hearts of unhappy women.

God's power to bring His personal love to "dead" women having no hope is displayed in His story of Sarah. Her fearful husband gave her twice to other men and hadn't faith to believe the promise of Isaac. Then came the man who knew Sarah secretly laughed and *knew her entire mind*, though she was inside the tent and out of his sight! This was not a natural man. *He had to be from God!* Therefore his promise was true! Her faith and her womb came to life!

QUESTIONS AND PRAYER: What are your ideas of the essential things a woman needs to find happiness?_____

_____

"I know him," replied the King gravely, but with just a hint of a smile. "I know him well. You do not exaggerate when you speak of his wretchedness. I have had to interfere and chastise him many times to try and correct his bullying propensities. But 'though I have chastened him sore I have not given him over unto death.'"

"No, no!" cried Grace and Glory imploringly, "don't ever do that, my Lord! Oh, I beg You, find some way to rescue and deliver him from himself, as You delivered me."

He made no answer for a little while, only looked at her very kindly and with a look of great contentment and happiness on His face. At last He spoke. "I am more than willing to do what you suggest," said He. "But, Grace and Glory, these unhappy souls we are speaking about will not allow Me into their homes, nor even permit Me to speak to them. I need a voice to speak for Me, to persuade them to let Me help them."

"I see what you mean," she cried joyfully. "We will go down with You and speak to them and show what You have done for us and what You are willing and able to do for them."

"Do you think they will listen to you?" He asked, smiling at her very gently as He spoke.

"No, I don't think it's at all likely—at least, not at first," she answered. "I was not at all the sort of person to make them want to listen to me. I did not behave at all lovingly to them, but You will tell me what to say. You will teach me and I will say it for You.

"O my Lord, let us make haste, and go down there. When they see what You have done for me, when they see Peace and Joy, I do think in the end they will want You to help them too. It is because they have lied to themselves about You and have persuaded themselves that You cannot do them good that they resist You and turn from Your help, but we will plead with them. Especially now, my Lord, when they are so unhappy and so despised by others. Their very misery and loneliness

Gap-Stander

READ: Hind's Feet... facing page & Exodus 32:1–14

"But now, if Thou wilt, forgive their sin—and if not, please blot me
out from Thy book which Thou hast written." —Exodus 32:32

"And I searched for a man among them who should build up the wall
and stand in the gap before Me for the land, that I should not destroy it; but
I found no one. Thus I have poured out My indignation on them; I have consumed
them with the fire of My wrath; their way I have brought upon their heads,
declares the Lord God." —Ezekiel 22:30–31

Jesus leaves us no room for compromise in confronting the bitter fruit of betrayal, persecution and injustice. He takes us far beyond forgiveness (Matt. 6:14–15) to the extreme other side. Mere forgiveness with "slack in the reins" neutrality is not adequate. We must be "in harness", pulling on the traces on behalf of those who wrong us. We must intercede with God on their behalf. "But I say to you, love your enemies, and pray for those who persecute you in order that you may be sons of your Father in heaven" (Matt. 5:44–45).

Obedience to this is easy to measure. If we cannot take the position of Moses on behalf of Israel, or of Grace and Glory on behalf of Craven Fear, or bake some cookies for someone who has injured us, we fall short. We are not free. We are captive by demonic spirits of our flesh warring against our souls. The Savior's work is not yet accomplished.

But Grace and Glory is free. She intercedes with the King for the man brutalized by spirits of torment. She is way beyond "not keeping an account of wrong suffered" (I Cor.13:5). She wants her enemy blessed; set free. Other things follow naturally.

"Then I heard the voice of the Lord, saying, 'Whom shall I send, and who will go for Us" (Isaiah 6:8)? Grace and Glory gives Isaiah's response, "Here am I. Send me."

QUESTIONS AND PRAYER: What are the two additional responses of Grace and Glory to her task? How should this apply to your actions for forgiving and intercession for those who have injured you?_____

_____

_____

[Please review her entrustment of her mouth to the King and also her urge to testify on His behalf (Ps. 30:1, 71:15–24, Luke 1:49)].

and sorrow will make them more willing to listen to news of Your grace and of Your desire to help them."

"True," He agreed, "that is just what I think. This is indeed a specially favorable time for us to go down and try to help them."

He rose to His feet as He spoke. She sprang up too, and all four stood joyful and radiant on the edge of the High Places, ready to go leaping down to the Valley again. Then Grace and Glory saw that the great waterfall quite close at hand was leaping down to the Valley too, with the tumultuous, joyful noise of many waters, singing as they poured themselves down over the rock lip:

> *From the heights we leap and flow*
> *To the valleys down below,*
> *Sweetest urge and sweetest will,*
> *To go lower, lower still.*

Suddenly she understood. She was beholding a wondrous and glorious truth; "a great multitude whom no man could number" brought like herself by the King to the Kingdom of Love and to the High Places so that they could now pour out their lives in gladdest abandonment, leaping down with Him to the sorrowful, desolate places below, to share with others the life which they had received. She herself was only one drop among that glad, exultant throng of Self-givers, the followers of the King of Love, united with Him and with one another, each one equally blessed and beloved as herself. "For He loves each one of us," she said to herself, "as though there were only one to love."

The thought of being made one with the great fall of many waters filled her heart with ecstasy and with a rapturous joy beyond power to express. She, too, at last, was to go down with them, pouring herself forth in Love's abandonment of Self-giving. "He brought me to the heights just for this," she whispered to herself, and then looked at Him and nodded.

Leap Downward

READ: Hind's Feet... facing page & **Philippians 3**

"Make my joy complete by being of the same mind, maintaining the same love, united in spirit, intent on one purpose. Do nothing from selfishness or empty conceit, but with humility of mind let each of you regard one another as more important than himself." —Philippians 2:2–3

"Go into the world and preach the gospel to all creation." —Mark 16:15

The crippled cannot leap downward. Those with casts, crutches or arthritis step upward more easily than downward. Grace and Glory has discovered her long journey upward was to enable her to leap downward! Like water whose secret she unraveled over the course of her journey, she has become like living water. By the "washing of water with the word" (Eph.5:26), she has become softened, fully conformed clay in the Master's hand.

Joined with a "multitude no man could number" (Rev. 7:9), like droplets "dressed in white", she reflects the dazzling light of our Savior. We know that all were previously transformed through death—individual, unique, personal death out of love for Christ (Rev. 6:9–11).

Married men, is your job, your play, your labor for yourself? No! It is a means to an end, on behalf of your wife (I Cor.7:33, Eph.5:25–29) and children. They need security and a man to demonstrate God's love and character. As God identified Himself as a Shield to Abraham (Gen. 15:1), a husband must be a shield for his wife. Away with fear, poverty and ruination! And for the unmarried? Boaz remained celibate while he gave physical, economic and emotional protection to Ruth (Ruth 2–4).

God also identified Himself to Abraham as an all-sufficient, more-than-enough breast (Gen. 17:1). This is the great function of women; as healers and nurturers. But they must have a breastplate. The man takes the risks, takes the blows and pays the ransom! Godly men are protectors, not attackers. The gospel starts with those closest to us. It is a great leap downward!

QUESTIONS AND PRAYER: How may men leap downward in service to Christ on behalf of their families? What must be broken and discarded? Would you take this to God with some serious fasting, prayer and self-scrutiny?_____

_____

Women, how may you work to enhance and affirm the men responsible to protect and lead you?_____

At that He began leaping and springing down the mountainside before them, bounding from rock to rock, always choosing, however, leaps which were within their power to follow, and sure footholds for less experienced feet. Behind Him went Grace and Glory, with Joy and Peace beside her, leaping down, just as the waters leaped and sang beside them. They mingled their voices with the joyful music of the many waters singing their own individual song:

> *Make haste, Beloved, be thou like an hart*
> *On mountains spicy sweet;*
> *And I, on those High Places where thou art,*
> *Will follow on hinds' feet;*
> *As close behind the hart, there leaps the roe,*
> *So where thou goest, I will surely go.*

That, as perhaps you know, is the last verse of the Song of Songs, which is Solomon's. But for Grace and Glory it was the beginning of a new song altogether.

A New Song

READ: Hind's Feet... facing page & **Philippians 2:5–11**

"So, then, my beloved, just as you have always obeyed, not as in my presence only, but now much more in my absence, work out your salvation with fear and trembling." —Philippians 2:12

"If you ask Me anything in My name, I will do it." —John 14:14

Grace and Glory starts a new journey, singing a new song. She has "put feet" to the word of God. She is no longer immobilized by fear and selfishness. Her initial obedience toward discipleship has now grown mature. Through growing trust and the consistent love of the Shepherd, Grace and Glory has become a radiant Bride, convinced of her Bridegroom's love and now set free, herself, to love others.

She goes with others having the same faith, making the same journey and outreach. One simply cannot remain alone. "If one can overpower him who is alone, two can resist him. A cord of three strands is not quickly torn apart" (Eccl.5:12). We see God's laws of self-protection and power in company for believers. (Matt.18:16, Lev.26:8, Deut.32:30).

Her security and freedom is based on the character of her Bridegroom; "the imprint of His name". Grace and Glory's success is already assured, predetermined by God's Word in Her (John 14:14). His work prepared beforehand in Grace and Glory now extends to others (Ephesians 2:10.)

QUESTIONS AND PRAYER: Consider how many women can't respond to God because they've never known Godly love through a father or husband. How many damaged wives, daughters and girl friends must there be who are "Much-Afraid" and seeking a man of character who would lay their life down for them? How many more innocent children and unborn will be sacrificed until the day a Godly man arrives? How will God deliver them without faithful men? Will He have to do it with you or without you? Write out your thoughts and prayers as best you can._____

_____

_____

_____

_____

_____

To order additional copies of

Have your credit card ready and call:

1-877-421-READ (7323)

or please visit our web site at
www.pleasantword.com

Also available at: www.amazon.com

BOOKS BY KARL DUFF

- *Restoration of Men (God's Rescue of Women and Children):* God provides healing, restoration, and protective accountability for men who find themselves ineffectual as husbands and fathers.
- *Lord and Scoutmaster:* The author relates humorous as well as educational true life adventures he had as a Scout and then as a Scoutmaster.
- *Leader's Guide for High Adventure:* This is a booklet of practical tips for leading Scouts or youth groups on extended backpacking or canoeing trips, based upon three decades of experience.
- *Still the Master of the Sea:* With signs and wonders God intervened in a modern hydrofoil warship program and changed a prideful naval officer. A remarkable testimony of miracles.
- *Teens, Sex, and Happiness:* God's design of male-female relationships is an important part of His plan for our lives. Youth must obey God's plan to find happiness and fulfillment. Includes discussion questions.

To order additional books, contact the author at:

Karl Duff
6112 Wynn Jones Road East
Port Orchard, WA 98366
206.871.1265

Place this order form in an envelope along with your check or money order.

QUANTITY	DESCRIPTION	UNIT PRICE	TOTAL PRICE
	Restoration of Marriage	$13.95	
	Restoration of Men	$9.95	
	Lord and Scoutmaster	$8.95	
	Leader's Guide for High Adventure	$3.00	
	Still the Master of the Sea	$10.95	
	Teens, Sex, and Happiness	$9.95	
	Bride of the High Places	$17.99	

Ship. (quant.) 1–2 3–5 6–9 10–14 15–19 20–25
Ship. Cost $2.50 4.00 6.50 10.50 13.25 16.00

Subtotal	
Less Discount	
Plus Shipping	
TOTAL DUE	

Name: _____

Address: _____

City/State/Zip: _____ Phone #: _____

Signature: _____ Date: _____

20% Discount for 5 or more copies

Printed in the United States
20215LVS00003B/33